D0929255

POPULATION GROWTH AND URBANIZATION IN LATIN AMERICA

The Rural-Urban Interface

POPULATION GROWTH AND URBANIZATION
IN LATIN AMERICA

The Rural-Urban Interface

Edited by

John M. Hunter
Robert N. Thomas
Scott Whiteford

SCHENKMAN PUBLISHING COMPANY, INC.
Cambridge, Massachusetts

Copyright © **1983**

Schenkman Publishing Company, Inc.
3 Mount Auburn Place
Cambridge, Massachusetts 02138

Library of Congress Cataloging in Publication Data

Population growth and urbanization in Latin America.

  1. Rural-urban migration—Latin America—Addresses,
essays, lectures. 2. Urbanization—Latin America—
Addresses, essays, lectures. 3. Latin America— Popula-
tion—Addresses, essays, lectures. I. Hunter, John
Melton, 1928-   . II. Thomas, Robert N., 1926-
III. Whiteford, Scott, 1942-   .
HB1990.5.A3P66   307'.2   80-28809
ISBN 0-87073-225-0
ISBN 0-87073-226-9 (pbk.)

PRINTED IN THE UNITED STATES OF AMERICA

CONTENTS

Preface . . . . *ix*

Introduction . . . . *xi*

Part I POPULATION GROWTH AND SOCIAL CHANGE . . *1*

Population Growth and Urbanization in Latin America:
The Next 20 Years
  Robert W. Fox *3*
Differential Population Growth in the Peruvian Altiplano
  Paul F. Brown *21*
Rural Stability and Forced Outmigration:
The Paradox of Agrarian Reform in Mexico
  Rodney C. Kirk *41*
The Urbanization Process in 19th Century Chile:
The Railroad and Rural-Urban Migration
  Robert Oppenheimer *57*
Social Indicators and the Quality of Life:
  An Internal Migration Example from Honduras
  Robert N. Thomas and John D. Stephens *76*
Population Growth and Composition in St. Vincent,
1861 to 1960
  Joseph G. Spinelli *91*

Part II DEVELOPMENT STRATEGIES
AND MIGRATION *97*

Decentralization of Urban Growth in Latin America:
Recent History and Some Current Experiences
  Emily Baldwin and Eric Chetwynd, Jr. 99
A.I.D.'s Rural Development Strategies in Latin America
and the Caribbean
  Clarence Zuvekas, Jr. 119
The Hydroelectric Potential of the Paraná River
and Prospect for Regional Economic Development
  J. Eliseo Da Roas 142
Industrial Shift and Labor Stability on a Government-
Administered Ejido Farming Development Project
in Southern Yucatán, Mexico
  Jacob J. Climo 158
Irrigation in Central Mexico and the Role of the State:
Dependency Relationships and Migration Patterns
  Laura Montgomery 167
Characteristics of Manufacturing Enterprises
by Locality Size in Four Regions of Honduras:
Implications for Rural Development
  Judith I. Stallmann and James W. Pease 184

**Part III URBANIZATION: THE RURAL-URBAN
INTERFACE** 201

From Squatters to Skyscrapers: New Directions
in Latin American Urbanization Research
  Robert V. Kemper 203
Urban Housing and Competition:
Responses to Rural-Urban Migration
  James F. Hopgood 218
The Lebanese Arab Community in Cali, Colombia
  Leila Bradfield 227
The Suburbanization of Campesinos
and the Metropolitan Crisis in Mexico City
  William Collins 243
Transcending Rural-Urban Boundaries:
A Comparative View of Two Labor Reserves
and Family Strategies
  Terry Hoops and Scott Whiteford 261

Urban-Rural Differences in the Selection Strategies
of Compadrazgo: A Controlled Comparison
Carl Kendall *281*

Part IV PERSPECTIVE *291*

Developmental Dilemmas And Paradoxes:
A Personal Philosophical Note
Peter Dorner *293*

PREFACE

The origins of this volume are the 1979 meeting of the Midwest Association for Latin American Studies held at Michigan State University with local leadership provided by the Latin American Studies Center. The theme—the volume's title—was chosen at least a year in advance and approved by the MALAS leadership. It offered both an important topic for consideration and the multidisciplinarity that conferences such as those of MALAS require.

Professors Robert N. Thomas and Scott Whiteford served as general program chairmen, and they secured fine session leaders who, in turn, sought out papers to contribute to the sub-themes of their respective sessions. In all, about forty-five papers were presented, relating in some way to the rural-urban interface.

It was our intent from the beginning to assemble from this conference a set of papers which would be at least moderately cohesive and provide new insights with respect to the topic of the conference. The present collection does that across a considerable array of disciplines—geography, history, anthropology, economics. The criteria for selection included: (1) the relationship of the theme of the paper to the central focus of the volume, (2) the quality and originality of the work itself, (3) the suitability of the paper for a multi- and interdisciplinary audience. Decisions, for the most part, were easy for us, the anthropologist, economist, geographer *qua* editors; but there were, as in most situations, the doubtful cases—fine papers which for one reason or another simply could not be included. And it was with considerable regret that some of the papers finally just had to be eliminated. We explicitly thank those contributors to the volume for their patience in uninformed waiting as well as for permitting us to include their work. We regret, too, those we could not include. For those who may seek to assign blame, our names appear alphabetically as a statement regarding shared responsibility!

There is a great list of people whom we should thank—those who contributed to the original conference and those who have similarly contributed to this volume. In any case, we can only report a portion of the visible part of the iceberg. Financial support by Michigan State University to the conference, the genesis of the volume, came from the MSU Development Fund; from the College of Arts and Letters and the College of Social Science; from the Office of the Provost and the Office of International Studies and Programs. Two people related particularly to the conference—as representatives of many—merit current recognition: Professor Betty Tyree Osiek, the then President of MALAS, for obvious reasons, and Mr. Marc VanWormer of MSU's Lifelong Education Programs, University Conferences and Institutes, who kept three amateurs on the right track and the conference flowing smoothly and successfully.

Finally, this is an occasion for the three of us to express our gratitude to Mrs. Diana J. Stetson, the LASC's secretary, who in a very small shop, bears much responsibility and thus deserves a great deal of the credit for whatever is accomplished.

John M. Hunter

INTRODUCTION

The importance of urban centers in Latin America dates from pre-Columbian times. They have served as power centers for population segments which have attempted to dominate rural areas politically, economically and culturally. Later, cities became the base of colonial control for the Spanish and the Portuguese, who brought with them a strong urban ideology from the Iberian penninsula (Nutini 1972:90). Many of the major cities in Latin America played a critical role in the extractive policies of the colonial nations. Since the colonial period, the countries of Latin America have become increasingly urbanized, but the pace of urbanization has been greatly accelerated during the last thirty years. In 1950, one of every ten Latin Americans lived in cities of more than one million inhabitants; but by 1980, the ratio for a much larger population is one of four in such cities. Over sixty percent of the population of Latin America lives in cities, and it is expected that by the year 2000, over seventy-five percent will be classified as urban. Excepting Cuba, Latin American nations have been unable or unwilling to stem the migration from the countryside to the city. The mass redistribution of population has profound social, economic and political implications for the future of Latin American society.

Explanations for the high rate of urbanization include a range of factors and processes. Much of the analyses have fallen into a "push/pull" framework in which lack of opportunities in rural areas and perceived advantages of the cities are seen as generating migration. The framework includes the micro-level of individual decision-making and considers factors such as sex, age, occupation and education. Demographic analysis is equally important. Population growth is viewed as an important factor increasing the pressure on resources and employment opportunities. On a more macro-level, the analyses have focused on factors which influence the distribution of services and the location of industry and other enterprises. Another important approach is historical-structural in nature. This perspective focuses on the penetration of national and international capitalism and the processes and interrelationships involved in that penetration. Articles supporting both of these approaches are included in this volume.

While most studies of urbanization assume that connections exist between the rural and urban milieu, most have been limited to examining processes in either the countryside or the city. This is partly due to limitations in time and resources for research, but is also a product of a rural-urban dichotomy that has pervaded the social science literature. This dichotomy represents a myth which is slowly being reinterpreted as new questions are leading to a reconceptualization. John Walton (1979:164) has suggested "a new unit of analysis based on distinctive vertically integrated processes passing through a network from the international level to the urban hinterland." Anthony Leeds (n.d.) and Douglas Uzzell (n.d.) question the utility of focusing on the differences between rural and urban localities and offer alternative analytical frameworks.

All of the articles in this volume examine linkages between the city and the countryside although their emphasis is bounded by locality as well. The volume is divided into three sections: 1) Population Growth and Social Change; 2) Development Strategies and Migration; and 3) Urbanization. Together the articles present the different faces of social change and the urbanization process in Latin America, including the rural as well as urban dimension.

POPULATION GROWTH AND SOCIAL CHANGE

During the last thirty-five years, skyrocketing population growth brought about by high fertility and declining mortality has created new concerns and aggravated old problems. During this period and in most Latin American countries, annual rates of population increase exceeded 3 percent while total population soared, reaching 360,000,000 in 1980. In 1980, average annual rates of population increase vary considerably throughout the region. For example, Middle America's rate still exceeds 3.0 percent with Honduras (3.5 percent) and Nicaragua (3.4 percent) having the highest rates. South America's rates vary from highs of 3.1 in Paraguay and 2.8 for both Brazil and Peru, to a low of 1.1 for Uruguay, 1.4 for Chile and 1.6 for Argentina. Although recent statistics indicate that the region's annual rate of increase has undergone a modest decline (to 2.6 percent in 1980), medium United Nations' projections indicate that by the year 2000, Latin America will contain nearly 600,000,000 people.

The articles in the first section of the book examine different dimensions of population growth and social change. In the lead article, "Population Growth and Urbanization in Latin America: The Next 20 Years," Robert W. Fox examines the specifics of the demographic problem and outlines national differences in population increase and urban growth rates. The rapid expansion of migrant population in principal cities in contrast to secondary and small urban centers poses another key problem. Most migrants bypass the smaller cities to head directly for their national capital or other major urban centers, thereby delegating the smaller centers to the social and economic backwaters. Fox further stresses the growing problem of urban unemployment as the labor market in major cities fails to keep pace with the exploding urban population.

In contrast to Fox's macro-view, Paul F. Brown's "Differential Population Growth in the Peruvian Atliplano" from intensive local research takes issue with the contemporary thesis that recent population growth in Latin America is primarily the result of decreasing mortality rates. An examination of population increase among the Aymara Indians of southern Peru suggests that the continued high rates of increase result from a conscious effort by parents to increase family size in order to increase the amount of farm-labor the family controls.

Rodney C. Kirk in "Rural Stability and Forced Out-Migration: The Paradox of Agrarian Reform in Mexico" explores another aspect of rural labor supply and demand. He notes the contradictory aspects of the ejido agrarian reform program where constraints placed on local reform committies by federal government lead to a lack of economic development. These controls, in turn, result in significant increases in unemployment and under-employment that provide the impetus for a dramatic increase in out-migration to Mexican cities and labor markets in the United States.

The next two chapters address the migrant component directly. In "The Urbanization Process in 19th Century Chile: The Railroad and Rural-Urban Migration," Robert Oppenheimer presents the urbanization process in mid-19th century Chile and analyzes the impact of railroad construction on the movement to the city. It is frequently assumed that little migration occurred during this period and that, generally, peasants remained in the countryside because of the low levels of industrialization and corresponding job opportunites. However, railroad data demonstrate that considerable movement did take place between farm and city, although this change in residence was frequently circular in nature: workers labored in the cities and returned to their farms during the harvest season. This contact with city life brought about by the expanding railroad network provided potential migrants with the necessary exposure to city-living that later would encourage a permanent move to Chilean cities.

"Social Indicators and the Quality of Life: An Internal Migration Example from Honduras" by Robert N. Thomas and John D. Stephens addresses the population redistribution issue in contemporary Central America and exposes the relationship between territorial social indicators and internal migration. Their findings suggest that most migrants who move to the capital city of Tegucigalpa come from other urban centers and specifically those cities which appear to be less socially and economically dynamic. The study also demonstrates the importance of rural participation in the move to the captial. Although distance is an important spatial variable that adds to the general explanatory power of their regression model, more prosperous agricultural areas found near the capital contribute proportionately more migrants to Tegucigalpa than do more impoverished, traditional, subsistence areas.

In the conclusion of "Population and Social Change" Joseph C. Spinelli's "Population Growth and Composition in St. Vincent, 1861 to 1960" presents a case study of the impact of population dynamics on this Caribbean island. The chapter divides the demographic history of St. Vincent into three distinct periods and discusses each: 1) foreign labor immigration in the post-slavery period: 1831 to 1881; 2) the era of emigration: 1881 to 1931; and 3) the period of rapid population growth: 1931 to 1960. The author incorporates an analysis of population distribution and composition in the context of the three time periods.

DEVELOPMENT STRATEGIES AND MIGRATION

The second section of the book focuses on the impacts of development strategies or projects on migration. While many studies have focused exclusively on migrants and their adaptation, a growing body of research places migration in a developmental context. Different types and rates of migration are viewed as symptomatic of particular patterns of development. Population redistribution is an important process interacting with other processes. It can be studied both in the context of the causal socio-economic change and in the context of effects on the socio-economic change. The authors in this volume have emphasized the processes responsible for the character of the regions or local ties which have both generated migration. Yet, there are significant differences in the assumptions underlying the analyses presented in this section. Jay Climo and Laura Montgomery take a dependency perspective emphasizing the dynamics of dependent capitalist development, similar to the historical-structural approach. In contrast, the other articles use a modernization approach to development which prescribes institutional or organizational changes to raise the standard of living and/or slow the pace of urbanization.

In "Decentralization of Urban Growth in Latin America: Recent History and Current Experience," Emily Baldwin and Eric Chetwynd examine a variety of strategies employed to slow rural-to-urban migration. Of particular interest is their detailed discussion of the successes and failures of the growth pole theory. They proceed to discuss the new approaches to rural development including the rejuvenation of small and medium-sized towns and the urbanization of the countryside through the provision of urban services to rural areas. They conclude by suggesting it is too early to determine how effective the truly integrative approach is in slowing migration to the cities. But, they suggest, there are ways to provide a greater variety of receiving centers for the potential migrants.

Many Latin American countries in their effort to develop rural areas have turned to international or foreign agencies for financial or technical assistance. One of the organizations most involved in this process is the Agency for International Development. Not without criticism, A.I.D. has played an important role in the development strategies of many Latin American countries. The article by Clarence Zuvekas, "A.I.D.'s Rural Development Strategies in Latin America and the Caribbean," is an important contribution to an understanding of A.I.D. programs. While acknowledging the effect of reformist programs is constrained without structural changes, Zuvekas points to strategies he feels increase the probability of satisfying basic human needs. Without questioning the A.I.D. philosophy, the article does examine changes in the development strategies and the reasons for these changes. The article provides a broad view of a range of policy issues from comprehensive agrarian reform to issues on credit, institution building, and pricing structures.

Many of the projects sponsored by institutions such as the World Bank and A.I.D. are large-scale. Eliseo da Rosa, in "The Hydro-electric Potential of the Parana River and the Prospects for Regional Development" examines the economic impact of one of the largest and most ambitious projects in Latin American history—the Itaipu dam and development project. A cooperative effort between Argentina, Brazil, and Paraguay, the project promises to generate massive population as well as production.

The last two papers in this section link the problem of underdevelopment to dependent capitalism and dependency. In his article "Industrial Shift and Labor Stability on a Government-Administered Ejido Farming Project in Southern Yucatan, Mexico," Jay Climo argues that despite the agrarian reform in the Yucatan, collective ejido labor organization shows a number of important similarities with earlier plantation labor organization. The agrarian reform brought about fewer changes than anticipated because the peasants remained constrained by their incorporation into the capitalist mode of production. Like their prereform forefathers the peasantry is characterized by underemployment, unequal statuses with differing privileges, and forced seasonal migration.

In many parts of rural Latin America access to water is as important as land ownership. National governments have developed elaborate and expensive irrigation projects in an effort to increase agricultural production. Laura Montgomery's article, "Peasant Irrigation Systems in Mexico: Implications for Production and Migration," analyzes the national economic and political context of irrigation agriculture in central Mexico. She suggests that the increased technological complexity of irrigation systems results in shifting control of the system away from the community to the central government and links water distribution to rural out-migration and migrant selectivity.

Another traditional view cast increasingly in doubt is that which associates only farming with rural areas and manufacturing only with the cities. Judith I. Stallmann and James W. Pease, in a search for means of reducing pressure on the cities, empirically examine four areas of rural Honduras and the presence and characteristics of rural industry there.

URBANIZATION: THE RURAL-URBAN INTERFACE

The urban explosion which has transformed the population distribution pattern in Latin America has created many new problems. Urban centers such as Mexico City, São Paulo and Buenos Aires are among the largest cities in the world while Latin America has the most urbanized population of any region in the developing world. Urban research in Latin America has expanded rapidly as the problems of urban growth attract increasing attention. In this section, Robert Kemper's article "From Squatters to Sky Scrapers: Reflections on New Directions in Latin American Research," examines how social science research in Latin America has shifted from a modernization perspective to a dependency perspective and how this change is reflected in the theoretical paradigms of urban research. He proceeds to discuss the implication of this change for the next generation of urban specialists and points out the need for multidisciplinary training and research efforts.

Robert Kemper's article sets the stage for a series of case studies which focus on a variety of urban problems. Housing, one of the central policy issues in urban Latin America and of primary concern to the urban poor, is the central topic of the article by James Hopgood, "Urban Housing and Competition: Responses to Rural-Urban Migration." The article compares two housing programs in the city of Monterrey, Mexico. One program is a private entrepreneurial effort organized by Monterrey's industrial elite, the other a federal government program with public housing a political as well as an economic issue.

Foreign immigrants are still arriving in Latin American cities where their impact may be considerable. Some immigrants come from other Latin American countries and others from Europe, Asia, or the Middle East. Immigrants can play an important economic role in their new homelands. Leila Bradfield's "The Arab Community in Cali, Colombia: A Success Story of Integration" focuses on the Lebanese who play an integrative role as middlemen minority between the upper and low sectors in Cali. Of special significance is the role of the women in the successful integration of the Lebanese.

The dislocation of large numbers of peasants and rural workers in Latin America and their move to the city is one of the most dramatic locational and social changes in contemporary Latin America. William Collins, in his article "The Suburbanization of Campesinos and the Metropolitan Crisis in Mexico City," contributes to our understanding of these processes by using data from Mexico City linking government urban service policy to the constant decision-making processes of migrants coping with problems of adjustment to urban living.

The article by Terry Hoops and Scott Whiteford, "Transcending Rural-Urban Boundaries: A Comparative View of a Labor Reserve and Family Strategies," also examines decision-making by low income families. Based on data from Queretaro, Mexico and Salta, Argentina, their article shows the importance of mixed household strategies in maintaining families through periods of unemployment, subsequently perpetuating a labor reserve for capitalist agriculture as well as industry. Their article concludes by indicating the linkages between the city and the countryside, suggesting they are part of the same system but organized in different ways.

In the final article, "Rural and Urban Dimensions of Compadrazgo," Carl Kendall examines the nature of compadrazgo (ritual kinship) in a Guatemalan city and village. His conclusions question the bifurcated distinction between rural and urban and suggest the need of new conceptual directions.

Peter Dorner's "Developmental Dilemmas and Paradoxes: A Personal Philosophical Note" is a fitting conclusion to this volume. His view is the broad one covering the issue of interdependency within and without the context of development. Development issues are examined in global context, and finally he underlines the importance of human minds and skills as critical components of expanded growth and well-being—wherever.

REFERENCES

Leeds, Anthony. "Forms of Urban Integration"—Social Urbanization in Comparative Perspective. Paper presented at the American Anthropological Meetings, Cincinnati, 1979.

Nutini, Hugo. "The Latin American City: A Cultural-Historical Approach." In: *The Anthropology of Urban Environments.* Edited by Thomas Weaver and Douglas White. Washington, D.C.: Society for Applied Anthropology Publication, 1972.

Uzzell, Douglas. "Conceptual Fallacies of the Rural-Urban Dichotomy." Paper presented at the American Anthropological Meetings, Cincinnati, 1979.

Walton, John. "From Cities to Systems: Recent Research of Latin American Urbanization." In: *Latin American Research Review* 14:1:159-169.

I
Population Growth and Social Change

POPULATION GROWTH AND URBANIZATION IN LATIN AMERICA: THE NEXT 20 YEARS

Robert W. Fox

In the early 1970's the first steps were taken by the Inter-American Development Bank to examine the relationships between population growth and urbanization in Latin America. This produced a long and fruitful collaboration with the U.S. Bureau of the Census' International Statistical Program Center, and in particular for me a close relationship with Jerry Huguet, with whom I recently co-authored a book on Central America. Our first effort in 1972 was a monograph called "Urban Population Growth Trends in Mexico" followed by similar reports covering more than half the countries of the region.

Like anyone's first experience with something important, memories of that monograph linger, for in it we had the audacity to project a Mexico City population of 32 million in the year 2000. My own first reaction on seeing this computer projection was to call Jerry and ask what had gone wrong, and my second reaction was to sit on the information for six months. But finally came the moment of truth, the monograph was printed and released, containing, among other projections, the one for Mexico City. With surprise and some relief, months later, I received a letter from John Grauman of the U.N. Population Division in which he stated that "strangely, though our methods of calculation are quite different, we come to similar results, and it is quite possible that in the year 2000 the world's biggest agglomeration may be Mexico City. While not exactly these figures, personally I believe that such cities will be of such orders of magnitude." Attached to the letter, and previewing a new U.N. population projection document, was a listing of the world's thirty largest urban agglomerations for the year 2000, noting for the latter year Mexico City at 32 million, and very similar to other projections we had made in the meanwhile, São Paulo at 26 million, Rio de Janeiro at 19 million, and Lima and Buenos Aires, both above 10 million.

That was five years ago. Today our observations (supported by a host of sample surveys on population trends and local readings on the growth of cities) tell us that Latin America is still rushing headlong to attain these projections. Not only are urban numbers being realized, but national projections are being realized as well. At the agglomeration level, for example, Mexico City with 8.6 million inhabitants in 1970 was projected at 13.6 million by 1980, but it now seems apparent that this one urban agglomeration will instead reach 15 or 16 million inhabitants by next year. An increase in an urban setting of this magnitude has never happened before, at any place, at any time.

To grasp this reality, the seven and one-half million population *net* increase for Mexico City alone in the ten-year period (1970-80) will be equal to the expected increases of *all* the European capital cities in the period: Sofia, Prague, Berlin, Budapest, Warsaw, Bucharest, Copenhagen, Helsinki, Dublin, Oslo, Stockholm, London, Tirana, Athens, Rome, Lisbon, Madrid, Belgrade, Vienna, Brussels, Paris, Bonn, Amsterdam, Geneva, as well as Washington, D.C. and Ottawa. This gives some idea of the scale, the dimensions, of what we are talking about.

And at the national level it is apparent that the Republic of Mexico, containing 49 million inhabitants in 1970, will reach the projected total of 68 million when the census count is tallied next year. And similarly, in country after country of the region we see our earlier expectations being fulfilled. In short, Latin America, a region of 160 million in 1950 passed 315 million in 1975, and by 1980 there will be some 365 million inhabitants in the area. Except for a rather rapid decline in the birth rate in Colombia, we have found no surprises in the past two or three years to modify birth and death levels that were plugged into the projections.

The notion of serious consequences·resulting from very rapid population growth not so long ago was marginal in the larger context of Latin American issues—an anomoly as it were. Our standard Latin American courses in the 1960's included political systems, social stratification and mobility, economic development with a stress on industrialization and import substitution, and agrarian reform. Now in the late 70's the topic of population growth is working toward the limelight, and deservedly so. It is no longer considered outside the area of key Latin American issues, but has earned a place as one of the major topics in the region. What I'd like to do here is to explain from a slightly technical viewpoint just why this topic deserves every bit of attention it can get.

I'll touch on three issues:

1) Population growth in Latin America, where it presently stands, the projections and the logic behind them, demographic inertia and the potential for reducing the current rate of growth.

2) Latin American urbanization, socio-economic issues related to rural to urban migration movements, and the pace of city growth.

3) Finally, a glance at the next major issue we will be facing: the rapid increase in the size of the (urban) labor force.

I begin on a premise I think we can all accept: *eventually* the rate of population growth in Latin America *must* fall substantially, but in the meanwhile there are ever increasing numbers to accommodate. A simple enough statement, but one still controversial in many quarters.

Logic tells us that eventually the rate of population growth will fall. If, for example, Mexico sustained her present 3.3 percent rate of growth through the end of the century, her present population of 65 million would total 134 million by the year 2000 (not far actually from what *is* projected), and 299 million just 25 years later.

Ansley Coale in a recent *Foreign Affairs* article on Mexico accentuated this point when he wrote "if fertility [in Mexico] were to be cut in half in 25 years beginning today, and were then maintained at no more than 50 percent of current levels, the population of Mexico would still be multiplied by 11 in 150 years. Multiplication by 11 would mean about 660 million, which exceeds the present population of India. On the other hand, to imagine the unimaginable of 150 years more in which fertility was not reduced is to think about a population multiplied by nearly 250 (to reach some 15 billion) or nearly four times the present total population of the world. These longer range calculations illustrate the undeniable point that the birthrate must eventually come down and come a long way down, if the low mortality that modern science and medicine can bring is to continue."

To cite two other examples: El Salvador's 4.5 million would number 9.4 million by the year 2000 under a continuation of the present 3.4 percent rate of growth, and 22 million inhabitants another 25 years later, and Brazil's would reach 229 million by the year 2000, and 468 million 25 years later.

Quite evidently, these rates *cannot* be sustained. What will probably happen, and in fact is now beginning to happen in small and moderate amounts, is that the birthrate is falling. The other two options leading to a drop in the rate of population growth are a rising death rate and net migration from a country. Since neither of these look plausible or desirable in large-scale terms, we look to a falling birthrate as the principal agent to a falling rate of population increase. However, as I detailed in the published reports,[1] to effectively bring about a much reduced rate of population growth from present levels takes a considerable amount of time because of what is called demographic inertia. Understanding this is essential, and I will review this shortly.

We can characterize Latin America by stating that it presently shows the highest rate of population growth of any of the world's major regions. The 1975 population of 315 million is fully expected to become one of over 600 million by the year 2000.

As we are aware, rates of population increase in the region are not homogenous. They range from a rather modest 0.9 percent increase in Uruguay and slightly higher for Argentina to exceptionally high rates of 3.2 percent and above found in several Central American countries, Mexico, Ecuador, and Peru. Mexico, for example, is the fastest growing nation in the world with 20 million and more inhabitants, while Brazil is the fastest growing in the world among all countries with more than 100 million inhabitants.

In discussing the "population problem" one has to differentiate clearly among countries. Argentina's "population problem" for example, is most appropriately associated with gerentology issues—retirement and social security systems—in addition to a *slow* rate of population growth. Uruguay's is most appropriately tied to a low birthrate, and particularly to high and public-borne costs related to socialization and education that nonetheless yield a high rate of emigration by young people. Bolivia's "population problem" is really tied to a very high infant mortality rate and spatial distribution patterns, that is, a crowded capital city and a densely settled altiplano along with empty lowlands.

Thus the average Argentinian or Uruguayan probably has little more understanding of the severity of the problem as it occurs in countries where rates are 3 percent and above than does the average Canadian or U.S. citizen.

Perhaps the impact of these enormously varying growth rates can best be illustrated by relating population totals and projections at two points for low growth and high growth countries. In one category (low growth) are Argentina and Chile. Argentina, with 16 million inhabitants in 1950, is projecting 34 million in the year 2000. Chile, with 6 million in 1950, is projected at 15 million in the year 2000. Among high growth countries, a considerably more striking situation prevails. For the six Central American countries (including Panama), their eight million population in 1950 should number 39 million in the year 2000. The Brazilian 1950 population of 52 million may well reach 202 million in 2000; while Mexico's 26 million in 1950 may well reach 129 million. Seen in another light, Mexico's projected net increase of 34 million in the decade 1990-2000 would equal Argentina's total population in the year 2000.

These figures are dramatic, but I am sure in the back of most minds right now is the thought, "Well, this just isn't going to happen." But we must note that midway through the period, 1950-2000, it *has* happened; that is, Central America's population *did double,* Brazil's *did* double, and Mexico's *did* double. Demographers like everyone else are startled by the experience of the past twenty-five years.

You may say that another redoubling is not going to occur for such reasons as the time period is too short for societies to develop the economic functions necessary to accommodate these great numbers, or that the required natural resource base simply does not exist, or that to sustain these great population numbers would do irrevocable and permanent damage to the carrying capacity of the earth's biological systems (grasslands, croplands, fisheries, and forests) as suggested by Lester Brown in his most recent book *The 29th Day*, or by Paul Ehrlich and company in their most recent work *Ecoscience*. A sociologist might go one step further and argue equally strongly against the feasibility of another redoubling of population numbers in the next twenty or twenty-five years because should this occur, the conditions will be met for *yet another* redoubling of numbers; that is, the demographic structure (wage and sex distribution patterns, fertility and mortality levels, etc.) would then be somewhat the same as they were twenty-five years earlier.

But today, sociologists and demographers and a growing number of planners and economists are concerned for this precise reason. That is, while demographic conditions are changing, they still are not much different now than they were twenty-five years ago. This message, i.e. the strong existing potential for another redoubling, fortunately is also starting to get through to leaders in the region, and in response most Latin American governments now have official policies to reduce the rate of population growth.

One may hope that these population policies, commissions, and programs that have been promulgated in recent years in Mexico, in El Salvador, and in the Dominican Republic among other countries will be effective. They may result separately, or in conjunction with societal changes in attitudes and values, in fertility rates dropping much, much faster than currently projected. But if a very real potential for yet another redoubling before the close of the century does exist on the one hand (and it does) while on the other hand there is increasing recognition at the national level (officially)that the birthrate must fall, one might ask whether there are any real obstacles to substantially reducing projected populations apart from successfully encouraging changing values and attitudes, extending health and family planning services particularly in rural areas, and legislating incentives or disincentives. The answer, of course, is "yes, there are obstacles," and here we turn to the question of demographic inertia and the absolute need to take a long-range view of this issue.

In a paper presented a few years ago in New Orleans to the Population Association of America, Victor Urquidi, the President of El Colegio de México, made a rather incisive statement, as follows: "I (Urquidi) venture to suggest also a peculiar reason for the neglect of the population factor (in Latin America). (It) is the unawareness, on the part of political and other leaders, of the significance of high rates of exponential growth. After all, 3 or 3.5 percent does not seem a very high number. When interest rates are 12 to 18 percent per year, a mere 3 percent is next to nothing. A doubling time of 20 years is not a meaningful concept for someone whose political view of the future does not extend beyond a six year term or the next military coup. Even economic planners, to the extent that they are close to decision making in Latin America, rarely see beyond 5 or 10 years, and tend to take population growth as a datum of minor significance and of no important variability."

I want to extend Urquidi's remark and suggest that most development planners, while aware a problem exists, have stayed unaware of the enormous forces that *will* produce further large increases. Forces that compound a rate of population growth are far different from a compounded rate of interest on capital investments. Capital, after all, can be withdrawn, and interest ceases immediately. But a population growth rate does not stop with a clear-cut consensus to bring about lower birth levels. It will slow down and eventually cease compounding, but this will occur over a period of generations. This eventual slowdown will occur not only as a function of individual couples deciding to have fewer children, but importantly also as a function of slowly shifting elements which operate within a clearly defined demographic structure. These include the increased life expectancy for populations in general which is still on the rise in Latin America, the near tandem relationship between falling birthrates and falling death rates (which will continue to be the pattern for several Latin American countries for awhile), and as a result of past fertility and mortality trends, age and sex structures in which the population majority is now under twenty years of age.

It is these particular elements that I wanted to serve as the bottom line in the reports: the notion of a demographic structure through which arresting population growth must be processed, and the long period of time necessary to bring this about.

At this juncture, I run the risk of preaching to the converted since many of you are fully aware of demographic inertia factors. Others, however, are not and since this is at the core of the population debate, I want to spend a minute or two examining these factors and show how they operate.

Let us take Central America as an example. As noted earlier, this region increased in population from 8.5 million in 1950 to around 19 million in 1975, and it should redouble in numbers to around 39 million by the year 2000, even while the birthrate falls by more than a quarter from present levels. The demographic evolution drill, if you will, is as follows:

Prior to 1940, or thereabouts, in Central America the traditional balance between both high birthrates and high death rates prevailed. If, in any measured period of time, there were 10 births and 7 deaths (and without appreciable net migration), the rate of population growth was held low. This *was* the situation and had been so. But in the post World War II period, given the dedicated efforts to reduce the death rate through the control of transmissible diseases, preventive health care and like measures, two events occurred: average life spans lengthened considerably, and the infant mortality rate dropped. From 1950 to 1975, the general mortality rate for Central America fell a full 50 percent. But the birthrate, exceptionally high to begin, stayed high (it actually did come down in several of these countries during the period, but only by about 15 percent). Thus, the traditional balance between both high birth and high death rates was broken. For every 10 births now there is something on the order of 2 or 3 deaths (and many of these deaths are among the older population which benefited initially from the mortality control some 30-40 years earlier).

Well, this much I think we all understand, but less understood is the fact that owing to these shifts in previous death and (to some extent) birth patterns, entirely new population structures have evolved.

This means that in projecting populations we have to consider:

1) A death rate in Central America that is still falling toward its anticipated minimum.

2) We assumed, and note this, a 28 percent overall drop in the birth-

rate in Central America over the 1970-2000 period, but a full 3/5ths of the falling birthrate should be offset by the still falling death rate (this is the near tandem relationship referred to earlier).

3) The next structural item is the increased life expectancy for the population in general, which actually may be presupposed from the expected decline in the general mortality rate.

4) The final item consists of the age structure in which almost half the Central American population is now less than 15 years of age. All in this group will enter their reproductive years of life in the coming 15-20 years, thus providing strong momentum for further large increases. The published reports go into this in more detail, but the point I want to make here is that a falling birthrate does not translate out into a fall of equal magnitude in the rate of population growth. Birthrate levels are but one ingredient in the mix. When all these structural items are studied in the context of the time necessary to slow this upsurge in numbers, I think most will agree that our projection path is realistic, operates within acceptable demographic tolerances, and unquestionably leads to the conclusion that enormous further increases will occur.

Let's further put these two elements together—demographic inertia together with the strong desire of a government to drastically reduce the rate of population growth—and see where it leads. Mexico is probably the Latin American country which is under more internal pressure than any other to reduce her rate of growth. You can attribute this to the country's very large population (presently 65 million) and her current rate of growth (around 3.3 percent per year), the quick pace of urbanization, the amount of arable land relative to population size, the staggering social costs attributable to education and health systems, to the high rate of unemployment and underemployment, and to rising expectations. Mexico has also come out strongly for a massive family planning program. This began in the Echeverría regime (1974) and has been reinforced in the current administration. Mexico is also the first Latin American country to have set quantitative population goals. In May of last year, President Lopez Portillo moved beyond the 2.5 percent population growth rate target already set for 1982 (an ambitious goal, I might add) to announce that program planning would now aim at reducing growth to 1.8 percent in 1988,

1.3 percent in 1994, and 1 percent in the year 2000. Consider for a moment what *enormous* changes these targets imply for modification of values and attitudes held by the Mexican population, the *enormous* shifts in reproductive behavior and the *costs* in providing social services in a country where there are 90,000 hamlets of less than 1,000 inhabitants apiece. Assuming all this comes about (and, incidentally, there is no doubt but that they are serious) what *may be* the final quantitative result for the year 2000 taking into account the inertia factor? Victor Urquidi noted last year that "if these trends prevail (that is, the continuation of a slightly falling growth rate) and a well coordinated and intensive program in family planning is followed . . . it would not be impossible to reach a total population of 110 million by the year 2000, instead of currently accepted projections of 126 to 140 million."

To finish on this point let me note that even if birthrates for each Latin American country slowed radically to the point where by year 2000 each family on average had two children, the region's population that year would—via the effects of demographic inertia—still number around 540 million rather than the 600-610 million currently projected.

It is within this context, national population growth rates and the realistic limits on altering these rates, that I turn to the next topic: Latin American urbanization patterns. What I want to do is quickly characterize the region's urbanization patterns, show their uniqueness, and point to reasons why I think the urban projections will be attained.

There is no precedent in the world's history for the sustained urban growth currently found in the region. It results from very high national level population increases in the majority of countries, combined with a massive rural to urban migration, processes begun in earnest in the 1950's.

In 1950, one in every ten Latin Americans lived in cities of more than a million inhabitants. At the present time, even while the total population has more than doubled, the ratio is almost one out of four.

Latin America is unique in its urbanization patterns. Most other developing countries have a much smaller proportion of their total numbers in a principal city or network of cities. The largest proportion of the population in most countries is well distributed throughout the rural areas in a small village pattern.

In India, China, Indonesia, and Burma, for example, which together hold about half the world's population, not more than 11 percent live in cities of over 100,000 population, according to the United Nations. For sub-Sahara Africa the regional average is just 12 percent. But in Argentina, Brazil, Chile, Mexico, Peru and Venezuela (among the countries studied) between 35 and 55 percent of the population resides in cities of this size, and in Colombia 45 percent. In Central America, population in cities over 100,000 is around 20 percent of the total.

The Latin American urbanization pattern, however, is beginning to emerge in other developing countries; the growth of monstrously large urban agglomerations such as Cairo, Jakarta, Karachi, or Lagos. Nonetheless, for all these cities, inside and outside Latin America, there is no model or experience on which to base our future expectations. New York City, London, Tokyo, Rhein-Ruhn, presently the largest cities, all took generations to arrive at their present size, while Latin American cities have mushroomed in a matter of a decade or two, and they should continue to mushroom.

A key characterization is the following: from mid-century to the present, Latin American cities experienced only a minor portion of their 1950 to year 2000 expected net increase. The 675 or so cities in the countries studied in our technical reports gained roughly 85 million inhabitants between 1950 and 1975, but are projected to gain another 165 million before the year 2000. In other words, only one-third of the urban growth for this half century had taken place by 1975. The remaining two-thirds is immediately in front of us. And this is completely apart from "new cities" that will form, e.g., those passing a certain minimum population threshold.

For the twelve countries studied, which contain most of the region's inhabitants, the total population will increase by a factor of four between 1950 and 2000, but the population of the cities will increase by a factor of seven. Actually, many of the cities of Brazil, Mexico, Peru and Venezuela in particular, will increase by a factor of ten or more times their size in 1950 during this period. Curitiba, in Brazil, for example, with a 1950 population of 157,000 is projected at 2,688,000 inhabitants by the year 2000.

Primate cities of the region, normally the capitals, we expect to continue to grow rapidly, adding huge populations in the coming years. Apart from the inevitability of national level population growth, they will continue to increase because:

1) Economic, political, social, and cultural functions of entire nations are concentrated in the capital cities or in dual principal cities such as Quito and Guayaquil in Ecuador or Tegucigalpa and San Pedro Sula in Honduras.

2) The rate of natural increase alone in most of these cities is near the national average. Historically, city populations until the 20th century only grew slowly if at all through constant rural to urban migration since the urban death rate was invariably higher than a city's birthrate, but now in Latin America with low urban mortality rates and as a result of two and three earlier generations of migrants in the cities who still maintain high fertility patterns, many large urban centers show rates of natural increase well in excess of 2.5 percent.

3) For numerous countries there is simply no effective growth alternative to the capital city. Arequipa, the second city of Peru, for example, is just 9 percent of the size of Lima; Quetzaltenango, is just 5 percent the size of Guatemala City. Seen in a slightly different light, were a conscious effort made to cut in half the 1970-1980 expected growth of Mexico City *and* the 16 remaining Mexican cities of over a quarter million inhabitants, and redistribute this population among the country's remaining 175 cities (over 20,000 inhabitants), these smaller cities would be swamped: they would double in size in just 10 years. As it is, the small cities are expected to increase on average by 50 percent during the interval, while the 17 dominant urban centers should increase by about 60 percent.

All of this points to the fact that there is little practical alternative to the continuation of rapid population growth among Latin America's major urban centers. The limited ability of secondary and tertiary cities to absorb much more than their proportional share of the burden also points to the weakly developed state of many national urban systems that are dominated by one principal city.

On this last point, let me add that cities of the second and third rank in Latin America are, nonetheless, growing at nearly the same pace as the capitals. The eleven capital cities studied, in addition to Rio de Janeiro and São Paulo in Brazil, rather than Brasília (a newcomer) increased from 18 to 42 million inhabitants between 1950 and 1970, and just these thirteen metropolitan areas are projecting 115 million inhabitants by the year 2000. That is a total increase of 540 percent. But the 46 secondary cities (those with 250,000 and more inhabitants) are projecting a jump from 10 million to 76 million in the 50-year interval. That's an increase of 660 percent. And the 567 cities of the third rank (from 20,000 to 250,000 inhabitants) are projecting an increase from 13 to 90 million inhabitants. That's a gain of 575 percent.

To speculate, I think for at least two reasons secondary and tertiary cities may have to grow faster than the projections show. First, it seems to me there must be a limit to the size of the largest metropolitan areas of the region, dictated by elements such as congestion, pollution, topographical barriers, limitations on water supply and on sewage disposal, and limitations dictated by diseconomies of scale. I cannot conceive of Mexico City growing to 32 million, but rather see this number as a warning flag. At one point or another, surely populations will be strongly directed to secondary and tertiary cities through such means as decentralizing capital city political and economic functions thus giving real meaning to regionalization schemes and providing incentives to locate industries and jobs away from the primate city. Today, in Mexico for example, one reads and hears the capital city's growth referred to as a cancer, the cancer of centralization, and it appears that Mexican authorities are at long last adjusting to the fact that remedial decentralizing action must be taken soon. Some months ago a new national decentralization plan was approved by the President of Mexico, but it remains to be seen if this administration will be any more successful than the last two in effectively carrying it out.

The second reason relates to the rural population and to the feasibility of attaining the rural projections. And this in turn ties to a whole range of issues related to rural social and economic systems as they presently operate. Our projections for the 12 countries show rural increases (rural arbitrarily defined as population outside cities of 20,000 and more) from a total of 80 million in 1950 to 114 million in 1970 and to 189 million by the year 2000. This projection, however, may well be too high.

For several countries such as Argentina, Chile and Venezuela no increases in the rural population are expected. This population should remain stable in absolute numbers. But for the remaining countries, moderate or large increases should occur. In Central America, for example, the rural population is projected to increase (outside cities of 10,000 and more) from 12 to 24 million (1970-2000), in Mexico from around 20 to 40 million, and in Peru from 7.8 to 10.4 million. But, these projections are, of course, based on a methodology in which the rural growth trends of the past are partially built-in.

However, a real question arises as to whether or not the rural exodus is still picking up steam, and if so, city population totals will be even higher than our projections show. Why the rural exodus should accelerate relates to push and pull issues that have been around for decades in Latin America. A good starting point on the push side is the pattern of land ownership and the land tenure system. In Central America, for example, just 7 percent of the cropland is worked by a full 55 percent of the agricultural population, while large holdings comprising 70 percent of agricultural land are controlled by less than 5 percent of the farming population. The number of landless farmers continues to increase and they exist under very precarious conditions while at the same time on large estates capital intensive investments in tractors and farm machinery lower the need for farm laborers. Rural families live in isolation with limited access to public health or education facilities, there is no potable water much less sewage disposal, or electricity. Unemployment is rampant, particularly for women.

Local rural communities are powerless with no taxation base or mandate for local project financing, and credit and banking facilities for small farmers are almost nonexistent. Add to this the strong limitations on personal fulfillment brought about by a rigid social stratification system, and key reasons for the urban migration in Latin America become abundantly clear.

At the same time, the population engaged in agricultural activities has declined throughout the region, showing a drop from about 54 percent of all those economically active in 1950 to a level of 41 percent in 1975. Industries and the service sector, both essentially urban oriented, have taken up the slack. In absolute terms, few increases among the population engaged in agricultural activities are expected. This is simply the continuation of a long-range trend underway for the last half century in Latin America. But it points to a dilemma in which a massive emerging labor force is caught in the middle. On the one hand, fewer and fewer people are willing to work in agriculture given, among other reasons, the rather miserable rural conditions, even while the present national and international hue and cry is that future investments be oriented to the agricultural sector. Quite understandably, raising agricultural production *is* a major goal in most of the countries although their rationale differs from place to place—to raise nutritional standards, to cut down on food import costs, etc.

But, I suggest there is a world of difference between raising agricultural production and improving rural levels of living. I would venture to suggest that the rediscovery of rural Latin America which is now in vogue has two chief elements at its base: a real need to increase food and livestock production on existing farmland and also to keep the population down on the farm and out of the cities.

As seen in employment policy and operational terms, it is currently expressed in the jargon as "raising the income and productivity of the rural poor." Four lines of reasoning have converged to bring about this focus.[2]

1) The strain of rapid urban population growth is showing in all the countries of Latin America, and the situation must be corrected. At the very least, the high rate of rural to urban migration must be slowed through (it is thought) developing rural employment opportunities.

2) In any case, manufacturing which is strictly urban-oriented cannot absorb the numbers coming into the labor market; capital costs are too high.

3) The agricultural sector in most countries, unlike the cities, does have "excess capacity," and by working to ameliorate inequities in social and economic systems in the countryside (land tenure conditions, etc.), rural areas can be redirected to intensified labor use and increased productivity.

4) Finally, it is thought that a flourishing agricultural base can support a network of decentralized cities and labor-intensive industries which should provide employment opportunities and ease the strain on the primate cities.

But increasing productivity and achieving "social and economic justice" are often competing goals when the relative ease with which production can be increased under "modernized" conditions is taken into account. Increased distributive justice for the subsistence class implies land tenure changes, effective social organization, the consolidation of small fragmented land parcels into economically viable units, training in more advanced systems of agriculture, the formation of agricultural buying cooperatives, the diffusion into rural communities of basic public services to raise education, health and nutritional levels, etc. In this competition, the latter group may on balance lose out, and in the form of a redundant labor force this large rural population will increasingly flood to the cities, and particularly to secondary and tertiary cities of the region. Just as one example, Tijuana, Mexico, which we projected at 566,000 in 1980 (up from 300,000 in 1970) has recently been projected by the Mexican Government at over 750,000 in 1980.

Accommodating the growing population is unquestionably the major social issue in Latin America today. This is the third and final topic, and I just want to spend a moment on it looking at one demographic parameter, the labor force dimension. *Most of the population explosion accommodation to date has been accomplished at the family level.* After all, 134 million (or 42 percent) of the region's total population of 318 million (1975) are children or adolescents under 15 years of age. In exceptional cases, by the way, this ratio creeps up to 45-46 percent (Mexico and Central America). Another way of expressing this is to say that the population explosion in Latin America to date has largely been a matter of Sr. y Sra. Sanchez and their six children at home, multiplied by tens of thousands of cases. The point I want to make is that the demands thus far that *this* young population has made on public services have been rather light in comparison to what is coming. In the rural sector the demands have been particularly light—some health services, some schooling at the elementary level, and that has been about it. Here, socialization costs are pretty well absorbed by the family and by rural communities, particularly indigenous communities. In urban settings the costs are higher, although not necessarily met by the public purse or met at all. Education and health services, housing, electricity, gas, water and sewage, transportation and communication needs—all these services have fallen short of meeting minimum needs.

But all of this, serious as it is, seems minor by comparison with the intractable issue of accommodating the growing labor force. We have a fairly good idea of its approaching size, since the population entering into the labor force during the coming 15-20 years has already been born. We are not so sure about a new dimension, women in the labor force. Their participation rate to date has easily been the lowest for any of the world's major regions.

However, the participation rate for women in Latin America cannot help but increase, and increase quickly as a product of urbanization, attaining a certain education level, having fewer children, and as a function of all the ingredients that contribute to social change. The ILO has projected that women in Latin America's labor force, numbering 23 million in 1975, will number 55 million by the year 2000.

Considering this pressure (which is closely tied to social change) and the further decline among those in agriculture noted earlier, it is in this context that I want to relate the ILO findings that even under present conditions of high unemployment and under-employment, Latin America must accommodate, and principally in her cities, a projected net increase of 97 million persons newly entering the labor market in the last quarter of the century. This compares to a total labor force of some 97 million in 1975.

To conclude, while rapid urbanization has represented the first sharp manifestation of Latin America's population explosion, the second sharply manifested aspect will be marked by the great numbers of youth seeking work in the cities in the coming years.

NOTES

1. Fox, Robert W. and Huguet, Jerrold W. *Population and Urban Trends in Central America and Panama*, Inter-American Development Bank, 1977 Washington, D.C. 224 pp. Fox, Robert W., *Urban Population Growth Trends in Latin America.* Inter-American Development Bank, 1975, Washington, D.C., 103 pp.

2. For a detailed and excellent statement on this topic, as well as the source of this categorization, see Kathleen Newland, "Global Employment and Economic Justice: The Policy Challenge," Worldwatch Paper 28, The Worldwatch Institute, 1979, Washington, D.C.

DIFFERENTIAL POPULATION GROWTH
IN THE PERUVIAN ALTIPLANO

Paul F. Brown

INTRODUCTION

Between 1954 and 1960, Harvard University, the Rockefeller Foundation, and the government of India spent approximately $1 million in the Indian district of Ludhiana in an attempt to lower fertility rates through the introduction of birth control devices (Mamdani 1972: 24-5). The social engineers of the project known as the Khana Study believed that the Indian people were ignorant of the effects of a large family; if peasants could only be "educated" to see how much better off they would be with fewer children, they would gladly adopt modern forms of birth control. The project was a failure. The crude birthrate dropped from 40 per 1000 in 1957 to 35 per 1000 in 1968, but the decrease was found to be the result of a rise in the age of marriage for Indian women and not due to the birth control campaign (p. 27-8).

The failure of the Khana Study stems from an assumption of the project planners, widely held by the western world, concerning the nature of population growth in many areas of the Third World, including much of Latin America. Freedman and Berelson (1974: 39) report that many peasant societies in the midst of socioeconomic change are experiencing population growth rates of 2.5 percent per year. In the majority of these cases, population growth is occurring, not because of increases in fertility, but rather because of decreases in mortality. Many demographers explain drops in mortality in peasant and pre-industrial societies undergoing sociocultural and economic changes by reference to one of two factors which are assumed to accompany the development process: (1) the importation and spread of western or cosmopolitan medical technology and the ensuing improvements in disease control, and (2) the upgrading of nutrition through economic and agricultural development (see Davis 1963, Demeny 1974, Hauser 1969, Tietelbaum 1974, and Young 1968). Implicit in this argument is the assumption that before the advent of modern (western) disease control, and economic and agricultural improvements, the naturally high birthrates of preindustrial populations were kept in check by equally high death rates resulting from disease and undernutrition. The introduction of cosmopolitan medicine and agricultural development schemes upset these Malthusian controls and give way to population growth. Thus, those factors which contribute to population growth are assumed to be largely beyond the cognition and control of preindustrial families.

This paper questions the western viewpoint concerning the nature of population growth. An examination of differential population growth among the Aymara Indians, peasant farmers and herders of the Andes of Southern Peru, suggests the following alternative hypothesis: population growth in preindustrial and peasant societies results from the conscious efforts of parents to increase family size in order to increase the amount of labor the family controls. The desire for more labor (and, thus, more children) is motivated by changes in social and economic conditions on the national level which have created new income opportunities for the peasants. While the opportunities do not offer permanent employment for the unacculturated rural segment, they do make small increases in income possible through temporary, often seasonal, wage labor.

In the case of the Aymara, I will show that changes in traditional patterns of agricultural production and the exploitation of new economic resources on the Peruvian coast have created a demand for labor within the nuclear family. This demand is being met by increasing the size of the family through a conscious effort to reduce infant mortality. Aymara parents are achieving higher rates of infant survival by suspending the indigenous population control mechanisms of abortion and infanticide.

I will begin with an examination of the population dynamics of two rural Aymara villages, Challapujo and Challacollo. The hypotheses of disease control, improvements in nutrition, and demand for labor will then be tested against the data I have for these two communities.

DIFFERENTIAL POPULATION GROWTH: CHALLAPUJO AND CHALLACOLLO

The majority of Aymara Indians are found in rural, non-nucleated settlements in the high plain or *altiplano* which surrounds Lake Titicaca in Southern Peru and Western Bolivia at an altitude ranging from 12,507 feet above sea level at the shore of the lake (James 1969:513) to over 13,000 feet (Dew 1969:36). The *altiplano* soils and climate combine to produce an environment in which available energy sources are limited (Thomas 1973), and environmental fluctuations from year to year are relatively severe. The soil is loose and spongy, allowing moisture to disappear rapidly from the surface. In those spots where natural depressions occur, the ground quickly fills with water during the rainy season and becomes so saturated that it is not usable for farming (Carter 1964: 15). Even when rainfall amounts are optimal for growing, the humus-deficient soil places a limit on the amount that can be grown. Soil analyses by Winterhalder, Larsen, and Thomas (1974: 99) in the *altiplano* reveal deficiencies of phosphorus, nitrogen, and organic matter. After three years of continuous cultivation, yields usually decrease to the point where the return for one's labor is not worth the effort (Carter 1964: 15).

Despite the difficulties of soil and climate, the Aymara have managed to thrive in the *altiplano* for hundreds of years. Centuries of trial and error have led to the development of agricultural practices which support at least 300,000 Aymara in Peru, and about twice that number in the Bolivian *altiplano* (Carter 1964: 1, Plummer 1966: 55).

During the past twenty-five years the Aymara way of life has undergone tremendous change. The picture of homogeneity and equilibrium in Aymara culture described by earlier anthropologists in the *altiplano* (see LaBarre 1948, and Tschopik 1946) has altered as new solutions had to be discovered by the Aymara for the problems of a rapidly changing social and physical world. More recent research by anthropologists (Brown 1978; Buechler and Buechler 1971; Carter 1964; Donahue 1972; Heath 1973; Hickman 1963; Lewellen 1978) has given us a very different picture of Aymara life.

A land-base shrinking with each new generation, the rapid growth of money markets, the expansion of job opportunities on the coast, and the construction and improvement of systems of roads and transportation have combined to produce fundamental changes in Aymara socioeconomic organization, population, family structure, and values.

The kind and extent of the reactions to these changes are not uniform in all Aymara communities. In some parts of the *altiplano,* centuries-old institutions and methods of problem-solving persist; in other areas with apparently similar environmental and social conditions, change and innovation at the expense of traditional ways of life are evident. One of the areas which exhibits differential change is population dynamics. An examination of the demographic characteristics of Challapujo (population, 533) and Challacollo (population, 202), two rural Aymara communities in the Department of Puno, Peru, demonstrates this.

The demographic data for the two communities show a crude birthrate of approximately 34 per thousand in Challacollo and 36 per thousand in Challapujo. These rates are low compared with the crude birthrates of 42 to 46 per thousand reported by James (1969: 450) for all of Peru. The Challapujeños experience a crude mortality rate of no less than fifteen to eighteen per thousand, while the Challacolleños show a rate of only eleven or twelve per thousand. Thus, Challacollo is growing at an annual rate of 2.3 to 2.4 percent, while Challapujo's annual rate of increase is only 1.8 to two percent.

Median age, another indicator of population growth, is also significantly different for the two communities. Challacollo has a median age of 15.2 years, while in Challapujo the median age is 19.3 years, indicating a faster growing population for Challacollo.

Perhaps the most striking difference between the two communities is in the area of infant and child mortality. In Challapujo, I found a child mortality rate of 37.9 percent for the first five years of life. Over 68 percent of these deaths occur during the first year. In Challacollo child deaths during the first five years of life average 31 percent, with only 39 percent of these occurring during the first year.

It is clear from the above data that Challacollo is experiencing a faster rate of growth than Challapujo. This situation raises questions concerning the cause of population growth in Challacollo. The data show that the Challacolleños are not having more children; rather, a higher percentage of their children are surviving. This is also shown by the fact that the average number of children per family is 3.55 in Challacollo and 3.16 in Challapujo. How is the survival rate of children being affected in Challacollo? Are the factors of disease control and improved nutrition responsible? Are Challacollo parents deliberately choosing larger family size? If this is the case, how are they affecting the survival rate of their children? The remainder of this paper will address these questions.

DISEASE CONTROL IN THE ALTIPLANO

Cosmopolitan medical treatment and drugs are available through health clinics and pharmacies in many towns in the *altiplano*. In addition, Peru's Ministry of Health has established local clinics in a number of rural communities in the *altiplano*. Thus, access to treatment of health problems is available to many Aymara, including the peoples of Challapujo and Challacollo. If disease control is behind Challacollo's faster growing population, then we might expect that the Challacolleños would show a higher frequency of use of cosmopolitan medical facilities than the Challapujeños. But, as Table I shows, there is no significant difference between Challacollo and Challapujo in the use of these facilities. Furthermore, in both groups over 75 percent of those questioned[1] report that they rely on traditional folk medicine.

NUTRITION

As I have shown elsewhere (Brown 1978: 57-65), the traditional diet of the Aymara contains enough proteins, vitamins, minerals and calories to maintain the populations of Challapujo and Challacollo above the level of malnutrition (see also Carter 1964: 22). Furthermore, if nutritional factors were responsible for the differences in population growth between the two,

TABLE I

USE OF MODERN MEDICAL FACILITIES: RESPONSES
TO SELECTED QUESTIONS

	Challapujo	*Challacollo*
1. When your children are sick do you take them to the local clinic or to a native curer?		
A. Local clinic	.29	.31
B. Native curer	.71	.69
2. *How many times during the past five years have you or your wife gone to the local clinic?		
Husband	.21	.19
Wife	.18	.20
3. When you are sick, what do you usually do?		
A. Go the the native curer and take natural remedies.	.46	.48
B. Go to the native curer and take natural remedies as well as medicines from the pharmacy.	.29	.26
C. Go to the native curer and take natural remedies as well as medicines, and sometimes go to the doctor.	.13	.07
D. Take medicines from the pharmacy and sometimes go to the doctor	.12	.19

*Responses to question 2 represent average number of times that adults in sample population have gone to local clinics. Responses to other questions in this table represent percentages of sample population.

then we would expect to find greater evidence of undernourishment in Challapujo. However, a recent study of Challapujo diet and nutrition by Mitchell (1979) reveals that the Challapujeños are not undernourished. Mitchell states:

> In spite of contradicting our standard indicators of good nutrition, the Challapujo diet does apparently meet daily needs. That is, obvious signs of undernourishment are not present. Kwashiorkor does not occur in the children. Other readily observable signs such as emaciation, depigmentation or roughness of skin or hair are also absent. Furthermore, normal healthy adults maintain normal body weight and activity level (p. 2).

Differential rates of infant and child mortality found in Challapujo and Challacollo also pose problems for the under-nutrition hypothesis. As Eckholm reports:

> Most deaths associated with infant undernutrition occur during or after weaning, as mother's milk is supplemented with or replaced by other foods. . . . As leading nutritionists Nevin Scrimshaw and Moisés Béhar observe, the mortality rate of children from one to four years of age—those in the postweaning period—is the best measure of malnutrition in a country (1977: 48-9).

During the first year of life, Aymara infants subsist almost entirely on mother's milk. Infants seldom go hungry since they are fed on demand. Aymara children breastfeed for two years on the average, with the addition of solid foods to their diet occurring during the second year (Buechler and Buechler 1971:24). Thus, if undernutrition were reponsible for the higher rate of childhood deaths found in Challapujo, we should find mortality to be highest after the second, or possibly the first, year of life. But, as I have stated above, it is during the *first* year of life that Challapujo children suffer the highest mortality—the period when they are receiving possibly the highest level of nutrition they will ever enjoy.

DEMAND FOR LABOR IN CHALLACOLLO

Another way of explaining population growth is to assume that parents have the ability to control consciously the size of their family. In this view, population growth is seen as the consequence of voluntary actions on the part of parents who desire more children.

The choice of family size is usually associated only with western populations which have access to modern birth control methods. Preindustrial populations are assumed to lack the means to affect either fertility or mortality. However, Benjamin White has recently questioned this assumption. In his study of population growth in Java, White concluded that population growth was the result of *conscious* efforts of Javanese parents to increase the size of their families by suspending indigenous population controls of infanticide and abortion (1973: 232). White found that the Javanese peasants were faced with the loss of labor need for subsistence production when the Dutch colonial government instituted a labor tax which required the Javanese to commit their labor to public projects. In order to maintain sufficient labor for their fields *and* meet the labor demands of the government, the Javanese decided to increase the size of their families by suspending the practices of infanticide and abortion. In this case, the added cost of raising larger families was offset by the need for more labor.

In a similar study, Mamdani (1972) demonstrated that peasants in Manupur, India, consciously attempt to have as many children as possible. Given the environmental conditions of life in Manupur, children produce more for the family than they consume. In the perception of Indian parents, the economic return from a large family exceed the cost of feeding more children.

The explanations given by White and Mamdani for population growth in Java and India are based on the "Demand for Labor" hypothesis. According to this hypothesis, social and economic conditions exist which select for large family size in order to increase the family's economic production. Under these conditions, a peasant family is confronted with the possibility of a decline in production (as in Java) or economic growth (as in India). In order to avoid the former or attain the latter, parents will consciously attempt to increase the family's labor supply.

The data for Challacollo and Challapujo support this hypothesis. As Table II shows, both the Challapujeños and the Challacolleños recognize that too many children can bring economic hardship to the family. Of greater demographic importance, however, is the fact that the two communities differ in their perception of what constitutes too many children. Obviously, the meaning of "too many children" depends upon what the members of the community consider to be a

TABLE II

DESIRED FAMILY SIZE: RESPONSE TO SELECTED QUESTIONS

	Challapujo	*Challacollo*
1. In your opinion what would be the perfect number of sons and daughters for a family?	*Average Responses*	
Sons	1.96	2.5
Daughters	1.5	1.97
2. *It is better to have a lot of children so that parents can be sure that someone will take care of them in their old age.	*% of Responses*	
Agree	.00	.16
In Part	.56	.40
Disagree	.43	.43
No response or don't know	.01	.01
3. It is better to have few children so that each one may have a better inheritance.		
Agree	.96	.71
In Part	.04	.22
Disagree	.00	.06
No response or don't know	.00	.01
4. *In order to be rich a person must have many children.		
Agree	.00	.10
In Part	.00	.32
Disagree	.93	.57
No response or don't know	.07	.01
5. A man who has many children is lucky because he has lots of help with the work of his fields.		
Agree	.04	.08
In Part	.33	.48
Disagree	.63	.44
No response or don't know	.00	.00

*Significant difference as measured by the chi square test at the .001 level of significance.

normal, adequate or ideal family size. Thus, while two groups may both agree that too many children create a hardship, the outcome in terms of family size will be different if one group considers, for example, five children ideal while the other sees three children as the most desirable number. Now, in the case of Challapujo and Challacollo, responses to the first question in Table II—ideal family size—show that the Challapujeños consider 3.46 children to be ideal, while the Challacolleños desire 4.47 children. Although this difference may appear to be small, it is substantial in terms of long-term demographic consequences. Furthermore, a significantly greater percentage of Challacollo parents consistently expressed less disagreement with statements that correlated wealth or other benefits with large family size.

The reason for these differences is found in the differential response of the two communities to change in social and economic conditions in Peru, leading to differential demand for labor. An examination of traditional Aymara production and the effects that socioeconomic change has had on this system will demonstrate this.

The Aymara nuclear family household is the principal unit of production. Throughout most of the year the members of the family supply all the needed labor and talent for traditional agricultural activities. However, during the periods of planting, weeding, and harvest, the nuclear family lacks sufficient manpower to complete the work within the strict time limits of the growing season set by the *altiplano* climate. The Aymara nuclear family can count on extra labor during these critical periods from the members of the family's kindred.

The members of the Aymara kindred are bound by the strong and enduring obligations of kinship to render assistance to one another under an ancient Andean system of labor reciprocity known as *ayni*. *Ayni* ("social duty" or "the obligation to return a benefit of favor") involves the direct exchange of labor between individual members of the kindred. *Ayni* debts cannot be reciprocated with money, nor can the labor be returned by helping with another task. For example, if a man helps another with planting, the person who receives help cannot cancel the debt by offering his assistance with, say, adobe-making. If help is given with planting it must be returned with planting, and it must be returned during the same growing season in which it is given. *Ayni* debts are repaid within a very short period of time, usually within a few days of receiving help. Careful records are kept—either written or mental—to ensure that both parties receive their fair share of labor.

Ayni relationships make sure that the nuclear family will receive all the additional labor it needs without increasing family size. This is critical in an environment such as the *altiplano* where large population densities cannot be supported. As described above, resources are limited and environmental fluctuations are severe in the *aliplano*. Under these conditions, the benefit derived from child labor can be quickly reversed if a family produces too many children. Thus, because of *ayni,* a family need not produce more children than it can afford; but it still has access to the extra labor it needs during critical periods of the year.

The expansion and improvements of roads and systems of transportation, and the growth of job opportunities on Peru's southern coast are having a profound impact on traditional Aymara practices, including *ayni* relationships. This impact is much greater in Challacollo than in Challapujo.

Every year thousands of Aymara men leave the *sierra* and head to the towns and cities of the coast in search of wage labor to supplement their incomes from agriculture. While this phenomenon touches practically every Aymara community in the *altiplano,* the length of stay and the type of work that is performed on the coast varies greatly from community to community. Differences in seasonal wage labor migration experiences are evident between Challacollo and Challapujo.

Because of historical and other factors, the majority of wage labor migrants from Challapujo work in the fields of the rice plantations near the coastal town of Camaná, while the Challacolleños work in construction in the town of Ilo. Since the Challapujeños work almost exclusively at the task of harvesting the rice, the amount of time they can spend on the coast is limited by the coastal growing season. The Challacolleños, on the other hand, are not limited in the amount of time they can spend at such jobs as carpentry and stone masonry. In addition, the Challacolleños earn more for their efforts than the Challapujeños.

The impact of seasonal wage labor migration upon *ayni* and other aspects of Aymara culture is, in part, a function of the amount of time that migrants are willing and able to spend on the coast. In Challapujo, wage labor migrants spend an average of 1.78 months on the coast. Since the majority of migrants make the trip during the slow periods of agricultural production in the *altiplano*, their absence has very little effect on the kindred's labor pool. During the critical periods of planting and harvest, the men are present to meet the kindred's labor needs.

The Challacolleños, on the other hand, spend an average of 4.78 months away from their fields. Many spend eight to ten months on the coast, only returning to Challacollo to visit friends and relatives during fiestas or to supervise the sale of their produce in the local markets. Consequently, many Challacolleños are absent during the critical periods of greatest labor need, when *ayni* relationships are the most important. Since they cannot return *ayni* labor, they are forced to hire laborers to work their fields in their absence. Although nothing prevents them from returning to Challacollo during planting and harvest, many of them see their time on the coast as more valuable than the time they spend in their fields. The money that a man has to spend on labor is much less than the amount he would lose if he returned to Challacollo for the long work of plowing and harvesting.

These shifts in the social and economic relationships of nuclear families in Challacollo have led to a demand for more labor and, thus, a desire for more children. The Challacolleños desire more children because they perceive that having a large family means more income. The following statement from a Challacolleño who spends much of his time on the coast explains the economic advantage of a large family:

> I can earn a lot of money as a bricklayer in Ilo. If I have to return to Challacollo for the planting or the harvest, I will lose money. A man can make more money in Ilo. Today the *mestizos* don't pay as good a price for produce as they did in the past. I always give money to my wife so she can pay others to work my fields. But a man with many sons doesn't have to pay for much help. His sons can do the work. My oldest son, Domingo, works with me in Ilo. Some day he will make a lot of money. My brother has many sons. He is lucky

because he takes Juan [his oldest son] to Ilo with him. His other sons [he has three others] stay in Challacollo and work the fields. He never pays for work in his fields.

There are few economic rewards to be had from a large family in Challapujo. Since the men can only spend one or two months working in the rice fields in Camaná, they are usually present in the community during the heaviest periods of field-work. Thus, they can count on the labor resources of the kindred for any assistance they require. In contrast, the breakdown of reciprocal labor in Challacollo has increased the labor needs of many households. The motivation for larger family size in Challocollo is clear: having more children means greater income from coastal wage labor and less expense in agricultural production.

SUSPENSION OF INDIGENOUS CONTROLS: THE MECHANISM OF POPULATION GROWTH

Thus far, I have outlined the major sociocultural variables which have created a demand for more children in Challacollo. Now, I will discuss the mechanism by which Challacollo parents achieve their goal of larger family size: the voluntary suspension of indigenous methods of population control. This section begins with a brief outline of these methods, followed by a discussion of the data for Challapujo and Challacollo which suggests that the differences in infant mortality between the two communities is the result of differences in the frequency of use of these methods.

Many centuries of life in the rugged *altiplano* have made the Aymara acutely aware of the need to maintain a balance between their meager resources and the number of their offspring. Like many other preindustrial societies, the Aymara developed population control mechanisms long before the advent of modern contraceptive devices, in response to the demands of life in a harsh and limiting environment. They manage their reproductive potential through a series of cultural practices which help keep population levels below the point of environmental deterioration, while still supplying the needed labor for their fields and herds. While some of these practices control reproductive rates by lessening fertility, the most effective measures are those which maintain high rates of infant mortality. A brief description of the two most important practices is given below.

Abortion

Aymara midwives are knowledgeable in the preparation and use of a number of locally available herbs which cause contractions of the uterus, expelling the fetus. The herbs taken to induce abortion include *ruta* (English "rue"), *altamira, it"apillu,* and *qarwa-qarwa.* These are usually taken in the form of a tea made from the herb. Carter (1977: 180) also reports the use of *wachanqa* (or *k'it"a ch'uai*), a locally available tuber. A few drops from the tuber are mixed with a cup of oregano to induce abortion. LaBarre (1948: 119) also reported herbal aborticants made from the orange flowers of a spring nettle, and the Buechlers (1971: 20) write that potions made from eucalyptus leaves, vaseline, and cane alcohol are also used. In addition, more and more Aymara women are using contraction producing drugs available in the town pharmacies.

Abortions are also induced through mechanical means. These include tying a belt tightly around the waist, carrying a heavy load, and being beaten (Buechler and Buechler 1971: 20). Voluntary abortions are also caused by vigorous dancing during fiestas accompanied by the consumption of large quantities of cane alcohol. The effectiveness of this method is shown by the observation of Mary Sloan, a missionary and trained midwife with 30 years experience in the *altiplano,* that miscarriages are much more frequent following a fiesta (1977).

Infanticide

Although infanticide is thought to be less desirable than abortion as a means of population control, it is still common in the *altiplano.* The women were very hesitant to discuss infanticide because of fear of supernatural sanctions which surround the death of an unnamed or unbaptized child. The Aymara are also aware of the attitudes of outsiders concerning the killing of unwanted children. Virtually no women reported using infanticide, but all informants (both male and female) talked about it in reference to other women in the community. In trying to discover what birth control practices exist in the *altiplano,* I asked the women what a woman does if she has a child that she does not want or cannot take care of. Many women were afraid to answer this question. However, of the 47 percent who did respond, over 70 percent answered that a woman intentionally kills the child.

Further evidence for the existence of infanticide is found in the ratio of male to female infants who die in the *altiplano*. According to Sloan, female infants are slightly stronger at birth than male infants. But in both Challapujo and Challacollo, 9.5 percent more female children died in early infancy than male children. Higher rates of female infanticide are expected, given the expressed desire of both groups for more male children than females (see Table II). Male children are desired over females because of the former's greater economic worth in the fields and on the coast.

Infanticide is achieved in a number of ways. Neglect of the newborn probably accounts for most of the cases of infanticide. The child is simply deprived of sufficient milk, or given sugar water as a milk substitute.

Many infants are also killed outright immediately after birth through both institutional and personal means. After the birth of a child, the infant is bathed in cold water and left uncovered. This proves fatal to many weak infants, especially during the winter months.

The next trial the newborn faces can also result in death. The baby is give cane alcohol to drink soon after birth. The Aymara believe this will strengthen the stomach and give the child protection against sickness during his or her lifetime. If only a small amount is given to the child the result is usually not harmful. However, if a woman does not want the child it is a simple matter to give it a fatal dose. Giving too much alcohol to a newborn is probably the most common form of intentional infanticide in the *altiplano*. The mother may also kill the child by smothering it with a blanket or by holding it too tightly against her breast.

Unwanted children may also be given away. The child may be given to a childless couple in the community, or sold to rich families from Arequipa or Lima who come up to the *altiplano* in search of cheap labor for their households. In most cases the practice of giving away children is actually another form of infanticide. Usually an unwanted child will be given to an older female relative who, lacking her own milk, will give the child sugar water. Of the women who responded to my question about what a woman does if she has a child she does not want, 30 percent mentioned the giving away of children.

While these practices are found in both communities, the data I have suggest that they are being used less frequently in Challacollo. As I stated above, the women in both communities were unwilling to discuss their own cases of the use of infanticide. Consequently, the exact frequency of occurrence of infanticide is unknown. However, other data supports the conclusion that it does not occur as often in Challacollo as in Challapujo.

Infanticide is normally performed immediately after birth, or, in the case of giving children away, within a few months after birth. Consequently, if infanticide is occurring less often in Challacollo, then a lower rate of infant mortality would be expected. This is, indeed, the case. As I mentioned previously, in Challapujo, more than 68 percent of all childhood deaths occur during the first year of life, while in Challacollo only 39 percent of childhood deaths take place during this period.

Similar differences are found in the frequency of abortions. Only 3.4 percent of the women in Challacollo who have ever had children reported voluntary abortions for the five year period of 1972 to 1977. But in Challapujo, 44 percent of the women reported abortions for this same period, with an average of 1.5 per woman.

CONCLUSION

The factors which influence population growth in Aymara society are not beyond the cognition and control of the people. In Challacollo, changes in traditional patterns of agricultural production brought about by the exploitation of employment opportunities on the Peruvian coast have motivated the people to increase the size of their families. As we have seen this is accomplished through the voluntary suspension of indigenous methods of population control. In Challapujo, on the other hand, the impact of wage labor migration on traditional systems of production is not as great. Consequently, parents have little desire to increase family size. Thus, they still rely upon abortion and infanticide to keep population growth within limits set by the conditions of life in the *altiplano.*

From the viewpoint of anthropology, it comes, as no surprise that population growth rates in Aymara society are not determined solely by so-called "natural" or unconscious factors. Many investigators have found that, even in the absence of modern forms of birth control, reproductive rates in preindustrial societies are not set by Malthusian controls alone. Brass (1970), Burch and Gendel (1971), Carr-Saunders (1936), Demeny (1974), Hackenberg (1971), Nag (1962), Polgar (1971), and Stott (1969), among others, have found that most primitive and peasant societies possess the means of limiting their reproduction through a wide variety of both unconscious and conscious cultural practices.

Benedict (1972: 74-80) describes age at marriage, the incidence of separation and divorce, absence of a spouse, widowhood and widow remarriage, polygamy, post-partum sexual abstinence, abstinence during certain seasons or ceremonies, and temporary or permanent celibacy as among the unconscious controls. Benedict includes voluntary sexual abstinence, contraceptive practices such as *coitus interruptus*, abortion, and infanticide among the conscious controls humans have used.

Hardin (1970: 15) has compiled a list of some of the many things which people in preindustrial societies have used for contraception:

> It is incredible what human beings have used for this purpose. An incomplete list of the astounding things used at one time or another would include: okra seed pod, tannic acid, various seaweeds, lemon juice, the root of spotted cowbane, castor beans (quite poisonous), marjoram, thyme, parsley, lavender, rosemary.
>
> Crocus, myrtle, camphor, black hellebore, a small ball of opium, elephant dung, crocodile dung, camel dung.
>
> Olive oil, cedar oil, copper sulphate, willow, fern root, cabbage blossoms, a piece of bark tied in three knots, tea made from gunpowder and foam from a camel's mouth.

The message is clear: the problem of population growth in Latin America and other areas of the Third World cannot be approached successfully without a perspective that includes the relevant sociocultural variables which affect the dynamics of population. We can no longer afford to repeat the mistakes of the Khana Study.

NOTES

1. The data were collected by means of open-ended interviews, a formal questionnaire, and structured interviews which followed the completion of the questionnaire. The questionnaire was administered to ninety families in Challapujo and twenty-nine families in Challacollo. This represents 77 percent of all families in Challapujo and 70 percent of the families in Challacollo. The size of the sample population was 405 (out of a total population of 533) for Challapujo, and 141 (out of a total population of 202) for Challacollo. The complete questionnaire is included in the appendix of Brown 1978.

REFERENCES

Benedict, Burton. "Social Regulation of Fertility." In *The Structure of Human Populations.* G.A. Harrison, ed. Oxford: Clarendon Press, 1972.

Brass, W. "The Growth of World Population." In *Population Control,* Anthony Allison, ed., pp. 131-151. London: Penguin Books, 1970.

Brown, Paul F. *"Fuerza por Fuerza*: Ecology and Culture Change among the Aymara of Southern Peru." Unpublished Ph.D. Dissertation, University of Colorado, Boulder, 1978.

Buechler, Hans C., and Judith-Marie Buechler. *The Bolivian Aymara.* New York: Holt, Rinehart and Winston, 1971.

Burch, Thomas K., and Murray Gendel. "Extended Family Structure and Fertility: Some Conceptual and Methodological Issues." In *Culture and Population: A Collection of Current Studies.* Steven Polgar, ed. Chapel Hill: Carolina Population Center, 1971.

Carr-Saunders, A.M. *World Population.* London: Oxford at the Clarendon Press, 1936.

Carter, William E. *Aymara Communities and the Bolivian Agrarian Reform.* University of Florida Monographs in the Social Sciences No. 24. Gainesville, Florida: University of Florida Press, 1964.

_____ . "Trial Marriage in the Andes?" In *Andean Kinship and Marriage.* Ralph Bolton and Enrique Mayer, eds. American Anthropological Association, Special Publication No. 7, pp. 177-216, 1977.

Davis, Kingsley. "Population." *Scientific American* 220: 45-56, 1963.

Demeny, Paul. "The Population of the Underdeveloped Countries." *Scientific American* 231: 148-59, 1974.

Dew, Edward. *Politics in the Altiplano: The Dynamics of Change in Rural Peru*. Austin: University of Texas Press, 1969.

Donahue, John M. "Circular Migration in Southern Peru: An Anthropological Perspective." Unpublished Manuscript. Program in Applied Anthropology, Teachers College, Columbia University, 1972.

Eckholm, Erik P. *The Picture of Health: Environmental Sources of Disease*. New York: W.W. Norton and Company, 1977.

Freedman, Ronald, and Bernard Berelson. "The Human Population." *Scientific American* 231: 30-9, 1974.

Hackenberg, Robert A., ed. *Population as a Field for Anthropological Research*. Boulder, Colorado: Institute of Behavioral Science, 1971.

Hardin, Garrett. *Birth Control*. New York: Pegasus, 1970.

Hauser, Philip M. "World Population Growth." In *The Population Dilemma*, Philip M. Hauser, ed., pp. 12-33. Englewood Cliffs, New Jersey: Prentice-Hall, 1969.

Heath, Dwight B. *New Patterns for Old: Changing Patron-Client Relationships in the Bolivian Yungas*, 1973.

Hickman, John M. "The Aymara of Chinchera, Peru: Persistence and Change in a Bicultural Context." Doctoral Dissertation, Cornell University. University Microfilms No. 64-3641, 1963.

James, Preston. *Latin America*. New York: The Odyssey Press. Fourth Edition, 1969.

LaBarre, Weston. *The Aymara Indians of the Lake Titicaca Plateau, Bolivia*. Memoirs of the American Anthropological Association, No. 68, 1948.

Lewellen, Ted. *Peasants in Transition: The Changing Economy of the Peruvian Aymara: A General Systems Approach*. Boulder Colorado: Westview Press, 1978.

Mamdani, Mahmood. *The Myth of Population Control: Family, Caste, and Class in an Indian Village*. New York: Monthly Review Press, 1972.

Mitchell, Winifred L. "A Reconsideration of Andean Nutrition." Paper presented at the Annual Meetings of the American Anthropological Association, November, Cincinnati, Ohio, 1979.

Nag, Moni. *Factors Affecting Human Fertility in Non-Industrial Societies*. New Haven: Yale University Publications in Anthropology, No. 66, 1962.

Plummer, John F. "Another Look at Aymara Personality." *Behavior Science Notes* 1: 55-78, 1966.

Polgar, Steven. "Culture, History and Population Dynamics." In *Culture and Population: A Collection of Current Studies,* Steven Polgar, ed., pp. 3-8. Chapel Hill: Carolina Population Center, 1971.

Sloan, Mary. Personal Communication, 1977.

Stott, D.H. "Cultural and Natural Checks on Population Growth." In *Environment and Cultural Behavior: Ecological Studies in Cultural Anthropology,* Andrew P. Vayda, ed., pp. 90-120. New York: The Natural History Press, 1969.

Thomas, R. Brooke. "Human Adaptation to a High Andean Energy Flow System." *Occasional Papers in Anthropology,* No. 7. University Park: Pennsylvania State University, Department of Anthropology, 1973.

Tietelbaum, Michael S. "Population and Development: Is a Consensus Possible?" Ford Foundation Reprint from *Foreign Affairs,* July, pp. 742-760, 1974.

Tschopik, Harry, Jr. "The Aymara." In *Handbook of South American Indians,* Vol 2, Julian Steward, ed. Bureau of American Ethnology. Washington, D.C.: Government Printing Office, 1946.

White, Benjamin. "Demand for Labor and Population Growth in Colonial Java." *Human Ecology* 1: 217-236, 1973.

Winterhalder, Bruce, Robert Larsen, and R. Brooke Thomas. "Dung as an Essential Resource in an Highland Peruvian Community." *Human Ecology* 2: 89-104, 1974.

Young, Louise B. "Forward." In *Population in Perspective,* Louise B. Young, ed, pp. v-xi. London: Oxford University Press, 1968.

RURAL STABILITY AND FORCED OUTMIGRATION: THE PARADOX OF AGRARIAN REFORM IN MEXICO

Rodney C. Kirk

This paper explores what initially seem to be quite contradictory characteristics of the *ejido* agrarian reform program in Mexico. The program was designed amidst ideological rhetoric of revolutionary reform yet only pragmatically implemented to pacify and stabilize areas where peasant unrest proved generally indomitable by other means. With the 1934-1940 presidency of Lázaro Cárdenas, new dimensions were added to the reform. Chief among these were, first, widespread implementation of the reform program throughout the national entity and, second, inclusion of support for the economic, social, and political development of the rural countryside. Since 1940, the rhetoric of reform and development has continued publicly but, as I hope to demonstrate, the program has actually resulted in neither the economic development nor the security and stability of the rural population but, rather, in a condition which I have termed elsewhere as "designed unemployment" (Kirk 1979). The constraints placed upon the agrarian reform communities, the *ejidos,* by successive administrations have resulted in a retardation of the productive development and the economic well-being of the ejido sector, have resulted in dramatic increases in unemployment and underemployment (ultimately throughout the nation), and have provided the impetus for a mounting migration from the rural areas of the urban centers of Mexico and to the labor market of the United States.

Despite the acclaimed "Mexican miracle" of industrial growth and increasing productivity in various other sectors of the Mexican economy, national unemployment and underemployment have increased to an estimated 50 percent of the workforce (Clement and Green 1978: 48-51), and the gap in income distribution has increased accordingly. Between 1950 and 1969, for example, the share of participation in national family income for the upper 20 percent of the population increased from 59.8% to 64.0%, while that of the lowest 20 percent of the population dropped from 6.1% to 4.0% (Nagel 1978: 11).

In exploring the political and economic factors which have impinged upon, and which have formed a part of, the setting or context for Mexican ejidos, I will begin by drawing chiefly from my own data concerning a collectivized plantation ejido in the north-central part of Yucatán. Following sections focus on noted parallels with the ejido experience in the northern areas of Mexico and the latter portion of the paper returns to a discussion of the impact of the ejido question upon the larger society and a review of the prospects for the ejidos, ejidatarios, and Mexico.

CASE STUDY: A YUCATEC PLANTATION EJIDO

The case community of San Antonio[1] is an ex-hacienda, collectivized, ejido land-reform community of approximately 300 people. It is located in what is considered to be the heart of the fiber-producing, henequen zone of northern Yucatán. Contemporary San Antonio has existed, and continues to exist, as the lowest productive appendage of the monocrop export economy of the state. For nearly a century, residents of this Yucatec-Mayan community have labored to supply the raw materials, the harvested henequen leaves, which are processed locally to extract a natural fiber used in Mérida to manufacture associated products (baler twine, etc.) for export.

Prior to 1937, the ejido lands and community itself were part of the larger holdings of Hacienda San Antonio. Together, these family-owned holdings formed an integrated production unit comprised of lands, labor, and a primary processing factory, or decorticating plant, separating the fiber from the pulp and skin of the henequen agave (Agave fourcroydes). Throughout much of this period, Mayan workers received, in return for wage labor *and* obligatory labor (*fagina* or *faena*) a house, a small plot of land to cultivate in their spare time, and "paper" wages in the form of "chits" or a credit account at the hacienda store (the *tienda de raya* or "company store"). Though debt peonage was officially abolished in 1914, the *tienda de raya* continued to inhibit out-migration by effectively preventing the necessary capital accumulation. The patrón and his administrators not only controlled all aspects of the cultivation of the fields and the production of the henequen fiber, but also regulated community life, rewarding those loyal and diligent workers and severely punishing others who acted contrary to the owner's image of "proper" productive and social behavior.

Early post-revolutionary reforms in northern Yucatán (during the period 1917-1925) affected primarily the larger towns, and only lands as yet unplanted in henequen or other crops were subjected to "redistribution." During this period the producing hacienda lands of San Antonio remained untouched and the "acasillados" or resident hacienda workers and their families were exempt from the provisions of the agrarian reform law. For San Antonio, the first reforms meant that the total holdings of the hacienda were reduced, but production and the core labor pool were essentially unaffected by the land reform legislation. (DAAC Archives)

THE FAILURE OF THE CÁRDENAS REFORMS

In 1937, Lázaro Cárdenas, then well into his six-year term of office, arrived in Mérida to announce a massive agrarian reform program. Full implementation of Cárdenas' program not only would restructure the distribution of land holdings and tenure, but also was intended to extend control over the industrial means of production to the ejidatarios. Cárdenas planned to create "integrated agricultural and industrial units" (Cárdenas 1937: 341), giving the ejidatarios land, federally supplied financial and technical assistance, and, more importantly, usufruct rights to, or complete ownership of, the fiber-producing decorticator factories of the expropriated haciendas.

At the end of Cárdenas' term of office, Canto Echeverría, governor of Yucatán, usurped federal control and transformed the entire henequen zone into one single ejido which he referred to as the "Gran Ejido Henequenero." This "gran ejido" was administered by a state organization, *Henequeneros de Yucatán*, which was run chiefly by the governor and an appointed board formed from the ranks of the ex-landowners. Of the few factories which had actually been expropriated under the Cárdenas reform (36 out of a total of 300), all but two were returned to their previous owners (Rodriguez 1966: 267). For the use of the now privately-owned decorticating factories, *Henequeneros* paid the ex-hacienda owners 52 percent of the fiber produced by the decortication of *ejido* leaves (DAAC Archives). For their efforts in the cultivation, weeding, and harvesting of leaves, the ejidatarios received revenue from the remaining 48 percent of the fiber extracted. From this amount were deducted the costs of *Henequeneros* administration: the various commissions charged for the management and accounting, and payment of the salaries of Henequeneros' employees (Ganzález Navarro 1970: 267; Rodriguez 1966: 279-280). Land reform, from one perspective, released the ex-haciendados from the obligations to maintain and provide for the workers and from the investment burdens and risks associated with the planting and maintenance of new henequen fields.[2] One author has concluded that the governor, through *Henequeneros,* had transformed the henequen zone not into a "Gran Ejido" but, rather, into a "Gran Hacienda" which even further intensified the patterns of exploitation of the Mayan peasant-proletarian (Benitez 1962: 136).

THE RESUMPTION OF FEDERAL CONTROL

In 1955, two events altered the structure of institutional control over henequen production and the labor force. Because of serious abuses by the state, the federal government resumed control of the henequen ejidos. In that same year, the Federal Agricultural Credit Law was passed to regulate relations between ejidos and the national ejido and agricultural credit banks. The law included sections which gave the Ejido Bank (Banjidal) absolute control over the productive exploitation of indebted "client" ejidos; it included provisions which divided the large collective ejidos, which were often able to exert considerable political and economic influence within a region, into smaller sub-groups (referred to officially as "grupos solidarios"); and it included prohibitions against collective or cooperative activities being organized which would link various ejidos together. The Agricultural Credit Law of 1955 (which is still in force in Mexico) has proved an intriguing vehicle used by the government to intensify control over the ejidos and to limit horizontal integration of ejidos into potentially powerful blocs.

During the period 1955 to 1963, charges mounted accusing the administrators of the Banjidal of skimming and defrauding the Mayan ejidatarios of an estimated 18 million pesos (Menéndez 1964). The official governmental response to the charges involved dissolving the Banjidal branch in Mérida, transferring the administrators to another part of Mexico, and installing a regional bank branch, the *Bangrario* (Banco Agrario de Yucatán, S.A.) to take the place of the Banjidal. This shift occurred in 1962, and since that time the regional bank has undergone two acronym changes and an impressive turnover in top and middle-level personnel. Charges of corruption and fraud are periodically levelled at the various Bangrario regimes, and it is difficult to assess what proportion of the charges are legitimate and what proportion express the resentment over local personnel and control being replaced from and by Mexico City.

By the first field work period, during 1970-1971, the Bangrario, as it was then termed, claimed that the ejido of San Antonio had incurrred a total debt of $500,000 pesos which had been carried over, with interest, from the earlier periods of both Henequeneros and the Banjidal. Although the elected officials of the ejido were never given an exact accounting of how this debt had accumulated, it meant nevertheless that they would never receive "profits" from their productive efforts.

For San Antonio, there exists nearly total dependence upon the regional Bangrario: the ejido receives a weekly work allotment sheet from the Bangrario which dictates the number of leaves to be harvested, the amount of land to be cleared, weeded, or replanted, the amount of work assigned for the repair of walls, and access road, etc. The Bangrario provides weekly compensation to the worker, charging these "wages" against the short-term "avío" account if the fields are in full production or against the long-term "refaccionario" account if the fields are under cultivation but not yet into full production. In the name of the ejido, the Bangrario contracts for the decortication of leaves in the local factory of the ex-hacendado (referred to as the *pequeño propietario*) and arranges for the transport, storage, and final sale of the fiber to the federally-controlled manufacturing complex of CORDEMEX (Cordeleros de México) in Mérida. CORDEMEX regularly classifies ejido fiber as low in quality and assigns low value to its "purchase" of the fiber from the Bangrario. Ejido fiber is derived by the same processes as employed by the factory owner on his own remnant holdings, but the ejidatarios consistently receive considerably less for their henequen fiber.

THE CONTRADICTIONS OF REFORM

Despite a reform ideology which stresses the social, political, and economic autonomy and development of the ejido communities,[3] San Antonio and other ejidos have been denied the benefits of compensation proportionate to productive effort. Work outside of that authorized by the Bangrario is neither permitted nor compensated and the indebted ejidos are prohibited from marketing their henequen fiber outside of the Bangrario itself. For nearly forty years, the ejidatarios have been exposed, on the one hand, to the public and official expression of reform ideology and the promise of massive changes in the general economic life and well-being of the ejidatario and, on the other hand, they have experienced only the receipt and deceit of wages paid for assigned tasks performed on a weekly basis. At the community level, the ejidatarios of San Antonio see themselves as captive wage-laborers in the employ of a succession of faceless, bureaucratic *patrones* rather than an actual hacendado. No longer tied to the land and a landowner by means of indebted servitude, the ejidatarios are presently the indebted "clients" of the controlling institution of the Bangrario.

Of the total 1971 worker population in San Antonio, the majority worked at least part-time for the pequeño propietario. Of the total estimated weekly income of $27 pesos per capita, fully one-half of that amount was gained from the employment provided by the propietario. A field estimate demonstrated that if the ejidatarios indeed controlled the decorticating factory of San Antonio, and received the owner's share of the profits, the *total* community income for 306 people, and from *all* sources, would at least double.

Presently, the henequen zone is generally characterized by

localized overpopulation (defined as a labor "surplus"), massive underemployment, and by underproductivity in the ejidal sector. It was estimated in an official publication (P.R.I. 1970) that there were at least 30,000 worker-families in the henequen zone that suffered from severe underemployment or under-utilization. This condition of "designed unemployment" was created by a program which allocated insufficient resources to support the ejidatarios *and* the siphon economy of the agencies of the state and federal governments and the ex-hacienda owners. Lacking incentives, production on many ejidos falls below that on the private holdings of the ex-hacendados (the legally protected "small holdings" or *pequeñas propiedades*). In the case of San Antonio, production on ejido lands fell only slightly below that on the private holdings. However, the small plots held individually by a few members of the ejido, and which were exempted from Bangrario control, produced a far greater yield of fiber per hectare than *either* the ejido or the private holdings (Kirk 1974).

Even projects which ostensibly were designed to improve the lot of the ejidatarios were executed in an exploitative and fraudulent fashion. During one field work period, the state and federal departments of agriculture, together with the ex-hacienda owner of the decorticating factory and private holdings, publicized the beginning of an experiment in truck-farming designed to improve drastically the economic and nutritional status of the ejidatario. An experiment was to be conducted which involved the raising of various vegetables on the fields which served as dumping grounds for the waste pulp (*bagazo*) from henequen processing. All agencies cooperating, a well was dug, a pump and extensive irrigation piping installed, and literally overnight, seedlings of various types were brought in from an agricultural research station and planted in the field. The day after the planting, state, federal, and United Nations officials were brought in from Mérida and shown the "magnificent" project. Once the officials left, the equipment was tested and it was discovered that the pump quickly taxed the reserves of the well and no irrigation in fact could take place. The seedlings, suffering from the lack of water and the trauma of being transplanted at too late a stage, all died. The official agencies lost interest but left their equipment. The propietario had the well enlarged, installed a smaller motor on the pump, and brought in new, appropriate seedlings. For a short time, about a dozen men from the community were employed by the project. The last time I visited the community in late 1976, only two men were working in the gardening "experiment" and they were from a town three miles distant. The owner believed the local workers were taking produce from the fields for their own use and thus lowering profits. The owner was selling the vegetables, which were of a high quality indeed, through the local *KOMESA* supermarket chain in Mérida. No workers from the community of San Antonio were employed in the latter stages of the project and the diet of no ejido family was improved because of this project. The project had actually displaced the few ejidatario families who had been raising vegetables in the waste field and using small gasoline pumps and buckets to water the plants. It is an additional fact that the decortication contract existing between the ejido and the factory owner specified that all fiber *and* waste products from decortication belonged to the members of the ejido. The factory owner was using the fertile waste pulp "belonging" to the ejido to profit personally through the truck gardening.

Nathaniel Raymond (1971, 1968), speaking to the tremendous exploitative constraints exerted by the state and federal institutions, noted considerable evidence for black-market dealings in leaves and fiber flowing surreptitiously from ejidos to the ex-hacendado propietarios. Leaves may be entered in the factory books as if they came from the propietarios' own lands or fiber may be shifted from one factory "pile" to another, leaving the impression that the ejido yield had simply declined. The effect is to inflate statistically private production and to deflate figures concerning ejidal production. The ejidatarios engage in these practices out of desperation, the owners engage in them out of the desire for both profits and the perpetuation of statistics which make the agrarian reform appear to be either a total failure or at the least, an unfortunate drain on the economy of the state and the nation.

YUCATEC REFORM: THE NORM

Striking parallels exist between the course of agrarian reform in Yucatán and that experienced in other areas within Mexico. A general assessment would be that the land reform ejido program has generally provided an insufficient resource base for even the minimal subsistence needs of the mass of the rural population. Despite outmigration, this problem has been aggravated by population growth and an ever increasing number of dependents existing on the ejidos. Stavenhagen (1978: 33) has concluded that a mass conversion of "subsistence plots" to "sub-family units" has occurred and, by his estimates, 84 percent of the farm units in Mexico may be identified as "sub-family units." The resulting meager resource base has forced and continues to force peasants and peasant-proletarians to seek supplementary income from a variety of other sources including part-time, temporary and/or seasonal employment in the regional private sectors; migrant or migratory labor, peasant-artisan or petty commodity production; or entry into the "tertiary" or service and commerce sectors of the Mexican *and* U.S. economies. (cf. Kirk 1976: 510; Littlefield 1978: 503-504; Singleman 1978: 53; Stavenhagen 1974: 130; Muñoz, Oliveira, and Stern 1979: 43-57; Whiteford and Henao 1979: 25-26, 30-31).

In my own research concerning the ejido land reform communities in the northeastern state of Tamaulipas (in the henequen zone surrounding Ciudad Victoria) I found further documentary evidence supporting the concept of "designed unemployment" as a feature of the agrarian reform. While analyzing archival materials (SRA Archives), I had the opportunity to examine the official pre-reform studies and calculations upon which expropriation and redistribution were based. In one particularly vivid case, the federal investigators calculated, in their 1932 report, that the total yearly costs to maintain an "average" peasant family (containing 3 adults and 3 children) amounted to $482.50 pesos per year. This amount included food, clothing, and "incidentals" categories. The investigators then recommended redistribution and specified an "average" plot size to be allocated to each head of household. Based on their own production calculations, the "average" ejidatario plot would have yielded a harvest valued at a total of $457.50 pesos per year, an amount $25 pesos *less* than the calculated minimal amount necessary to maintain the family unit. There was no attempt at providing leeway or flexibility to compensate for either fluctuations in the family size, nor for any seasonal variation in either the crop yield or the market conditions for the sale of such crops. In all of the documents studied, which represented official reports preparatory to reform, the basic question was never "how much land can a peasant cultivate? " but, rather, "what is the absolute minimal amount of land required to maintain a peasant family?" For the government to employ this criterion in the calculation of "basic" ejidatario plots and then to later criticize the peasants for failing to progress under the reform is simply ludicrous.

It should be clear at this point that what is often identified in the literature as a "peasant" or a "rural, dualistic," or a "precapitalist" economy is actually an economic structure which creates and perpetuates an inexpensive and highly elastic (perhaps "vulnerable" is a more appropriate term) labor supply which is made only nearly self-sufficient. Capitalist sectors of both Mexico and the United States have long utilized segments of these lower socioeconomic classes without the necessity of either enterprise or government directly assuming the burden of providing for the maintenance and reproduction of the work force. From the perspective of the U.S. economy, we can understand the attractiveness of the "cheap" *bracero,* green or white card holder, or undocumented *mojado* worker: growers, ranchers, and entrepreneurs pay little more than the temporary maintenance costs of the laborers. Once the contract period has ended, the worker is returned to Mexico, returned to survive as well as possible within an alternate, yet dependent economic sphere until the start of the next contract period. (Bustamante 1975; Burawoy 1976.)

Cynthia Hewett de Alcántara's study, *Modernizing Mexican Agriculture* (1976), provides ample evidence supporting the notion of "designed unemployment" and the intended failure of the agrarian reform program in Mexico (its failure to promote much real socioeconomic change in the rural sectors). Due to space constraints, only a few of her major points will be summarized below.

1. Following the termination of Cárdenas' term in office (post-1940), federally supported irrigation projects benefited the private sector more than the ejido sector. By the 1960's, 4.5 percent of the users controlled 35.5 percent of the irrigated farming area in Mexico

(1976: 13-16).

2. During the period from 1940 to 1950, the credit resources of the ejidal credit bank remained constant while credit provided the private sector more than doubled, increasing eight-fold by the 1970's (1976: 60).

3. High yielding "miracle" or "green revolution" seeds which were developed or acquired with public funds were made available first to the private sector, together with the needed fertilizers and insecticides (1976: 60).

4. When ejidatarios finally received such seeds from the Banjidal, they were frequently outdated seed varieties which no longer had an adequate germination rate and which were already known in the private sector to be susceptible to local varieties of rust (1976: 205).

5. Of those ejidos operating in the state of Sonora which were clients of the Banjidal, most were charged high prices for inferior supplies obtained through the bank, and were charged high fees, again via the bank, by the owners of agricultural machinery who were contracted by the Banjidal to work on the ejido lands (1976: 209).

6. Banjidal control over Sonora ejidos and delays and abuses in the fiscal relations between bank and ejido, forced many to sell at a loss on the black market in order to obtain needed cash (1976: 209-210).

7. The Banjidal operated to break up or prevent the formation of cooperative movements which attempted to link ejidos together over a region (1976: 194, 217). One large Sonoran collective ejido had attempted to pursue through the courts their charge that the Banjidal had defrauded them of 5 million pesos through manipulation of the ejidal cotton harvest. It is clear that small ejidos or individual ejidatarios would have been unable to pursue this complaint beyond the offices of the bank itself (1976: 217).

8. Commenting on the atmosphere of "corruption and disorganization" which accompanied the few attempts of the Banjidal to capitalize the ejido sector, Hewett notes "a rapid and spectacular rise in ejido debt." With the capital supplies and machinery obtained from the private sector and usually at high prices, Hewett concludes that "One might almost see the process as the transfer of wealth from the ejido and the public sector (through subsidies) to the private sector, through the forced provision of costly inputs to captive buyers." (1976: 208)

PROSPECTS

Unfortunately is is easy to recommend changes and program goals which would be expected to alter the nonprogressive course of agrarian reform. It is also unfortunate that such recommendations are extremely difficult to implement in a country controlled and influenced by such powerful national and international vested interests. It is clear that the immediate problem to be tackled is that of unemployment and under-employment. Francisco Alba calculated the 1970 under-employment rate to have varied between 37 percent and 45 percent of the work force and translated this figure into between 4.9 and 5.8 million underemployed in Mexico (Alba 1978: 506). Nagel, taking into account present population growth, calculated that 32 million new jobs would be needed by 1990 for Mexico to achieve anything approaching full employment of its labor force (Nagel 1978: 12).

The "green revolution" has been identified by some investigators as tending to accentuate income inequality in Mexico (Evans and James 1979: 12). Indeed, the ejidatarios I interviewed in the area of Ciudad Victoria, Tamaulipas, referred to the projects of the federal Secretaría or Department of Agriculture not as the "Revolución Verde" but as the "Robolución Verde" or "Green Robbery." Certainly for agricultural science to benefit the ejidatarios, emphasis should be placed on the development of strains of wheat, corn, beans, etc. which will provide increased yields in the drylands regions and in the absence of the other material inputs of special fertilizers, insecticides, etc.

More recently, the massive petroleum reserves are indicated as holding the promise for future Mexican development. The massive international debt and continuing unfavorable balance of trade increase the chances for a further denationalization of the Mexican economy. Curiously enough, as recently as 1973, PEMEX, the national petroleum company, was a net petroleum *importer* (Looney 1978: 83). Mexico must exercise caution in the form in which development capital is raised, and in the manner in which the petroleum is to be exploited.

Investment in the development of a petrochemical industry oriented towards production for the export market could be disastrous. Studies have indicated that this tremendously automated industry generates few jobs for the high investments required. Evans and James (1974: 14) state that $100 million invested in petrochemicals creates indirectly 1,000 jobs, while that same investment amount would create an estimated 102,000 jobs in clothing, 56,000 in footwear, and 49,000 jobs in wood furniture construction. They conclude that "it thus appears probable that the planned major investments in petrochemicals will be severely detrimental to employment to the extent that they are financed with capital which would have found other uses." One desirable goal might be to develop an industry scaled to meet national demands and the products utilized as material support for internal development of other sectors of the economy.

Limiting the emphasis on the expansion and export of crude oil and refined products may stabilize and improve the position of the peso to such an extent that tourism and tourist services become too "expensive" for many travelers. The capital acquired from petroleum must be marshalled by the government and utilized in quite cautious ways. The challenge for the 80's and beyond has certainly presented itself to the people and government of Mexico. They hold a natural resource which may, depending upon the way in which it is used, either create a new "Mexican miracle" of development and progress to the benefit of the majority of the population, or it will destroy the facade of democracy and wipe out the rhetoric of revolutionary reform which has become such an automatic characteristic of political life and which has come to be so meaningless for the ejidatarios, the unemployed, the underemployed, and those caught in the web of designed unemployment.

I prefer to attempt optimism for the future of Mexico, but many students of Latin America find this difficult. Evans and James (1979: 20), in an outburst of pessimism, stated that:

> Hoping that declining population growth, the petroleum boom, industrialization along the border, or various single trends or policies will rescue the situation within the next twenty years is akin to hoping that a brick in the toilet will save the day for water conservation.

NOTES

1. The original research (1970-1971) in Yucatán was funded by grants from the Department of Anthropology and the Latin American Studies Center, Michigan State University, East Lansing. Subsequent research field work in Yucatán (12/74-1/75, 11/76-12/76) and Tamaulipas (7/76-11/76) was supported, in part, by grants from the Faculty Research and Creative Endeavors Committee, Central Michigan University, Mt. Pleasant.

2. The henequen cactus, Agave fourcroydes, must be planted and cared for over a period of approximately 6 years until the plant is mature enough to allow for the periodic harvesting of the leaves. A total of 6 to 8 leaves may be harvested during each of two annual cutting cycles and over the approximately 18 years of life remaining a plant. At the end of its life-cycle, the agave sends up a flowering stalk and dies. This is a difficult plant to cultivate as it obviously involves several years of investment (at least in weeding operations) without capital return upon that investment.

3. Speeches by politicians and officials rarely fail to include some aspect of reform ideology and the ejido. The following is an example of the rhetoric used, in this case, by the Mexican Secretary of Agriculture upon the inauguration of the Banco Agrario de Yucatán, S.A. The speech was given at the ejidatarios' "Casa del Pueblo" in Mérida, Yucatán. The original Spanish is used since this conveys more completely the false drama of the moment;

> Esta es, compañeros campesinos, a grande rasgos, LAS NUEVA REFORMA AGRARIA DE YUCATAN que está siendo puesta en marcha por el Presidente López Mateos.
> La integración de una economía más human, más técnica, más nacional; la integración vertical del ejido hacia etapas de la industria, hace que el pan se reparta en mejor forma, que haya mejor justicia social en Yucatán. Muchas Gracias. (Puga y Castillo 1962: 13)

REFERENCES

Alba, Francisco. "Mexico's international migration as a manifestation of its development pattern." International Migration Review, 12: 502-513, 1978.

Benítez, Fernando. *KI, El Drama de un Pueblo y una Planta.* México: Fondo de Cultura Económica, 1962.

Burawoy, Michael. "The functions and reproduction of migrant labor." *American Journal of Sociology* 81: 1050-1087, 1976.

Bustamante, Jorge A. *Espaldas Mojadas: Materia Prima Para le Expansión del Capital Norte-Americano.* México: El Colegio de México, Centro de Estudios Sociológicos, 1975.

Camara, Fernando and Robert Van Kemper. *Migration Across Frontiers: Mexico and the United States.* Albany: Latin American Anthropology Group/Institute for Mesoamerican Studies, S.U.N.Y., Albany, 1979.

Cárdenas, Lázaro. "Discurso, acuerdo y mensaje de Lázaro Cárdenas." In González Navarro 1970: 336-342, 1937.

Clement, Norris and Louis Green. "The political economy of devaluation in Mexico." *Inter-American Economic Affairs,* 32: 47-75, 1978.

DAAC Archives. *Expedientes de los Ejidos de Ixil, Mocochá, Y Baca.* Yucatán: Departamento de Asuntos Agrarios Y Colonización (en Mérida).

Evans, John S. and Dilmus D. James. "Conditions of Employment and income distribution in Mexico as incentives for Mexican migration to the United States: Prospects to the end of the century." *International Migration Review,* 13: 4-24, 1979.

González Navarro, Moisés. *Raza Y Tierra: La Guerra de Castas Y el Henequén.* México: El Colegio de México, 1970.

Hewett de Alcántara, Cynthia. *Modernizing Mexican Agriculture: Socioeconomic Implications of Technological Change 1940-1970.* Geneva: United Nations Research Institute for Social Development (UNRISD), 1976.

_____ . *Ensayo Sobre La Satisfacción De Necesidades Básicas Del Pueblo Mexicano Entre 1940 Y 1970.* México: El Colegio De México, Centro De Estudios Sociológicos, 1977.

Kirk, Rodney C. "Productive alliance in an ejido of acasillados." Paper presented at the Annual Meetings of the American Anthropological Association, Mexico City, November, 1974.

_____ . "El compadrazgo y la reforma agraria: cambios de patrones en San Antonio, Yucatán." América Indígena 36: 499-515, 1976.

_____ . "Agrarian reform and designed unemployment." Paper presented at the CIBOLA Anthropological Society Annual Meetings, Brownsville, TX, March, 1979.

Littlefield, Alice. "Exploitation and the expansion of capitalism: the case of the hammock industry of Yucatán." *American Ethnologist,* 5: 495-508, 1978.

Looney, Robert E. *Mexico's Economy: A Policy Analysis with Forecasts to 1999.* Boulder: Westview Press, 1978.

Menéndez Rodríguez, Mario. *Yucatán O El Genocidio.* México: Fondo de Cultura Popular, 1964.

México. Ley de Crédito Agrícola. In: *Ley Federal De Reforma Agraria.* Colección Porrua, Leyes Y Códigos de México. México: Editorial Porrua, S.A. (335-374), 1976.

Muñoz, Humberto, Orlandina de Oliveira and Claudio Stern. "Internal migration to Mexico City and its impact upon the city's labor market." In Camara and Kemper 1979: 35-64, 1979.

Nagel, John S. "Mexico's population policy turnaround." *Population Bulletin* 33: 3-39, 1978.

P.R.I. (Partido Revolucianario Institucional). *Bases Preliminaries para un Plan Integral de Desarrollo Económico Y Social de Yucatán.* Mérida: P.R.I. Monograph, 1970.

Puga y Castillo, Juvencio. *El Ejido Integral Henequenero de Yucatán.* Mérida, 1962.

Raymond, Nathaniel. "Land reform and the structure of production in Yucatán." *Ethnology* 7:461-470, 1968.

_____ . "The Impact of Land Reform in the Monocrop Region of Yucatán, Mexico." Unpublished Ph.D. Dissertation, Ann Arbor: University Microfilms, 1971.

Rodríguez, Antonio. *El Henequén: Una Planta Calumniada.* México: B. COSTA-AMIC, 1966.

Singlemann, Peter. "Rural collectivization and dependent capitalism: the Mexican collective ejido." *Latin American Perspectives* 5: 38-61, 1978.

SRA Archives, *Expedientes de Varios Ejidos de Victoria Y Güemez, Tamaulipas.* Tamaulipas: Secretaría de la Reforma Agrária en Ciudad Victoria.

Stavenhagen, Rodolfo. "The future of Latin America: between underdevelopment and revolution." Latin American Perspectives 1: 124-148, 1974.

_____ . "Capitalism and the peasantry in Mexico." *Latin American Perspectives* 5: 27-37, 1978.

Whiteford, Scott and Luis Emilio Henao. "Agriculture, irrigation control and selective labor migration: the case of the Tehuacan Valley." In Camara and Kemper 1979: 25-33, 1970.

THE URBANIZATION PROCESS IN 19TH CENTURY CHILE: THE RAILROAD AND RURAL-URBAN MIGRATION

Robert Oppenheimer

Economic development and internal migration in post-World War II Chile have been the subjects of numerous studies.[1] They concentrate on Santiago and the growth of industry in the city. Little attempt has been made to analyze internal migration historically, especially in the 19th century. In studying railroads and railroad workers in mid-19th century Chile, for example, I found more movement by laborers, specifically in a rural-urban context, than had been anticipated or mentioned in the historiography.

Consequently, this presentation has two objectives. First: to describe the general pattern of urbanization that was taking place in mid-19th century Chile, and analyze the role and impact of the railroad in this process. The form which urbanization took in Chile is not dissimilar from other Latin American nations in the same period.[2] Second: to show the importance that the use of such supplemental material as railroad statistics and data can have on our understanding of migration and other demographic patterns.

We must first establish a set of geographic and chronological parameters and present an overview of the economic conditions in Chile and the region being studied.

The region encompasses the seven provinces of the northern Central Valley (Aconcagua, Valparaiso, Santiago, O'Higgins, Colchagua, Curico, and Talca). This region includes the Capital and only metropolis in 19th century Chile, Santiago; and Valparaiso, the nation's major port. The first key rail lines were constructed in this region. The Ferrocarril de Santiago a Valparaiso (FCSV) began construction in Valparaiso in 1852 and reached Santiago in 1863, and the Ferrocarril del Sur (FCSur) was built from Santiago south 250 kms. to Talca between 1856 and 1875.

Generally, the time sequence covers the period from the early attempts to form railroad companies in the 1840s to the end of the War of the Pacific (1879-83). From the standpoint of the railroads the latter date is a significant one because it marks the formation of the National State Railway Agency (Ferrocarriles del Estado—FFCCE) that operated and owned both Central Valley lines.

In mid-century Chile, railroad construction was part of a general economic growth trend that centered on the import-export trade. From the discovery of the Chañarcillo silver lode in 1832, mineral exports became the mainstay of the Chilean economy. In the late 1840s and early 1850s large deposits of silver and copper ore were discovered in the Norte Chico and Santiago regions. By the mid-1850s Chile was the world's leading producer of copper. Foodstuffs, especially wheat and flour, were also important exports in the 19th century. Exports of foodstuffs in Chile's traditional colonial market, Peru, increased considerably as the Peruvian export economy expanded. From 1849 to 1855 Chile was a major supplier of food to the California and Australian gold rushes. At the same time a more permanent market opened in the Atacama desert mining region. Finally, in the 1860s Chile began to ship large quantities of wheat to Great Britain and continued to do so until the late 1870s.[3]

Santiago and Valparaiso were the focal points of much of Chile's economic activity. By the mid-1850s virtually all the commercial houses, mining enterprises and export oriented businesses were operated from offices in the capital or port, though much of the actual production took place in other regions of the country. Valparaiso was the major port for imports, exports, coast-trade and customs revenues, while Santiago was the financial center and locale for much of Chile's light industry. From the 1830s the national bureaucracy in Santiago, which relied heavily on customs duties for its revenue, took an active role in the expansion of the national export economy. From the

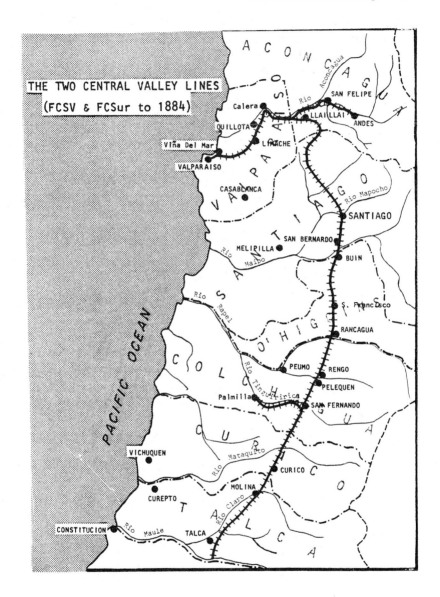

THE TWO CENTRAL VALLEY LINES
(FCSV & FCSur to 1884)

1830s to 1900 customs duties accounted for approximately 60 percent of government revenues and seldom fell below 50 percent.[4] Generally, the Central Valley regional economy followed the pattern of the nation, but there were intra-regional variations. The region became a major supplier of wheat. However, while the Curicó, Talca and Colchagua regions reached peak production capacity after the 1860s, Aconcagua had peaked by 1865 and rose little after this date. Santiago, on the other hand, switched from wheat to vegetables.[5]

By the late 1840s increased economic activity made the need for improved transportation within the Central Valley increasingly obvious. Because there were no navigable waterways, canals were impractical, and the attempts to improve road systems for various reasons were unsuccessful. Construction and maintenance of roads simply could not keep up with increased use and demand. Discussions on the possibilities of building rail lines in Chile began in the early 1840s, and finally the government and a group of Chilean entrepreneurs formed the FCSV company in 1852.[6]

Part of the economic expansion was a slow, but steady urbanization process.[7] While the Chilean population from 1865-1895 increased by approximately 48 percent, the northern Central Valley region grew by about 30 percent. The regional population as a percentage of the whole declined slowly, but remained at a level of between 45-50 percent. (see Table 1) Much of Chile's increased population in 1885 and 1895 was a result of the annexation of territory from Chile's victory in the War of the Pacific.

TABLE 1
THE POPULATION OF CHILE AND THE CENTRAL VALLEY BY CENSUS

Year	Chile	Central Valley (7 Provinces)
1854	1,439,120	
1865	1,819,223	928,257 (51%)
1875	2,075,971	1,011,295 (48.7%)
1885	2,507,005	1,142,356 (45.5%)
1895	2,695,625	1,210,066 (44.9%)

However, the urban population of the Central Valley rose at a more rapid rate than that of the nation. By 1895 almost 45 percent of the region's population was in urban centers of 2,000 inhabitants or more. (see Table 2)

TABLE 2
PERCENT OF URBAN POPULATION FOR CHILE AND REGION, 1865-95[8]

Year	Chile	Central Valley
1865	21.9%	28.9%
1875	26.0	34.8
1885	28.6	38.9
1895	34.2	44.8

The bulk of the increase was in Santiago, Valparaiso and the provincial capitals. Between 1865-75, Curicó's provincial population remained relatively stable, but the provincial capital's population almost doubled. From 1875-1885 Talca's provincial population increased 21 percent, and its capital by more than 34 percent. Interestingly, the FCSur reached the town of Curicó in 1868 and Talca in 1875.[9]

Both the number of urban centers within the Central Valley and the urban population more than doubled between 1865 (14 cities with 268,511) and 1895 (30 cities with 542,279). The urban population was concentrated in the provinces of Valparaiso and Santiago. From 1865 the province of Valparaiso had an urban population of more than 60 percent greater and Santiago province more than 50 percent greater than in 1875. However, the overall percentages of these two provinces relative to the region remained virtually unchanged throughout the period. (see Table 3)

TABLE 3
URBAN POPULATION OF THE REGION, SANTIAGO AND VALPARAISO
(cities), 1865-1895

Year	Region	Santiago	Valparaiso
1865	268,511	115,377	70,438
1875	351,795	150,367	97,737
1885	442,014	189,332	104,952
1895	542,279	256,403	122,447

The urban centers of 20,000 or more, including Santiago, received the largest share of the urban population increase. Their rate of growth was significantly greater than the total population or the rural population. This is important to the northern Central Valley in that virtually all the urban centers with over 20,000 inhabitants were in the region.[10]

The indications are that urbanization was underway in Chile

by the second half of the 19th century, and process, no doubt, was enhanced and accelerated by specific events such as the California Gold Rush and the War of the Pacific, but was also part of the general economic growth of the period. In a sense, we have the beginnings of the process of the transfer of the labor force from rural to urban areas and the dominance of Santiago and Valparaiso, even to the present, in urbanization. As a result of the data presented above, my own research and the work of others, a number of questions arise about the migrants and the process of migration. What motivated the migration? Was it a selective process? How much mobility was there?

While many causes were obviously involved in individual migration, the main factors center on the economic and demographic conditions within the Central Valley. Through much of the period, there was an excess of rural labor in the Central Valley. This labor force migrated to other regions of Chile and Central Valley cities to find work in the copper mines, on crews of the railroad and other internal improvement projects and in urban construction. Many Chileans also emigrated to find work as laborers on railroad construction projects in Panama or Perú. In Perú, for example, Henry Meiggs recruited 25 to 30,000 Chilean workers to labor on the construction of Perú's railroads in the late 1860s and early 1970s. From the 1850s to the 1870s thousands of Chileans labored on the construction of the FCSV, FCSur and the Chillan-Talcahuano line.[11]

There were also the problems of wages and production. With the exception of the harvest, wages for rural laborers remained at about 25 centavos per day plus food rations. Railroad workers received rations, living quarters and a peso a day. Meiggs promised laborers food and 62 centavos a day and attracted almost 30,000 Chileans to Perú. Vagrancy also became a problem in the Central Valley in mid-19th century. Finally, production increases were accomplished by putting more land into cultivation or by more efficient use of resources. As arable land ran out, technology was introduced. In both cases greater numbers of rural laborers were forced to emigrate. Passenger movement on the Central Valley railroads confirms the relationship between migration and rural economic conditions. In any given year strong correlations can be made between migration from province to city and provincial production: greater production creates less migration and lower production accounts for more migration.[12]

Not unlike the more recent migration experience described by Herrick and the Instituto de Economia,[13] the process in mid-19th century was a selective one. A comparison of census data and the railroad company records demonstrates that the lines' employees can be considered indicative of the migrant being hired in the urban areas. Most of the migrants would seem to be young men (15-45 years old). While many moved with their families, most left home to work for short periods in the cities, only to return to the countryside for harvest and planting. For example, Central Valley railroad construction was annually slowed or shut down during the three months of harvest (Jan.-March).[14] The migrants had some education and often an artisan skill. The pay records show that the majority could sign their names, though many had others sign for them or used an "x." Most of the lower echelons of the railway artisans (smiths, carpenters, boilermakers, mechanics apprentices and others) were usually migrants. The railroad civil engineers often indicated that these workers either came to the cities with the artisan expertise or the sufficient education or aptitude to quickly learn the skills.[15] Mechanics, I assume, would have to have some ability to read and understand some basic mechanical concepts.

Finally, by reviewing the role of the railroads in the migratory process we not only begin to understand the importance of this technology in connecting rural and urban Chile, but it also gives us insight into the amount of migration taking place.

The movement of passengers was one of the more important services of the Central Valley lines, especially between Santiago and Valparaiso. The railroads were immediately able to reduce the time and cost of passenger travel within the region and to improve the comfort and reliability of such travel. Therefore, mass use of railroads by passengers, especially third-class, was almost instantaneous. There was a consistent increase in the total number of passengers moved annually, the number of trips per inhabitant, utilized capacity and the number of passenger-fares.

Compared to a horse-drawn coach trip, the rail line significantly improved travelling conditions between Santiago and Valparaiso. In the early 1860s a horse-drawn coach trip between the port and capital took 14 hours, leaving daily, except Sundays, from both cities at 4 a.m. and arriving at 6 p.m. Travel accounts described the trip as long and arduous, and in the winter often twice as long if attempted at all. The trip from Santiago to Valparaiso cost 10 pesos per person (plus meals). After the completion of the FCSV in 1863, a similar rail trip took 6 hours and 40 minutes and cost from 2.50 to 5 pesos. By 1870 the express reduced the trip to 5 hours and 20 minutes and by 1872 to 4½ hours, but the ticket rates remained the same until after the War of the Pacific. For a peasant a 2.50 peso ticket was expensive, but most travelled shorter distances.[16]

A horse-drawn coach trip from Santiago into the Central Valley took as long as two or three days, without delays, to Talca (250 kms.), and the cost ran to 20 pesos plus meals and lodging. In 1863 the train reached San Fernando in 4 hours and 25 minutes and by 1868 reached Curicó in 6¼ hours. The train trip to Talca took 7½ hours in 1875 and cost from 2.25 to 6 pesos.[17]

From 1855 to 1885 the number of passengers travelling on the FCSV rose by almost 25 times and from 1864, the first full year of operation, to 1885 increased more than four-fold, and the number of passengers per kilometer of track from 1864 to 1885 rose from 1,647 to 5,604. From the completion of the line, passenger traffic declined from the previous year on only four occasions—in 1866 during the War with Spain in which Valparaiso was under constant bombardment, and three years (1877-79) during the severe depression of the 1870s.[18]

On the FCSur from 1857 to 1885 the number of passengers carried increased almost six times but never reached the quantities of the FCSV. In fact, the number of passengers per kilometer of track decreased considerably over the years indicating that passengers were taking shorter trips or more intra-provincial travel occurred. The average daily travel rose from 374 passengers in 1857 to 2,190 in 1885. Before 1868, the number of passengers per year fluctuated depending to a great extent on the economic conditions within the northern Central Valley.[19] This confirms the notion that migration was strongly influenced by economic conditions. Though the cities may also have been suffering during a depression, there would still seem to be more opportunity for workers than in rural areas.

TABLE 4
THE NUMBER OF PASSENGERS/KM. OF TRACK IN SPECIFIC YEAR, FCSUR

1857-58	6,823 passengers/mr. of track	1868	1,277
1862	2,010	1885	2,728

Source: Informes-FCSur, 1858-1885.

During the period, the FCSV carried more than 16 million passengers and the FCSur more than 10.5 million. The overwhelming majority travelled by third class (67.9% on the FCSV and 71.67% on the FCSur). In the years before the completion of the FCSV third class passengers accounted for over 80 percent of railway travellers. From the completion of the FCSV in 1864 an increasingly greater portion of the traffic on the line was between Santiago and Valparaiso. As a result, the percentage of the third-class passengers, most of whom travelled between the city and rural provinces, declined. Since the FCSur serviced the more distant rural provinces at increasingly less expensive rates, the rate of third-class travel on the line remained constant.[20]

From 1865 to 1885 passenger traffic per inhabitant of the northern Central Valley tripled from .58 trips per person per year to 1.81, and relative to the population of Santiago increased from 4.75 to 11 trips per person per year. With few exceptions, the first quarter of each year was the period of the heaviest passenger travel. This phenomenon resulted from the summer harvest season in the Central Valley, when most fundo owners and their families and urban day-laborers returned to the countryside.[21] The owners went for vacation and to oversee the harvest, and the laborers returned to visit their families, participate in the harvest, and partake in the traditional festivities of the season.

Most passengers travelled to and from the major stations. On the FCSV from 1864 to 1875 the three main stations (Santiago, Valparaiso and Quillota) accounted for almost 55 percent of all passengers. In 1874 on the FCSur 176,451 passengers left Santiago for points south, of a total of 534,647. The difference between in- and out-migration by rail from most stations on both lines, particularly from Santiago, was often zero or nearly zero. Considering the growth of Santiago during the period at between 25 and 30 percent per decade or 25,000 to 35,000 persons per decade, the migratory pattern was astonishing. In the decade from 1865 to 1875 the annual in-out migration by rail of Santiago ranged from 100,000 to 200,000 passengers per year, and the majority travelled third class.[22] Though there were, no doubt, some multiple trips, the probability was that they were limited by the modes of transport and distance. This was especially true of non-rail traffic. The amount of movement was amazing in a city with a population of 100,000 to 150,000 persons.

Consistently the numbers of travellers leaving Valparaiso and Santiago was greater than the number entering the city by rail.[23] Among other reasons for this circumstance is an important economic one. This would indicate that workers who may have come to the city without funds were able to return to the countryside for harvest by rail because they could afford to do so. The implication is that the figures presented above on the possible in-out migration annually for Santiago was at the very least equal to the numbers leaving the capital by rail. This is the case because some people enter and do not leave, others enter by rail and leave by some other means or, most likely, migrants enter and leave by non-rail transportation. Though the capital and port dominated travel, a relatively large percentage of passengers moved between smaller urban areas in the provinces. This would help to account for the increase in population of the smaller provincial cities.

The migratory pattern of mid-19th century Chile set a precedent that would continue to the present. The process established Santiago and Valparaiso as the dominant urban industrial centers and this would be magnified in the 20th century. Traditional historiography often assumed that little migration took place in this period and that peasants remained relatively sedentary because of the low levels of industrial production. The urban process was slow, but the cities grew at a steady pace. However, railroad data shows there was significantly more migration than is indicated by the growth of the urban population. This early stage of rural-urban migration was often not one of permanent settlement. Workers labored in the cities, but often returned to the rural areas for harvest. This is yet another example of the use of mixed strategies of economic activity by the peasant family to meet its needs in the ever expanding market economy. Many migrants in the late 19th and early 20th century, who would permanently settle in the city, probably had contact with the city in the earlier period, and this early contact helped to alleviate pressures of urban dislocation in the later period.

The migration centered on Santiago and Valparaiso, but also a number of provincial capitals in the Central Valley. The migrants came for many reasons, but dominant factors were fluctuating rural conditions, excess labor force in the rural areas, the need for labor in the mines and in urban areas, and higher wages in urban centers. The process was also a selective one with most laborers males between 15 and 45 with some ability to read and write and some artisan skills.

The railroad was an important, but not essential, factor in this migration. Rural laborers would have, and did, find other means of moving to the cities, but since the railroad was available, it was often used. The railway made personal travel accessible to a large portion of the population that previously found travel difficult. The lines reduced the cost and time of travel and improved the comfort and reliability of a trip compared to its competition. Whatever other effects the railroads had on the Chilean economy and society of the mid-19th century, they provided an improved consumer service, travel, to a vast majority of the population. Finally, the use of railroad data along with census materials adds a new dimension to our understanding of the process of rural-urban migration in 19th century Chile.

NOTES

1. Bruce Herrick, *Urban Migration and Economic Development in Chile* (Cambridge, Mass. MIT Press, 1965), is the best of these studies, along with others from University of Chile faculties such as the Instituto de Economia.

2. Richard E. Boyer and Keith A. Davies, *Urbanization in 19th Century Latin America: Statistics and Sources* (Los Angeles, UCLA Latin American Center, 1973).

3. *Estadística Comercial de le República de Chile* and Alberto Hermann, *La Produccion en Chile de los Metales i Minerales mas Importantes desde La Conquista hasta fines del Año 1902* (Santiago, 1903).

4. *Estadistica Comercial: Resumen de la Hacienda Publica desde 1833 hasta 1914* (London, 1914); The location of businesses was taken from *Matricula de Patentes* and *El Mercurio*.; The *Memoria* of the Ministry of Interior annually published in the 1840s and 1850s the cost of the maintenance of roads and tolls collected.

5. Oppenheimer, Chap. 2; Anne Hagerman Johnson, "The Impact of Market Agriculture on Family and Household Structure in 19th Century Chile" *Hispanic American Historical Review*, Vol 58, 1978, pp. 634-35.

6. See note four for information on roads. Robert Oppenheimer, "Chilean Transportation Development: The Railroads and Socio-Economic Change in the Central Valley, 1840-1885" (UCLA, Unpublished Ph. D., 1976), Chap. 3.

7. The population figures are taken from the Census of 1854, 1865, 1875, 1855, 1895; Carlos Hurtado Ruiz-Tagle, "Population Concentration and Economic Development: The Chilean Case" (Harvard Univ. Unpublished Ph.D. 1966); and Markos Mamalakis, *Historical Statistics* (Mimeographed, n.d., Vol. II, "Demography". I will use the provincial figures based on the 1960 geographic divisions. The figures from the three sources differ depending on how the geographic divisons were made. Also, the census data is not meant to be considered absolute. The accuracy of this data is questionable, but gives a good measurement of general trend. My own research as well as that of others indicates the need for the census figures to be checked against other sources. See Robert McCaa, "Chile Social and Demographic History", *Latin American Research Review*, Vol. XIII, No. 2, 1978, pp. 104-126.

8. Urban is to be defined as 2,000 or more inhabitants.

9. Brian Loveman, *Chile* (New York, 1978), p. 163; Appendix I, Oppenheimer, Chap. 5. The data on urban population are from Hurtado Ruiz-Tagle, Table 8.

10. Appendices I and II. In 1865 and 1875 all the cities with 20,000 or more people were in the Central Valley, while Concepcion will be added in 1885 and 1895 and Iquique in 1895.

11. Oppenheimer, Chap. 5 and 6; Loveman, p. 163.

12. Hagerman Johnson, p. 637; Loveman, p. 164; Oppenheimer, Chaps. 5 and 7; Arnold Bauer, *Chilean Rural Society* (London, 1975), p. 156.

13. Herrick and the Instituto de Economia, *La Poblacion de Gran Santiago* (Santiago, 1959), and *La Migracion Interna en Chile en el Periodo, 1940-1952* (Santiago, 1959).

14. Hagerman Johnson, passim; Oppenheimer, Chap. 5. Since the rail industry was a major urban employer in mid-19th century Chile, the comparison is a good one.

15. Oppenheimer, Chap. 6.

16. Oppenheimer, Chap. 7.

17. Oppenheimer, Chap. 7; Talca information is from the *Archivo del Ministerio de Interior*, Vol. 738, "Itinerario del Ferrocarril del Sur", March 18, 1875.

18. Appendix II.

19. Appendix III.

20. Appendices II and III.

21. The data on monthly travel was found sporadically in the Informes of the FCSV and FCSur; Calculations were made from the population figures in the tables and appendices and the passenger counts in the appendices.

22. Appendix IV; *Informes FCSV-1864-75* and *Informe-FCSur-1874*.

23. Appendix IV.

BIBLIOGRAPHY

Censuses

Oficina central de estadística. *Censo jeneral de la República de Chile levantado en abril de 1854.* Santiago: Imprenta del Ferrocarril, 1858.

—————. *Censo jeneral de la República de Chile levantado el 19 de abril de 1865.* Santiago: Imprenta Nacional, 1866.

—————. *Quinto censo jeneral de la población de Chile levantado el 19 de abril de 1875.* Valparaíso: Imprenta del Mercurio, 1876.

—————. *Sesto censo jeneral de la población de Chile levantado el 26 de noviembre de 1885.* 2 vols. Valparaíso: Imprenta de la Patria, 1889-1890.

—————. *Sétimo censo jeneral de la población de Chile levantado el 28 de noviembre de 1895.* 4 vols. Valparaíso: Imprenta Guillermo Helfmann, 1900.

Comisión central del censo. *Censo de la República de Chile levantado el 28 de noviembre de 1907.* Santiago: Sociedad Imprenta y Litografía Universo, 1908.

Other Documents

Archivo del Ministerio del Interior, Vol. 738.

Ferrocarril de Santiago a Valparaiso. *Informes de la Junta Directiva del Ferrocarril de Santiago a Valparaiso presentado a los Accionistas de Esta Empresa.* Santiago, for the years 1853-1881.

Ferrocarril del Sur. *Informes de la Junta Directiva del Ferrocarril del Sur a los Accionistas de la Empresa.* Santiago, for the years 1856-1883.

Matricula de Patentes de Santiago. 1873.

Matricula de Patentes de Valparaiso. 1873.

Ministerio del Interior. *Memoria 1845-1860.*

Oficina Central de Estadística. *Estadístic Comercial de la Republica de Chile,* Years consulted, 1844-1885.

Resumen de la Hacienda Publíca desde 1833 hasta 1914. London, 1914.

Books and Articles

Bauer, Arnold. *Chilean Rural Society.* London, 1975.

Boyer, Richard and Keith Davies. *Urbanization in 19th Century Latin America: Statistics & Sources.* Los Angeles: UCLA Latin American Center, 1973.

C.E.L.A.D.E. "Preliminary Report on Nuptiality, Fertility and Mortality based on Histories of Chilean Families." Mimeo, unpublished. Santiago, 1978.

Hagerman Johnson, Anne. "The Impact of Market Agriculture on Family and Household Structure in 19th Century Chile." *Hispanic American Historical Review,* Vol. 58, 1978, pp. 625-648.

Hermann, Alberto. *La Producción en Chile de los Metales i Minerales mas Importantes desde la Conquista hasta fines de Año 1902.* Santiago, 1903.

Herrick, Bruce. *Urban Migration and Economic Development in Chile.* Cambridge, Mass.: M.I.T. Press, 1965.

Hurtado Ruiz-Tagle, Carlos. "Population Concentration and Economic Development: The Chilean Case." Harvard Univ. Unpublished, Ph.D., 1966.

Instituto de Economia. *La Poblacion de Gran Santiago.* Santiago, 1959.

————— . *La Migración Interna en Chile en el Periodo, 1940-1952.* Santiago, 1959.

Loveman, Brian. *Chile.* New York, 1978.

Mamalakis, Markos. "Historical Statistics on Chile." Mimeographs, n.d., 4 Vols.

McCaa, Robert. "Chile Social and Demographic History." *Latin America Research Review,* Vol. XIII, No. 2, 1978, pp. 104-126.

Oppenheimer, Robert. "Chilean Transportation Development: Railroads and Socio-Economic Change in the Central Valley, 1840-1885." UCLA Unpublished, Ph.D., 1976.

El Mercurio, 1840-1885.

APPENDIX I
YEARLY GROWTH RATES OF POPULATION LIVING IN CITIES OF DIFFERENT SIZES,
INCLUDING AND EXCLUDING THE EFFECT OF AN INCREASE IN THE NUMBER OF CENTERS

PERIOD	Rate of growth of population living in centers with 2,000 to 20,000 inhabitants	Rate of growth of population living in the centers that had 2,000 to 20,000 inhabitants at the beginning of the period	Rate of growth of population living in cities with 2,000 or more inhabitants excluding Santiago	Rate of growth of the centers that had 20,000 or more inhabitants at the beginning of the period, excluding Santiago	Rate of growth of Santiago	Rate of growth of rural population	Rate of growth of total population
1865-75	3.2	0.6	3.3	3.3	2.7	0.8	1.4
1875-85	2.0	1.6	5.9	0.7	2.3	1.5	1.9
1885-95	2.1	0.7	2.8	1.9	3.1	0.0	0.7
1895-07	1.2	2.1	4.4	2.2	2.2	1.1	1.5
1907-20	0.7	0.9	2.6	1.0	3.3	0.5	1.1
1920-30	2.1	1.6	2.6	1.5	3.2	0.4	1.4
1930-40	0.6	1.1	2.4	0.8	3.2	1.1	1.6
1940-52	1.8	2.3	2.6	1.5	2.9	0.0	1.4
1952-60	0.7	3.9	5.8	2.9	4.4	0.8	2.8

Source: Table 8 of Hurtado Ruiz-Tagle

APPENDIX II
TOTAL NUMBER OF PASSENGERS CARRIED ON THE FCSV
AND THE PERCENTAGE BY CLASS, 1855-1885

Year	Passengers Carried	Percentage of First Class	Percentage of Second Class	Percentage of Third Class
1855	52,115	29.8%	70.2%	a.
1856	81,912	31.4	58.3	10.3%
1857	140,562	6.9	16.1	77.0
1858	201,530	3.7	8.6	87.7
1859	207,115	3.3	9.4	87.4
1860	203,459	4.0	10.0	86.0
1861	194,968	3.6	9.6	85.5
1862	164,394	4.9	9.6	85.5
1863	224,376	8.1	14.0	77.8
1864	303,027	12.6	18.6	68.8
1865	346,506	11.3	18.6	70.0
1866	328,733	12.7	13.9	73.4
1867	349,557	15.2	14.2	70.6
1868	385,655	15.2	14.6	70.2
1869	442,894	15.5	15.6	68.9
1870	462,466	15.6	16.5	67.9
1871	511,075	17.0	17.6	65.5
1872	608,466	18.0	18.0	64.0
1873	697,002	19.3	19.0	61.7
1874	747,488	21.0	19.3	59.7
1875	749,398	21.8	19.5	58.7
1876	753,849	22.9	20.1	57.0
1877	689,198	22.6	21.9	55.5
1878	598,676	-	-	-
1879	597,725	22.6	20.1	57.3
1880	662,815	24.1	19.6	56.3
1881	847,415	24.6	20.1	55.3
1882	1,009,238	-	-	-
1883	1,093,439	25.4	19.1	55.4
1884	1,183,033	24.0	20.4	55.6
1885	1,283,262	24.9	21.6	53.5

Source: *Informes–FCSV, 1855-1883; Memorias–FFCCE, 1884-1885.*

a. In 1855 there was no third class service. Whenever no data was given, none were available.

APPENDIX III
TOTAL NUMBER OF PASSENGERS CARRIED ON THE FCS
AND THE PERCENTAGE BY CLASS, 1857-1885

Year	Passengers Carried	Percentage of First Class	Percentage of Second Class	Percentage of Third Class
1857[a]	36,467			
1858	147,332			
1859	354,105			
1860	370,713			
1861	-			
1862	269,373	10.4%	b.	89.6%
1863	264,530	9.1	1.6%	89.3
1864	189,842	8.6	2.9	88.5
1865	201,428	10.2	13.2	76.6
1866	181,965	10.2	13.5	76.3
1867	191,152	11.1	12.7	67.2
1868	236,620	14.6	14.9	70.5
1869	273,513	15.3	14.2	70.5
1870	298,943	15.3	12.7	72.0
1871	316,595	16.6	12.0	73.4
1872	360,901	14.7	11.4	73.9
1873	502,878	14.7	11.4	73.9
1874	534,647	14.8	11.3	73.9
1875	509,883	15.7	11.0	73.3
1876	492,827	-	-	-
1877	428,191	17.8	10.8	71.4
1878	404,488	19.9	9.9	70.2
1879	348,979	21.4	9.5	69.1
1880	418,149	20.4	10.0	69.6
1881	547,053	19.2	9.5	71.3
1882	644,764	19.5	7.7	72.8
1883	734,840	17.2	6.6	76.2
1884	777,759	18.0	7.0	75.0
1885	799,328	18.5	7.1	74.4

Source: *Informes-FCS, 1857-1883* and *Memorias-FFCCE, 1884-1885.*

a. The data for the years 1857 and 1868 were actually given from September to September, but were adjusted to a January to January basis.

b. In 1857 there was no second class, and whenever no data are given, none were available.

APPENDIX IV
PASSENGER TRAFFIC TO AND FROM SANTIAGO AND
VALPARAISO ON THE FCSV (1864-1875) AND THE FCS (1877-1883)

FCSV	To Valparaiso	From Valparaiso	To Santiago	From Santiago
1864	86,825	105,083	35,631	37,276
1865	99,423	116,027	36,006	37,751
1866	100,263	109,079	30,801	37,790
1867	108,948	127,074	38,253	44,439
1868	124,808	139,001	42,466	47,999
1869	135,658	158,037	49,399	54,207
1870	138,538	160,899	49,657	58,596
1871	165,429	158,841	56,312	66,284
1872	177,309	202,409	63,904	73,601
1873	202,344	230,396	74,788	85,656
1874	196,303	245,482	70,653	83,203
1875	201,373	241,415	69,007	87,868

FCS	To Santiago	From Santiago
1877	133,457	130,934
1878	-	-
1879	-	-
1880	136,778	128,473
1881	170,369	168,265
1882	189,475	197,330
1883	201,662	204,070

Source: *Informes de FCSV and FCS.*

SOCIAL INDICATORS AND THE QUALITY OF LIFE: AN INTERNAL MIGRATION EXAMPLE FROM HONDURAS

Robert N. Thomas
John D. Stephens

There is an emerging interest in the systematic monitoring of the well-being of nations. The "social indicators movement," has generated a large volume of literature (Wilcox, *et. al.*, 1972) in response to a concern that "quality of life" is not adequately reflected in conventional indicators such as gross national product (GNP) or per capita income. Although discussion generally focuses on time series of national aggregates, some efforts have been made to develop subnational indicators (Russet, *et. al.*, 1964). These efforts reflect dissatisfaction with national indicators which do not provide adequate information on which to base regional social and economic planning decisions.

Social indicators are intended to be indicative of human well-being. Selection and weight of criteria may vary with culture, ideology, and personal predisposition. However, certain fundamental human needs are recognized—food, clothing, and shelter—the satisfaction of which is a necessary condition for physical survival. There are other emotional or psychological needs which are independent of a specific culture. While all societies have their own distinctive wants, it is useful to identify existing consensus regarding general, social indicators.

Since a social indicator may be any variable or parameter relevant to understanding the way in which a society operates, a *territorial* social indicator is any such measure applied to sets of geographical units (e.g., nations, regions, and smaller areal units) so as to permit areal comparisons. The development of territorial social indicators provides considerable scope for geographic research.

MIGRATION AS A TERRITORIAL SOCIAL INDICATOR

The genesis of migration lies in dissatisfaction with one's contemporary environment. Disparity of opportunity to enjoy levels of living in terms of income or the physical or social environment provides the main motive force behind migration which is rapidly becoming, if it is not already so, the most dynamic population change component in developing societies. It represents a process of human adjustment to the social, economic, political, and physical environment and, as such, has considerable potential as a territorial social indicator of human well-being.

In Latin America, rates of internal redistribution of populations are increasing. Although internal migration is a fact of immediate importance to the economic, social and political life of Latin American countries, not enough is known about its extent and even less is understood about the causes and processes of population movement at the national level. This stems partly from the intrinsic difficulties of collecting migration data and partly from the scarcity of intensive, coordinated, or comprehensive empirical work. Given these deficiencies, population censuses must play a vital role in the development of migration analysis. Administrators, development planners, and research workers, the users of migration data, are almost entirely dependent on this source of information for anything other than localized studies.

In many Latin American censuses, little or no direct information pertaining to internal migration is published. In the case of Honduras, the most recent official census (Dirección General de Estadística y Censos, 1964) provides only tabulations of place of birth by place of residence. The data are tabulated by *departmento,* a level of aggregation which tends to hide significant spatial variations in change of residence within these administrative units.

URBANIZATION AND URBAN MIGRATION
IN HONDURAS

Honduras has approximately 2.9 million people, an average population size for Central American countries. The current birthrate is 49.3 per thousand inhabitants, one of the highest in Latin America (CELADE,1975a). The most recent estimate of natural increase is 3.5 percent per year which is high compared to other Latin American countries and the world. At this annual rate of growth, the doubling time for the Honduran population is less than twenty years.

The process of urbanization in Honduras is relatively recent. Approximately three in every ten Hondurans reside in urban areas. As late as 1971, 67.7 percent of the population was still classified as rural (CELADE, 1975a). Historically, what was once a primate city size distribution has evolved into a rank-size distribution so that today, the majority of economic wealth and prosperity is concentrated in the two largest centers in the urban system, Tegucigalpa and San Pedro Sula (Figure 1).

Tegucigalpa, the capital and major urban center, is a city of about 250,000 residents. Its population is increasing at a rate of 6.4 percent annually and will double in less than ten years. Well over half of this increase can be attributed to internal migration rather than natural increase (CELADE, 1975a). The second major city in Honduras is San Pedro Sual which has a population of slightly more than 100,000 inhabitants. The annual growth rate for this north coast city is over ten percent, more than six percent of which is the result of internal migration.

RESEARCH PROBLEM

This research focuses on one trend in migration common to most Central American republics; the disproportionately large volume of migrants destined for the largest city. In the case of Honduras, this urban center is Tegucigalpa, the national capital. The characteristics of the migrants who relocate to the capital city are of secondary importance for our present purposes. The overriding concern is to develop a methodology to identify areas of potentially high outmigration in developing societies whose population is still largely rural. Thus, we attempt to identify territorial social indicators which reflect the migration-promoting characteristics of contemporary physical and social environments.

RESEARCH HYPOTHESES

From pertinent internal migration literature and a knowledge of the social and economic environment of Honduras, the following hypotheses concerning migration to Tegucigalpa are proposed.

(1) The first indicator chosen is that of accessibility to Teguci-galpa. The measure of accessibility reflects the actual highway distance between the geographical center of a *municipio* and Tegucigalpa, which is weighted according to the quality of the road surface.* Hypothesis: an inverse relationship exists be-tween accessibility and the volume of migration to Tegucigalpa.

(2) A second characteristic of migration to the large urban centers is observed throughout Latin America. Inter-urban migration is important, involving literate and skilled or semi-skilled persons moving to the largest cities from other, smaller cities (Herrick, 1970). This migrant has already experienced urban ways of life, so problems of further adjustment in the big city are lessened.

Inter-urban migrants to the largest city frequently have higher educational attainments and substantially greater skills than rural-urban migrants destined for smaller centers (Herrick, 1970). Thus, a general index of the urbanization of a *munici-pio's* population may well serve as a proxy for the aggregate education level or occupational skills of that population. Hypothesis: the relative volume of migration to Tegucigalpa is thought to be directly associated with the general degree of urbanization in Honduras.

(3) Areas other than the primate city experiencing large shares of urban *growth* are likely to have attracted and absorbed a considerable volume of inter-urban and rural-urban migrants. They would not be expected to provide significant numbers of migrants to the capital. Rather, those *municipios* which have sustained declines in urban population over time would be the more likely source of migrants. This second category of growth includes urban areas increasing in size at a decreasing rate as well as those having absolute losses in urban population. Hypothesis: an indirect relationship exists between the rate of urban growth during 1961-1970 and the volume of migration for that period.

---

*A paved highway calculated on a one kilometer to one kilometer basis. Each kilo-meter of unpaved surface was calculated on a two for one basis, assuming a greater friction of distance from the unpaved surface. For a precedent in the literature see: Robert N. Thomas, "The Migration System of Guatemala City: Spatial Inputs," *The Professional Geographer*, 24/2:105-112 (May, 1972).

(4) A fourth variable considered important to an understanding of the migration to the capital is the density of farm laborers, or agriculturalists, per unit of land. Much of Honduras is characterized by high rates of rural natural increase, a large proportion of the rural-agricultural population in the *minifundio* and/or landless employee class, and a large share of the agricultural land held by *latifundistas.* In fact, in countries where the distribution of land is extremely unequal (e.g., Honduras, Chile, Peru, and Bolivia), *minifundios* represent on the order of 60-80 percent of all farms and 0.7-4.0 percent of the country's total agricultural land, and average 1.0-1.7 hectares in size. *Latifundios,* on the other hand, comprise 0.5-2.0 percent of the units, encompass 75-95 percent of the land, and have an average size of 2000-4000 hectares (Shaw, 1975). Thus, employment opportunites for a large proportion of agricultural labor are limited because of the institutional system of land tenure. With rapid rural population growth and limited opportunties, high rates of rural emigration are expected. However, it is our premise that these emigrants move over relatively short distances to more prosperous rural areas or small urban centers, and thereby do not contribute significantly to the volume of migration directed to Tegucigalpa. Hypothesis: the greater the density of agriculturalists per square kilometer of farmland, the lesser the volume of migrants to the capital.

(5) A fifth hypothesis established a pattern of association between the number of migrants to Tegucigalpa and the more advanced agricultural areas of Honduras. We postulate that the more prosperous and developed a *municipio* is agriculturally, the greater will be the number of migrants generated by that *municipio* (Brunn and Thomas, 1972).

Agricultural productivity is believed to be associated with net migratory flow toward the capital for at least two reasons. First, the labor force employed in agriculturally more modern areas is relatively transient compared with labor living in the subsistence areas (CELADE, 1975b). Secondly, the channels of communication and resulting information flows are likely to be more widespread between large urban places and agriculturally prosperous regions. Therefore, the probability of migration is likely to be greater between areas having these characteristics and the capital city. In this context, prosperity and stage develment are defined in terms of agricultural productivity per hectare of farmland; the sum of all field crops, produce, and livestock measured in cwt's (hundred weights) per hectare of land under cultivation and in pasture.

(6) The economic desirability of avoiding unemployment has suggested a job opportunity hypothesis that predicts net migratory flows toward places with low unemployment rates. This hypothesis regards low measured rates of unemployment as deceptive because they ignore disguised unemployment and underemployment in agricultural activities. Realizing this weakness in the data and the fact that the unemployment rate for the city of Tegucigalpa is one of the highest in Honduras, we propose the use of a differential between unemployment rates of a given *municipio* and Tegucigalpa, where positive values apply to those administrative units having rates of unemployment exceeding that of the capital. The sixth hypothesis: as the differential unemployment rate for a given area increases, we would expect a concomitant increase in the number of migrants from that area.

ACQUISITION OF RELEVANT DATA

Data pertaining to the six hypotheses described above were obtained for the 278 *municipios* from various government census documents (Dirección General de Estadística y Censos, 1965 and 1969).

Data documenting the volume and characteristics of the migratory flow to Tegucigalpa are unavailable. Origin destination tables of internal migration, classified by small administrative areas, are not published in the official census documents of Honduras. In fact, the only indirect evidence pertaining to migration trends is given within tables cross-classifying the then current location of the population by department of birth (Dirección General de Estadística y Censo, 1964).

The unavailability of data necessitated a sample survey of households in Tegucigalpa. The required migration data were collected during the summer of 1970 through a stratified random sample of 1,000 family heads of households. This represented a 2.5 percent sample of all households in the city. For the purposes of sampling, the city was divided into 39 units having approximately equal populations. Within each unit, somewhat similar socioeconomic conditions prevailed. The sample was then stratified according to the populations of the 39 areas and, within each, households were selected randomly.

For each individual, a migration history was acquired, including the respondent's place of birth and last place of residence before moving to Tegucigalpa. For each person moving to the city between 1961 and 1970, his or her last *municipio* of residence was recorded. A frequency table was then developed indicating the number of respondents residing in the i-th *municipio* prior to moving to Tegucigalpa. These migration data were converted into rates per thousand population of the *municipio* of origin (Figure 2).

MULTIPLE REGRESSION MODEL

In order to accurately assess the degree to which variations in the territorial indicators estimated variations in migration rates, a linear stepwise multiple regression model was developed and tested. In the statistical model, migration is used as the dependent variable. The migration measure represents the number of migrants to Tegucigalpa per thousand population by *municipio* of last residence. The six indicators of migration form the set of independent variables.

The matrix of simple correlation coefficients among all variables is given in Table 1. In all cases, the signed relationships between migration and the independent variables are in the hypothesized directions. As for the relationships among the six indicators of migration, the low correlation coefficients suggest their relative independence.

The results of statistical estimation of the multiple regression equation tend to support the hypotheses. Overall model estimation is modestly high—over 60 percent. In order to determine the relative importance of the various independent variables, a stepwise multiple regression procedure was invoked. The stepwise technique "searches out" the greatest contributors to the total variance and effectively rank-orders them.

Results from the stepwise multiple regression are given in Table 2. The accessibility measure, weighted highway distance, accounts for the majority of statistical variation in the dependent variable. Upon entry of the urban growth and urban proportion indicators, the coefficient of determination increases by 11.1 percent and 5.8 percent, repectively. As the fourth and fifth variables enter, it can be observed that little of the remaining variance can be attributed to functions of agricultural productivity and density of agriculturalists. The differential unemployment measure was statistically insignificant and, thus, did not meet the criteria for entry. The Beta coefficients, which provide an indication of the relative causal independence of variables, are relatively high for the first three variables entered. But, the Beta coefficient for accessibility clearly dominates all other indicators.

A basic assumption of least squares regression is that the error terms, or unexplained variance, in the regression model are independent under the null hypothesis. In applications of multiple regression, where the data have a geographic ordering, the regression model requires the error terms to be independent spatially under the null hypothesis. In order to ascertain whether or not the residuals from the regression model are void of spatial autocorrelation, the conventional isopleth map of the residuals was generated (Figure 3). Although the map depicts the areal distribution of residuals with considerable accuracy, it is necessary to determine what, if any, significant spatial trend is embedded within the distribution. It is useful to suppress some of the detail, and to summarize the situation by extracting general trends in the pattern of observations as they vary over distance. This can be accomplished by the fitting of trend surfaces to the distribution of residuals. (Smith, 1975).

An attempt was made to fit a linear trend surface to the pattern of residuals. The closeness of fit is shown by a coefficient of multiple correlation (R) of 0.191. Thus, the surface accounts for only 3.6 percent of the areal variation in migration residuals, measured by R^2. However, since the coefficient was not found to be statistically significant at the 0.05 level, additional attempts were made to fit higher-order surfaces of non-linear type to the residuals. The results are summarized in Table 3. As successively higher order curvilinear surfaces are computed, the proportion of variance accounted for increases. Despite the increases, the percent of explained variation by the cubic surface amounts to only 16.9 (Figure 4).

Trend surface analysis can only describe the degree of regularity within the pattern of residuals; it cannot explain them. The results do indicate, however, that the null hypothesis of spatially independent error terms cannot be accepted. The existence of a trend, albeit small, suggests that other indicators, critical to a more complete understanding of migration flows to Tegucigalpa, have been overlooked.

SUMMARY

In summary, 63 percent of the statistical variation in the dependent variable, migration rate by last place of residence, was accounted for by five of the six indicators at the 0.05 significance level. Or, well over half of the spatial variation of the place of last residence of migrants can be attributed to the five territorial indicators chosen.

The statistical model illustrates that the last residences of the migrants are primarily urban places that are accessible to the capital city. Furthermore, these urban centers are experiencing either limited growth or absolute declines in population. Of the migrants whose last place of residence is not urban, the majority originate in relatively prosperous agricultural areas and not the poor and densely settled agricultural regions of Honduras. Thus, the migration system of Tegucigalpa cannot be described by the simple rural-urban process that is frequently mentioned in Latin American population literature.

TABLE 1
MATRIX OF SIMPLE CORRELATION COEFFICIENTS

	Y	X_1	X_2	X_3	X_4	X_5	X_6
Y	1.000	-0.669	0.417	-0.511	-0.329	0.310	0.219
X_1		1.000	0.168	0.069	0.266	-0.094	-0.114
X_2			1.000	-0.030	0.080	-0.208	-0.193
X_3				1.000	0.252	-0.075	-0.015
X_4					1.000	-0.083	-0.224
X_5						1.000	0.248
X_6							1.000

TABLE 2
RESULTS OF THE STEPWISE MULTIPLE REGRESSION

Independent Variables Given by Order of Entry

Step	Variable	Multiple R	R^2	Change in R^2	r	Beta
1	Accessibility (X_1)	0.669	0.4486	0.4486	-0.669	-0.703
2	Urban Growth (X_3)	0.748	0.5595	0.1109	-0.551	-0.416
3	Urban Population (X_2)	0.786	0.6178	0.0583	0.417	0.354
4	Agricultural Productivity (X_5)	0.791	0.6257	0.0079	-0.389	-0.129
5	Density of Agriculturalists (X_4)	0.794	0.6304	0.0047	0.310	0.091

TABLE 3
TREND SURFACE ANALYSES OF RESIDUALS FROM REGRESSION

Order of Surface	Total Variation	Standard Deviation	Variation Explained By Surface	r	R^2
Linear	175.67	0.83	6.32	0.191	0.036
Quadratic	175.67	0.77	10.74	0.247	0.061
*Cubic	175.67	0.73	29.71	0.411	0.169

*Significant at the 0.05 level.

REFERENCES

Brunn, Stanley D., and Robert N. Thomas. "Socio-Economic Environments and Internal Migration: The Case of Tegucigalpa, Honduras." *Social and Economic Studies*, 21(4), 463-473, 1972.

Centro Latinamerican de Demografía (CELADE). *Encuesta Demográfica de Honduras. Resultados y Elaboración de Datos.* Pulicaciones, Series A, 129 (2). San José, Cost Rica: CELADE, 1975.

Centro Latinoamerican de Demografía (CELADE). *Encuesta Demográfica de Honduras. Resultados y Elaboración de Datos.* Publicaciones, Series A, 129 (2). San José, Costa Rica: CELADE, 1975.

Dirección General de Estadística y Censos. *Censo Nacional de Honduras, Características Generales y Educativas de la Población.* Tegucigalpa, Honduras: Dirección General de Estadística y Censos, Secretaría de Economia y Hacienda, 1964.

Dirección General de Estadística y Censos. *Población Total en Cabeceras Municipales y en Aldeas y Caseríos: 1967-1970.* Tegucigalpa, Honduras: Dirección General de Estadística y Censos, Secretaría de Economía y Hacienda, 1969.

Herrick, Bruce. "Urbanization and Urban Migration in Latin America: An Economist's View." In F. F. Rabinovitz and F. M. Trueblood, eds., *Latin American Urban Research,* Volume I, Beverly Hills, CA: Sage Publications, Inc., 1970, pp. 71-82.

Organization for Economic Cooperation and Development (OECD). *List of Social Concerns Common to Most OECD Countries.* Paris: OECD, 1973.

Russet, B. M., *et al. World Handbook of Political and Social Indicators.* New Haven, CN: Yale University Press, 1964.

Shaw, R. Paul. "Land Tenure and the Rural Exodus in Latin America." *Economic Development and Cultural Change*, 23(1), 123-132, 1975.

Smith, D. M. *The Geography of Social Well-Being in the United States.* New York: McGraw-Hill, 1973.

_____. *Patterns in Human Geography.* New York: Crane, Russak and Company, Inc, 1975.

Wilcox, L. D., *et al. Social Indicators and Societal Monitoring: An Annotated Bibliography.* Amsterdam: Elsevier, 1972.

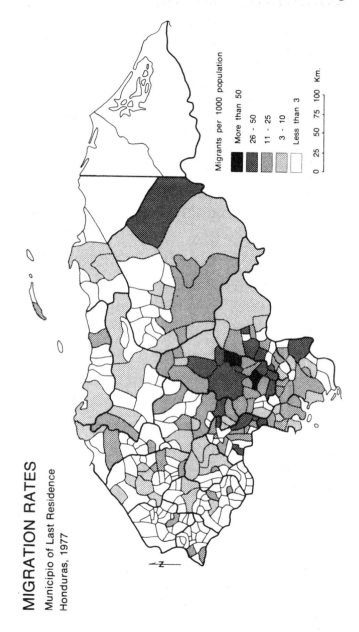

MIGRATION RATES

Municipio of Last Residence

Honduras, 1977

Migrants per 1000 population

More than 50

26 - 50

11 - 25

3 - 10

Less than 3

0   25   50   75   100   Km.

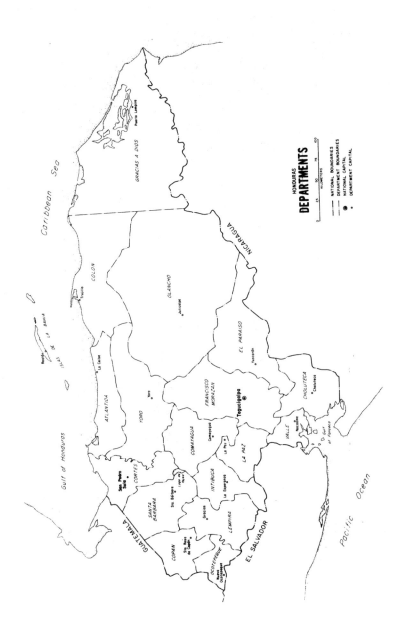

HONDURAS
DEPARTMENTS

NATIONAL BOUNDARIES
DEPARTMENT BOUNDARIES
NATIONAL CAPITAL
DEPARTMENT CAPITAL

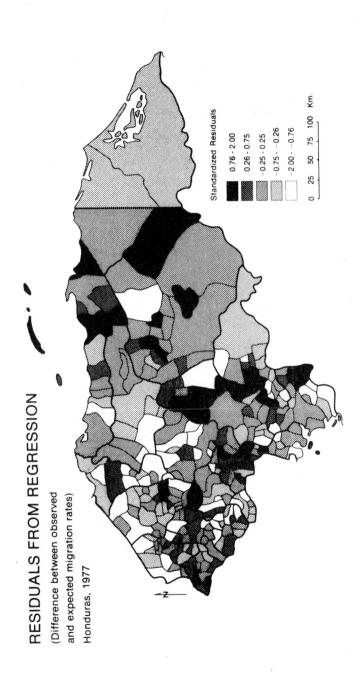

RESIDUALS FROM REGRESSION

(Difference between observed
and expected migration rates)

Honduras, 1977

Standardized Residuals

0.76 - 2.00
0.26 - 0.75
-0.25 - 0.25
-0.75 - -0.26
-2.00 - -0.76

0   25   50   75   100   Km.

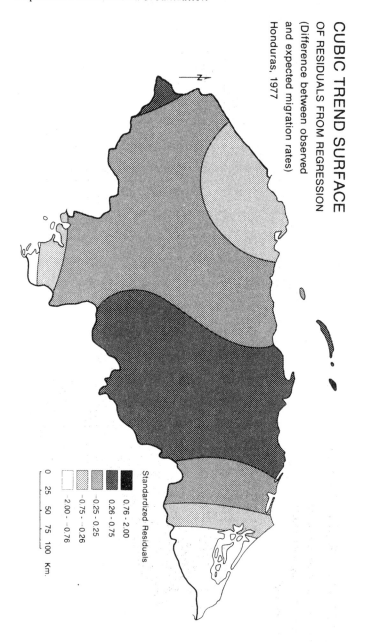

CUBIC TREND SURFACE
OF RESIDUALS FROM REGRESSION
(Difference between observed
and expected migration rates)
Honduras, 1977

Standardized Residuals

0.76 - 2.00
0.26 - 0.75
-0.25 - 0.25
-0.75 - -0.26
-2.00 - -0.76

0 25 50 75 100 Km.

N

POPULATION GROWTH AND COMPOSITION IN ST. VINCENT, 1861 TO 1960

Joseph G. Spinelli

St. Vincent, in the eastern Caribbean, is representative of other small Caribbean islands in the process of socio-economic development. With only 150 square miles in area including its Grenadine dependencies, St. Vincent has nonetheless experienced a history of overlapping monocultural cash crop regimens. Population growth, in turn, has closely followed the fortunes of the Vincentian economy.

St. Vincent's demographic history of the last century and a half is divided into roughly three periods: 1) post-slavery, foreign-labor immigration: 1838 to 1881; 2) emigration: 1881 to 1931; and 3) rapid population growth: 1931 to 1960.

FOREIGN LABOR IMMIGRATION

With the end of slavery in 1838, the sugarcane planters in St. Vincent became concerned with obtaining abundant and cheap labor, as many ex-slaves opted to withdraw from estate work. As a result, the first official census was taken in 1844 to determine the number of people in the colony. The population was estimated to be 27,248.

The legislature sought to increase the pool of laborers by importing indentured agricultural workers, and between 1844 and 1880, 5,575 indentured workers were brought to St. Vincent. There were 3,138 Portuguese Madeirans and "liberated" Africans landed between 1844 and 1862, and 2,429 East Indians between 1861 and 1880. It was during the latter period that St. Vincent's sugar industry was partially restored by the actions of the West Indian Encumbered Estates Act of 1857, which brought many abandoned estates into production. By 1881, the census enumerated 40,548 people in St. Vincent, an annual rate of population growth of 1.07 percent since the first census.

ERA OF EMIGRATION

The interval between 1881 and 1931 included some of the worst economic and natural disasters in St. Vincent's history. These induced considerable out-migration. Increasingly, losses in sugar production in the last quarter of the century resulted in a steady outflow of Vincentians to more prosperous environments in the circum-Caribbean region, especially to Trinidad. A severe hurricane in 1898 and the Soufrière volcanic eruption in 1902, with its great losses of life and property, caused additional heavy out-migration; the annual rate of net migration between 1891 and 1911 was –18.9 per 1000, the highest ever recorded by the official censuses. The population losses from emigration were so great that population increased (from 40,548 to 47,961) at an average annual rate of only 0.3 percent between 1881 and 1931. Natural increase was estimated to be 40,420, yet the change in the total population in this fifty-year period was only 7,413, or only 18 percent of that expected from natural increase.

RAPID POPULATION GROWTH

Between 1931 and 1960, however, St. Vincent experienced the most rapid rate of growth in its census history: 1.7 percent per year. A combination of high fertility and declining mortality—despite periodic out-migration—accounted for the "explosive" growth rates after 1931. From 47,961 in 1931, the population grew to 79,948 in 1960. This would have been considerably larger had laborers not emigrated during the Second World War or during the brief existence of the West Indian Federation. For example, between 1947 and 1959, natural increase amounted to 28,000, while net migration amounted to a *loss* of 11,220. This means that 40 percent of the natural increase was "neutralized" by out-migration. Had St. Vincent experienced no emigration and had it grown at the annual rate of natural increase for the year 1957 (4.2 percent), the population would have doubled in only seventeen years.

SPATIAL DISTRIBUTION AND DENSITY

The spatial distribution of the population has changed very little since the early nineteenth century. Most of the population has been, and still is, concentrated below the 1,000-foot contour level. The ruggedness of the topography above 1,000 feet has effectively eliminated such lands from continuous exploitation. Only 56 percent of the main island's area can be effectively used. The main concentrations of population have been along the Windward and Leeward coasts and the lower reaches of the interior valleys; density increases towards Kingstown at the southern end of the island.

The calculation of population density (total population divided by total area) results in a population density of 182 persons per square mile as far back as 1844, 535 per square mile in 1960 and 629 per square mile by 1970. By including only the accessible portions of the "main" island of St. Vincent (the area below the 1,000-foot elevation), the *effective* density of population increased from 339 persons per square mile in 1844 to 1,002 per square mile in 1960 and 1,119 by 1970. This presents a more realistic measurement of crowding in the island bringing the real density closer to that experienced in Barbados, the most densely settled island in the formerly British Caribbean.

POPULATION COMPOSITION

Important population characteristics including (1) age, (2) sex, (3) race, (4) rural-urban residence, and (5) occupational status are comparable through various censuses.

In general, the population has been characterized by its extreme youthfulness. For the population under 20 years of age, there has been relatively little change between 1861 and 1960. In 1861, 50 percent of the population was under 20 years of age and in 1960 this had increased to 58 percent. The 1970 census showed 62 percent.

Most of the change in age composition has been confined to the younger working-age groups, 20 through 39 years of age. These are the ages most selective of migrants leaving the island. Above 40 years of age, there has been little fluctuation over the last century or so.

When age and sex are taken togeher, the out-migration

streams were predominately young male adults between 1881 and 1931. It was only after the Second World War, especially in the late 1950's that young female adults began leaving, first to Trinidad and Tobago and later, in the early 1960's to Great Britain and Canada.

St. Vincent's "young" population is the result of both heavy emigration of young adults and the high fertility experienced after the world trade depression years of the 1930's. Consequently, the economic burden of dependency on those remaining adults has been high throughout the post-slavery era. From a minimum of seventy-two "dependents" (those under fifteen and over sixty-four years of age) per 100 working-age persons in 1911, the total dependency ratio increased to 115 in 1960, with 91 percent of the 1960 dependency ratio made up of children under fifteen years of age. By 1970, the dependency ratio had increased to 127, with youths still accounting for 91 percent of the total.

St. Vincent has also experienced a declining sex ratio (the number of males per 100 females). This tendency results from the very high sex ratios during slave days which declined after the importation of slaves into the British West Indies was abolished in 1808. Thereafter, the higher mortality of the aging ex-slaves plus the low fertility rate among the predominately black population caused the sex ratio to fall so that by 1844 (the time of the first official census) there were only 86 males per 100 females.

The period of foreign labor immigration reversed this trend briefly, raising the sex ratio to a high of ninety in the census years of 1861 and 1871. After 1871, the heavy out-migration experienced for the next fifty years once again lowered the sex ratio to a low of seventy-six in 1921. The high fertility rates after 1931 and the worldwide restrictions on migration caused St. Vincent's sex ratio to increase from eighty-three in 1946, to eighty-nine in 1960; and to ninety by 1970. St. Vincent, thus, is still characterized by its extreme youthfulness and its female sex dominance.

For more than 200 years, the overwhelming proportion of the island's population has been black ("African" or "Negro"), clearly the result of the period of slavery when only relatively few "whites" and "mixed" operated the sugar estates or worked as free men in the towns and villages.

From a maximum of 90 percent black population in 1812, this proportion declined slowly but steadily as the "mixed" (or "colored") segment increased. In 1861, when the East Indians began arriving, the black component of the population accounted for 71 percent of the total, while the "mixed" group (which included the East Indians) accounted for 20 percent of the population. Thereafter, as late as 1960, these figures varied only a few percentage points at each census. The "white" (or "European") population decreased from a maximum of 11 percent in 1787 to a minimum of slightly more than 2 percent in 1960.

None of the censuses has satisfactorily taken account of settlement sizes. The terms "urban" and "rural" have never been used; instead, in the 1940 and 1960 censuses, so-called "small towns" were set aside from their rural environs. Although this practice was more satisfactory than earlier ones, it still failed to distinguish urban and rural characteristics. If settlements possessed "certain institutions or facilities" and had 2,000 inhabitants or more, they were designated as "small towns" for census purposes.

St. Vincent, in effect, is a "rural" island. The only settlement that can be judged "urban" is Kingstown, the capital and primate city. Other "small towns" are still agriculturally oriented, as many residents work in their fields during the day and return to their village homes in the evening. Life in most villages is distinctly rural in character.

It is helpful to group the occupations listed in the censuses from 1861 to 1960 into three broad industrial categories: (1) primary activities, (2) secondary activities, and (3) service activities.

Although the size of the labor force has increased over the last century, it has decreased as a percentage of the total population, from 64 percent in 1861 to only 29 percent in 1960. Since the end of large-scale emigration in the first quarter of the twentieth century, the sex ratio of all the industrial groups has shown an increase. The greatest increase was in secondary occupations (small-scale manufacturing, carpentry, and construction). Between 1911 and 1960, the sex ratio of this group increased from 86 to 256, while that of the primary group (agriculture) increased from 86 to 177. Although the sex ratio increased for service activities, it was much lower—from 50 in 1911 to 99 in 1960.

During the twentieth century, males have been much more active in the labor force than females, at all ages, despite their smaller numbers. For example, between 1861 and 1931, the percentage of the labor force engaged in the primary sector remained relatively constant at about 60-65 percent. Thereafter, it declined as more workers entered the secondary and service sectors of the economy, reaching a low of 42 percent by 1960. About 32 percent were in service jobs. Much of this change was the result of younger workers shifting out of farming and into the more attractive jobs, a trend that will continue as the government stimulates more economic diversification, especially in tourism, government employment, and construction.

II
Development Strategies and Migration

DECENTRALIZATION OF URBAN GROWTH
IN LATIN AMERICA:
RECENT HISTORY AND SOME CURRENT EXPERIENCES

Emily Baldwin and Eric Chetwynd, Jr. *

Since World War II the process of urbanization in Latin America has been progressing at a rapid pace. While some countries now are more urbanized than others and there are differential rates of urbanization, all have had to face the reality of rapidly growing cities. Average urban population growth rates of four percent and more per year have been common in Latin America in the last several decades and are expected to continue in many countries for several decades more (Fox, 1975; Beier, 1975). At this rate, urban populations double every eighteen years. While rapid urbanization is a marked characteristic of all less developed areas of the world at present, Latin America is by far the most urbanized (Portes and Browning, 1976:3), and some of its cities rank among the largest in the world.

PRIMACY AND URBAN STRUCTURES

Population increase is in large part responsible for this rapid urbanization. As a country's population increases in absolute numbers, existing towns and cities acquire more residents as well. But beyond the population increases are economic, social, and political factors which fuel the process of urbanization in Latin America, i.e., the massive influxes that have migrated from the rural regions to the major cities in search of work, training, health and medical care, and an opportunity to parti-

---

*The opinions expressed in this paper are the authors', and in no way reflect the views or policies of the United States Agency for International Development.

cipate more actively in national development (Lander and Funes, 1975: 333; Fox, 1975:x).

Many Latin American countries have developed around a single urban center that more often than not has been the administrative, economic and social—if not geographic—center of the country. While other urban centers have existed within each country, their ability to influence and attract population, investments, and control has typically been weak in comparison to the primate city. The dominance of the major city has been due to the concentration of population, wealth, and economic activity, compounding itself as the primate city seemed to offer advantages over the smaller cities (Lander and Funes, 1975: 333).

This dominance of the principal city in the national urban system is frequently referred to as "primacy" and normally is measured in terms of population differential. A commonly used index of primacy is the ratio of the population of the largest city to the combined population of the next three largest cities. A standard Gini coefficient also has been used as an index of primacy (Chetwynd, 1976: 125-126).*

In comparison with other less developed areas of the world, Latin America has by far the highest primacy, as shown in the table below:

	1950-60		1960-70	
	Gini	Primacy	Gini	Primacy
Latin America	.45	2.67	.48	2.92
Africa	.27	1.44	.31	1.67
Asia	.24	1.50	.28	1.67

In other words, primacy in Latin America is approximately 60 percent higher than in either Asia or Africa, and this pattern

---

*The Gini coefficient for Primacy serves as a measure of the degree of equality between the actual distribution and a hypothetical rank-size distribution. It is obtained by summing the area under a curve generated by the actual city size distribution and the area under the city-size distribution rank-size curve. The former is subtracted from the latter and the difference is divided by the area under the rank-size curve. The higher the Gini coefficient, up to a maximum of 1.0, the greater the degree of divergence between the hypothetical rank-size curve and the curve depicting the actual city size distribution.

has held true at least over the two recent decades from 1950-1970 (Chetwynd, 1976:174).

THE CHANGING STRUCTURE OF URBAN SYSTEMS

Despite the extreme primacy of Latin American urban structures over time, recent evidence does suggest that the trend may be changing. Fox (1975:x), for example, states that a "changing structure of urban systems, characterized by a rapid increase in the number of secondary cities," has begun to emerge. Many of these smaller secondary cities now match or even exceed the growth rates of the primate cites. In a study of six of the larger and more populous countries,* Fox (1975) found that non-primate cities of 250,000 inhabitants or more were expanding most rapidly, accounting for 20.4 percent of Latin American urban residents in 1960 and for a projected 31.1 percent by 1980. During the same period, smaller cities (those with 20,000-250,000 inhabitants) declined somewhat in their percentage of urban population although their absolute populations increased.

In summary, cities of all sizes are growing, as would be expected with rapid natural population increase, but the largest secondary cities are exerting a proportionately larger influence on the changing urban system.

Peru provides an example of the growing importance of the larger secondary cities within the national urban system in the more populous Latin American countries. In 1940, Peru had no city outside of the Lima metropolitan area with a population of even 100,000. By 1972, the city of Arequipa had surpassed the 250,000 population mark, accounting for 5.4 percent of the nation's urban population. By 1980, two more cities, Trujillo and Chiclayo, will have joined Arequipa in having more than 250,000 people, the three cities together accounting for an estimated 12.5 percent of the total urban population (Fox, 1972). Mexico and Brazil offer even more dramatic examples of secondary city growth. Each of these countries had eight cities of 250,000 inhabitants or more (approximately 23 percent of the urban population in both countries) outside of the Mexico City, Rio de Janeiro and São Paulo metropolitan

---

*Argentina, Brazil, Chile, Mexico, Peru, Venezuela.

areas in 1960. Yet by 1980 this city-size group is expected to have grown to 27 cities (37.3 percent of the total urban population) in Mexico and 25 cities (32.3 percent of total urban population) in Brazil (Fox, 1975:15).

This growth of larger secondary cities (i.e., those over 250,000) is characteristic of both the larger Latin American countries and the Central American countries and Panama. In Central America, those cities with populations of 250,000 or more are exclusively the capital-primate cities; and only San Pedro Sula possesses a size and urban growth rate sufficient to make it a secondary city (100,000 or more inhabitants) of consequence. It is, instead, the smaller cities of the region—those with populations between 10,000 and 50,000—which are growing most rapidly. In 1950, Central America and Panama together had only 26 cities of 10,000 to 50,000 inhabitants; but by 1980, the number of cities in this size category is expected to have grown to 95. Some of these smaller cities (e.g., David, Panama, and Escuintla, Guatemala) have growth rates not only above the national average but also above the primate city's growth rate. Despite their relatively small size, these cities have grown rapidly enough to maintain a roughly constant proportion of their nations' urban populations over time, representing 24.6 percent of the urban population in 1950 and 25 percent in 1980. In marked contrast to the growth of these smaller cities in Central America, the number of relatively large secondary cities (with populations between 50,000 and 250,000) has changed hardly at all in thirty years. With the exception of San Pedro Sula, the larger urban centers exhibit surprisingly low rates of growth in comparison to the national average and in comparison to the smaller cities. As a result, the percentage of national urban population represented by the larger secondary cities has dropped precipitously—from 54.5 percent of the total urban population in 1950 to 12.2 percent in 1980 (Fox and Huguet, 1977).

Despite the relatively rapid growth of certain secondary cities, many are still dwarfed in absolute size by the primate cities.

Accordng to a United Nations survey, no Latin American country desires a reversal of its overall urbanization trends, but most find the current spatial distribution of population inappropriate and favor a deceleration and redirection of their urban growth patterns (United Nations, 1979: 72-77). A concern over the size and rapid growth of the primate city has spawned a variety of decentralization and regionalization plans by the Latin Amercian countries.

THE MOTIVATION FOR DECENTRALIZATION AND REGIONALIZATION

Concern over the size and growth of the primate city is widespread, but the cause of the concern varies depending upon countries' circumstances and philosophical outlooks. These differences have resulted in a variety of approaches for altering the current urban structure. Some countries, for example, have been concerned primarily with the social and political consequences of a primate city's dominance. A fear of a country's dependence upon one large city has prompted some governments to attempt interventions in the urban structure. As one illustration, the Cuban government has consciously stopped the growth of Havana while promoting the growth of much smaller cities in order to extend equal benefits to as much of the population as possible (Acosta and Hardoy, 1972: 172; Landstreet, 1975: 137). This has been achieved through a variety of means. Among the most important are the funneling of investments away from Havana and toward smaller cities (limiting new jobs in Havana and creating jobs elsewhere), the restriction of residence permits and ration cards in Havana, and the construction of a series of new towns aimed at integrating agricultural and industrial projects at the village level (Landstreet, 1975).

Other countries, while not as anti-primate city as Cuba, simply have been unable to cope with the rapid influxes of people to the primate city and have undertaken decentralization to ease the socioeconomic pressures on the major centers. Peru, for instance, has tried to offer urban alternatives to Lima in an attempt to reduce the problems in that city. This has been accomplished primarily through regional allocation of industry primarily to Arequipa, and through some re-allocation of investments, both public and private (Webb, 1975).

Other countries have been more concerned with purely economic questions than with socio-political questions. Brazil, for example, has been concerned primarily with stimulating a high rate of economic growth and, as a consequence, has wanted to draw on as many of its national resources as efficiently as possible. Given the area of Brazil, the promotion of urban decentralization has been undertaken to exploit a large portion of the country's resources while minimizing the economic drain of large concentrations of underproductive labor in the major cities (United Nations, 1970: 86-113; Harrigan, 1975). Brazil developed dramatic programs to direct development and population movement into the country: the creation of Brasília, and construction of the Trans-Amazonian Highway and the Rio-Brasília Highway, and the establishment of several regional development institutions. These were notable parts of a concerted effort to decentralize and to move inland, particularly away from the Rio-São Paulo area. Brazil's emphasis on economic growth with heavy reliance on the private sector has resulted in much of its decentralization efforts being unplanned and rather haphazard. In addition, many of the expected results of the minimal decentralization plans have not been forthcoming as private investors have failed to respond as expected to government incentives and programs. A similar pattern occurred in Mexico recently where a reliance on private investors to stimulate economic growth and development has lead to an ever greater concentration of activity and wealth in a few major urban centers (Barkin, 1975).

Simultaneous concern for the socio-political consequences and for the economic consequences of primate city growth has become apparent. Strong desire for national integration, in response to the frustrations of historical primate city-nation dichotomies motivates urban decentralization. With varying degrees of commitment and energy many Latin American countries have begun formulating and implementing plans designed to address what is felt to be a lack of national integration or a severely underdeveloped and imbalanced urban hierarchy.

RECENT HISTORY OF DECENTRALIZATION EXPERIENCES

Latin American spatial planning had some isolated beginnings as early as the 1930's in Puerto Rico (Pico, 1962; Findley, 1979) and 1940's and 1950's in Mexico and Brazil (Cardenas, 1972 ; Stohr, 1975). The construction of Brasília in the late 1950's was one of the earliest attempts to decentralize a national urban structure by forcibly moving the administrative control of Brazil away from the traditionally large and growing cities and into the hinterland (Stohr, 1975: 173). However, most of the initial attempts at urban decentralization and regional planning were uncoordinated, and lax. In most cases, it was not until the major cities in each country began to grow enormously in absolute size in the 1960's and 1970's that more systematic planning of the national urban structure was attempted.

Growth Poles

Some of the early efforts at nationwide decentralization centered on the "growth pole" strategy which identified potentially growing secondary cities distant from the primate city and designated them as "growth poles." Rather than "decentralization," the strategy associated with concentration of efforts on the growth poles is more appropriately "deconcentration" or "decentralized concentration." Typically, the "growth poles" chosen were relatively large, existing cities which were to receive increases in public infrastructure (ususally transportation and communication improvements) and government incentives (tax credits, subsidies, construction of publicly-owned heavy industry) designed to encourage private investments. Some "growth poles," however, were new cities, such as Brasília, built explicitly to serve as countermagnets to the primate cities.

Emphasis on industrialization in growth and development during the 1950's and 1960's usually determined that a growth pole's "potential for growth" meant its industrial capacity and promise. Thus, the increasing concentration of population in urban centers was considered good and necessary in order to industrialize and develop as long as the urban population could be concentrated in several cities instead of just one or two (Gilbert, 1975: 242). This strategy was seen as offering rural out-migrants an alternative to migration to the primate city through provision of modern sector employment and services in cities closer to home.

Several countries in Latin America implemented growth pole-influenced programs in the 1960's and early 1970's. As part of a strong nationalistic drive toward economic growth and development, Venezuela formulated one of Latin America's earliest

growth-pole plans. A coordinated national policy of decentralization was undertaken in the early 1960's although construction of Ciudad Guyana had begun several years earlier as an
isolated project to take advantage of rich natural resources in
the hinterland. The growth poles identified in the national plan
were cities already showing high growth potential. A ranking of
"core regions" was made, naming Caracas, Valencia, and Ciudad
Guyana "national metropoli" with several other existing major
cities as second and third order centers (Friedmann, 1966;
Rodwin, 1972). This plan was urban-oriented and, with the
exception of Ciudad Guyana, supported the already existing
urban hierarchy.

Chile, as another example, in the late 1960's designated
Concepción, Valparaiso, and Antofagasta as countermagnets to
the growth of Santiago. Unfortunately, the government's
"published plans did not specify fully the advantages to be
obtained by the deconcentration strategy, and they indicated
only some of the roles of the growth poles, such as geographic
specialization and absorption or rural migration" (Lozano,
1975b: 304). State-owned industries were built and infrastructure monies directed toward the growth poles named, but
Santiago continued to receive the lion's share of both public
and private investments. As a result, the government of this
period "ended up contributing to the regional trends [it] criticized" (Lozano, 1975: 308; Friedmann, 1971).

Colombia also initiated a growth pole-influenced decentralization policy. In the late 1960's, Colombia defined levels of
urban centers and the function of each; in this sense, the
Colombian plan resembled that of Venezuela. In particular,
"Bogotá was considered to be of singular importance and was
classified as the 'National Metropolis.' Next in importance were
the three 'Metropoli of Equilibrium,' Medellín, Cali and Barranquilla, which it was hoped could act as countermagnets to the
dominance of Bogotá. To help them in this role, manufacturing complexes were to be developed and high-level urban
services . . . established" (Gilbert 1975: 257).

Despite its emphasis on industrial development and large
urban centers, the Colombian program did include provisions to
improve the socio-economic conditions of smaller cities and the
rural areas. The approach, however, was overtly pro-urban and,

among other policies, made no attempt to slow rural out-migration, concentrated on investment in a few large-scale industries in the major cities, and directed most of the infra-structure investments toward those same major cities (Gilbert, 1975).

In short, the growth pole approach enjoyed a short-lived popularity as it often did not directly address some of the fundamental needs of decentralization. Critics noted that the people and resources of the rural areas were still not being effectively integrated into the national sphere. That is, the growth pole strategy frequently was a stop-gap measure, aimed primarily at easing the pressures of industrialization and modernization on the primate city. It often lacked a "regional" vision of integrating a geographical area into a national working system. Growth poles met some needs of the surrounding popu-lations, but the primate cities frequently continued to project the image of uniquely satisfying the widest variety of needs. Thus, while some rural-urban migration may indeed have been directed away from the primate city through this strategy, it has apparently been "small and undesirable" in many coun-tries (Findley, 1977: 101). In addition, objections on several fronts were substantial enough to weaken the popularity of the growth pole approach. Among these objection were: (1) ideolo-gical problems, the "growth poles" being perceived as perpetu-ating the urban-dominant pattern of the primate city; (2) theo-retical problems, the difficulty of transferring growth pole ideas from paper to reality and from developed country to less developed country; and, (3) political problems, some regions being selected for growth, others were consciously excluded; (Conroy, 1973; Lozano, 1975b: 313). The objections to the growth pole approach and the continued dominance of many primate cities despite growth pole policies weakened support for this particular decentralization approach.

The Rural Emphasis

Attention in the 1970's, particularly on the part of develop-ment assistance donors, began to turn away from the cities and toward the rural areas in an attempt to stem the tide of migra-tion at its source. Land reform, agricultural credit, assistance plans, rural health and education programs, and infrastructure construction have all been implemented in varying degrees to make rural areas more attractive. As several authors (Rhoda, 1979; Findley, 1979) have noted, however, purely rural strategies to curb rural out-migration have been ineffective. In fact, they frequently have had an opposite effect, stimulating rather than reducing migration. For example, rural education programs have often raised expectations of rural youths to higher levels than can be attained at home. At the same time, they have reduced the rural-urban cultural "distance," thereby increasing the flow of migrants to the cities in search of fulfillment. Even some programs directly related to agriculture, particularly Green Revolution and farm mechanization programs, have stimulated migration by reducing the need for farm labor, and therefore, leaving fewer employment opportunities in the rural areas. Even though countries turned to rural development in the early 1970's, urban areas still received more attention. The flow of large private and public investments, and the concentration of influential men and women always keep urban problems nationally and internationally visible.

An Integrated Approach

The decline in popularity of the growth pole and of purely rural development strategies has been accompanied by a relatively recent rise in popularity of a more "integrated" approach which combines elements of these two previous strategies. One of the earliest advocates of a more integrated rural-urban plan was Chile's Allende administration. A pioneer plan, the Allende program lacked somewhat in clarity and coherence, but it nonetheless served as a forerunner of much of the decentralization planning now taking place by stressing "the rejuvenation of small and medium-sized towns" and the urbanization of the countryside through provision of urban services to rural areas" (Lozano, 1975a). More recently, many government policies dealing with decentralization focus on the market town and/or rural service center as the critical link between the rural areas and the national urban system. On the one hand, these market towns/service centers perform the marketing, service, and other "urban" functions for farmers which many rural development programs lacked; on the other hand, they help to draw the rural areas into the national development process, an objective which many growth pole programs failed to achieve. It develops the link between rural and urban areas, rather than focusing on one to the exclusion of the other. The object is to provide farmers with greater access to marketing, urban services, and off-farm employment opportunities close to home so they may no longer need to move to the city (Findley, 1970). The purpose of this approach is two-fold: one, to stimulate development in the rural areas of the country, and two, to retain the population in the rural areas by curbing migration incentives.

Many Latin American countries are now looking to some form of this integrated approach for their decentralization policies. Since the authors are most familiar with those countries working with the U.S. Agency for International Development (A.I.D.) on this approach, the examples used here will concentrate on A.I.D. programs. This is not to say, however, that other countries are not working on similar plans.

RURAL-URBAN INTEGRATION

Throughout Latin America, countries are turning to development policies which combine rural and urban functions in small urban centers. A.I.D. has encouraged and supported such programs. In the Dominican Republic, for example, "the primary focus of A.I.D. programs will continue to be on rural areas and the rural poor, including villages, market towns, and small cities, and will emphasize provision of markets, services, employment, and balanced growth . . ." (Benjamin, 1979).

The government of Costa Rica recognized the existing and future problems it faces in allowing San José and the surrounding plateau area to grow unabated. For this reason, in 1976 Costa Rica established an urban and regional development planning system to draw the rural areas into the national economy and decision-making process. Priority has been given to the northern and Atlantic regions of the country, and more specifically, to six of the poorest areas which will receive development support in part for an example to other areas. The emphasis is on the support and development of regional urban centers which can provide non-farm employment opportunities as well as agricultural services. A.I.D. is supporting the policy through a loan to be used to promote greater rural self-reliance through technical assistance and income-producing demonstration projects (CDSS, 1979; ABS, 1978, 1979).

Panama is perhaps one of the best examples of a recent government attempt to formulate and implement an integrated decentralization policy. This policy is motivated by the belief that "lack of access" is the key to rural poverty, therefore to urbanward migration (CDSS, 1979: 40). The "Growth and Service Centers Project" now in progress is "based on the idea that regional development can be stimulated by improving the provision of services and function by urban centers to their hinterlands" (Rhoda, 1978: 346). By providing marketing credit and technical services, developing infrastructure and transportation, and stimulating agricultural processing in care-fully selected secondary cities in Western Panama, the govern-ment hopes to promote agricultural expansion and off-farm employment alternatives, thereby improving rural incomes, drawing farmers into the national economy, and deterring some migration.

Specifically, the Panamanian program focuses on two "growth centers," David and Chitre-Los Santos, which will serve as the location of agriculture-related industry and transportation centers, and six smaller "service centers," designed to link the villages to the growth centers. Since the population of Western Panama is very dispersed, this strategy is intended to concen-trate activities around a series of small cities which can meet local needs efficiently and offer alternatives to migration (AID/Panama; Quarterly Economic Review of Nicaragua, Costa Rica, Panama, 1976, 1977: Rhoda, 1978; CDSS, 1979; Miller, 1979).

A.I.D.'s "Integrated Regional Development Loan" to Peru serves "to assist the [Government of Peru] to improve its regional and urban planning capability and to provide a finan-cing mechanism for identified priorities of selected intermediate cities and market towns." This loan supports Peru's recognition of the need to strengthen rural-urban linkages in the form of marketing, supply, transportation, extension and other services to the rural areas. The efforts in Peru are, for the time being at least, concentrated on selected areas of the sierra and jungle regions away from the more urban coastal region. One major emphasis is on institution building, that is, on establishing and strengthening a national system for regional development.

Simultaneously, high priority will be given to several regional centers to develop the actual infrastructure and services needed as demonstration areas (ABS, 1978: AID/Peru Project Paper, 1979).

A.I.D. also is assisting in integrated decentralization projects in several other South American countries. In Bolivia, A.I.D. is working with the Departmental Development Corporations (DDCs), regional planning agencies which report to the central government but which also retain a large amount of independence. The DDCs were initially created to carry out urban development projects within each region, but, with increased interest in rural development in recent years, they have now expanded to include such projects as rural infrastructure and agro-industries. The expanded activity reflects an increasing awareness that most urban centers are not integrated with nearby rural areas. The A.I.D. decentralization efforts in Bolivia encourage the development of rural-urban linkages through the strengthening of market towns and rural service centers, but the DDCs maintain the final word on exactly how and to what extent this will be carried out. Since the project is yet new, the form the decentralization policies will take is yet unclear (CDSS, 1979; AID, Mission to Bolivia, 1979).

One of the more innovative attempts to decentralize the urban structure has been implemented in Paraguay. As it was initially conceived, at least, the "Market Town Development Plan" was intended to be "bottom up" decentralization (Rhoda, 1977), that is, the local authorities were to play the major role in design and implementation of projects to develop their area's most needed urban services. Ideally, emphasis was to feature local participation and input with a minimum of interference from high authorities. The national government's Municipal Development Institute (IDM) was to have some control over local programs, but its primary purpose was to supply technical assistance, training, and advice upon the request of the local authorities. While the project was designed to "finance small municipal development subprojects (e.g., market places, water supplies, health centers)," rural poor were the major target. This municipal development project was, therefore, being carried out in conjunction with rural road construction and agro-industry development projects, all designed to improve agriculturalists' income opportunities. The project has encouraged the growth and strengthening of small urban centers outside Asunción which the government hopes will prevent large migration to the capital and will improve the rural standard of living (Rhoda, 1977). Paraguay continues to implement this program, but without U.S. support which limits our access to information for current evaluation.

Colombia, Brazil, and Venezuela are also pursuing urban decentralization policies. These countries, however, while dominated by one or two very large cities, have a more balanced urban system already in existence than those countries already discussed; and their policies, however interesting, cannot be covered here.

EVALUATION OF INTEGRATED DECENTRALIZATION

The integrated approach to decentralization is too new in most countries to permit evaluation of its success relative to previous decentralization policies. Whatever its success, the approach is not without its problems.

Its emphasis on local participation and planning inevitably places tremendous strain on both local and national institutions in the LDCs. On the one hand, the highly centralized nature of many Latin American governments has frequently prevented the development of local institutions for local decision-making. On the other hand, the details of planning at the local level require more of central planners than they can or should deliver.

In addition, the integrated approach requires a cross-sectoral coordination foreign to most Latin American governments which are accustomed to planning for development on a ministry-by-ministry basis. Integration implies major interministerial coordination.

Integrated decentralization focuses on some of a nation's most neglected areas. The rural hinterlands and small towns have historically not been the recipients of much investment, public or private. Despite growing commitment to public investment, success will still depend in large part on the private sector. Because of the amount of work needed to improve these previously neglected areas and the relatively high risks involved, the support of the private sector is by no means guaranteed.

Being new, the integrated approach implementation is not

particularly well-defined. Each country and perhaps even each region must develop a strategy suited to its own needs. Lack of knowledge and shortages of skilled planners make the tailoring of decentralization plans to each local area difficult and risk-prone.

CONCLUSIONS

The realization that past development policies which have emphasized either rural or urban development in isolation have been ineffective in reducing either poverty or urbanward migration has led to a search for other, more effective, development strategies. The current trend toward rural-urban integration in decentralization policies addresses issues which are necessary and appropriate. Decentralization, however, does not carry the same policy prescription to all countries. In accordance with the needs, goals, resources, and circumstances of each nation and of each region, different policies for decentralization need to be developed.

"Decentralization" and "integration" are interrelated, yet independent, concepts. That is, there is a distinction between the form of an urban hierarchy and its function. Urban decentralization may be a prerequisite for integration in many countries, but planning for an urban hierarchy, in the absence of "vigorous social restructuring and participation of all members of society in the benefits of economic growth" (Geisse and Coraggio, 1972: 58) would seem to avoid the central issue.

The integrated approach can by no means be viewed as a panacea and as a guarantee to reduce rural-urban migration. In fact, Rhoda (1979: 1-2) states that "migration is usually stimulated by activities which foster rural-urban integration . . . ." In Findley's view (1979: 50), "it appears that 'slowing the rural-urban drift' is an unrealistic and inappropriate goal for integrated rural development schemes. A more accurate reflection of the dynamics of rural development and migration would be 'increasing migration options.' " That is, while rural residents may continue to migrate toward urban centers, an integrated development approach will, hopefully, at least, offer a number of urban alternatives to the primate city (Rhoda, 1979: 21). In this way, some of the population pressures felt by the primate city may be eased while individual migrants are able to pursue off-farm employment alternatives.

The literature indicates (Rhoda, 1979; Findley, 1979), that people will continue to migrate from rural areas. This shift in rural-urban population proportions should not necessarily be viewed with alarm. The concern instead lies with the distribution of the urban population and the nation's ability to cope with that distribution. Most Latin American countries have, in the last few decades, begun to translate their concern over the large size and rapid growth of their primate cities into realizable policies to direct growth and migration toward smaller urban centers. However, the current emphasis on integrated development through the promotion of market towns and service centers which link rural and urban areas is, as yet, too recent to permit evaluation of its impact. Policies in most countries are still in the formulation stage; in other countries where implementation has begun, it will be some time before the effects can be seen and analyzed. Only then will there be some indication of whether or not such policies have indeed been able to redirect a significant amount of the rural-urban migration flow toward smaller secondary cities or if the attraction of the primate city remains predominant. Further, even if the early indications are that migration patterns have shifted away from the primate city, it will take much longer to assess whether the long-term results of integrated decentralization differ from those in the short-run. That is, even if integrated policies successfully divert migration to secondary cities in the short-run, there remains the possibility that those migrants may make a later move to the primate city as part of a step-wise, or stage, migration (Rhoda, 1979; 46).

Finally, migration forms only a part of urban growth in Latin America (Fox, 1975; Rhoda, 1979). Natural population increase will continue to play a dominant role in urban growth for years to come, and an alteration in migration trends alone will not solve the problems of the primate cities. Whatever form decentralization policies take and whatever success they achieve, they can at best be seen as a partial solution to the problems of rapid urban growth.

BIBLIOGRAPHY

Acosta, Maruja and Jorge E. Hardoy. "Urbanization Policies in Revolutionary Cuba," pages 167-177. In Guillermo Geisse and Jorge Hardoy, editors, Latin American Urban Research, Volume 2, Regional and Urban Development Policies: A Latin American Perspective. Beverly Hills: Sage Publications, 1972.

Barkin, David. "Regional Development and Interregional Equity: A Mexican Case Study," Wayne A. Cornelius and Felicity M. Trueblood, editors, *Latin American Urban Research*, Volume 5, *Urbanization and Inequality: The Political Economy of Urban and Rural Development in Latin America.* Beverly Hills: Sage Publications, 1975

Beier, George, et al. *The Task Ahead for the Cities of the Developing Countries.* IBRD: Bank Staff Working Paper, No. 209, 1975.

Benjamin, Aaron L. "Report on a Proposed Urban Development Strategy for the Dominican Republic." Draft paper for AID/LAC/DR, 1979.

Cardenas, Cuauhtemoc. "Regional Rural Development: The Mexican Rio Balsas Commission," pages 143-150. In Guillermo Geisee and Jorge Hardoy, editors, *Latin American Urban Research,* Volume 2, *Regional and Urban Development Policies: A Latin American Perspective.* Beverly Hills: Sage Publications, 1972.

Chetwynd, Eric Jr. "City-Size Distribution, Spatial Integration and Economic Development in Developing Countries: An Analysis of Some Key Relationships." Dissertation, Duke University, 1976.

Conroy, Michael E. "Rejection of Growth Center Strategy in Latin American Regional Development Planning," *Land Economics,* XLIX: 1 (November): 371-380, 1973.

Findley, Sally E. *Planning for Internal Migration: A Review of Issues and Policies in Developing Countries.* Washington: U.S. Bureau of the Census, U.S. Department of Commerce, 1977.

_____ . "Rural Development Programs: Planned versus Actual Migration Outcomes." Paper prepared for UN/UNFPA Workshop on Population Distribution Policies and Development Planning, Bangkok, September 4-13, 1979.

Fox, Robert W. *Urban Population Growth in Peru.* Washington: IDB, 1972.

_____ . *Urban Population Growth Trends in Latin America.* Washington: IDB, 1975.

Fox, Robert W. and Jerrold W. Huguet. *Population and Urban Trends in Central America and Panama.* Washington: IDB, 1977.

Friedmann, John. *Regional Development Policy: A Case Study of Venezuela.* Cambridge: The MIT Press, 1966.

————. "Urban-Regional Policies for National Development in Chile." Francine F. Rabinovitz and Feliciy M. Trueblood, editor, *Latin American Urban Research,* Volume 1, Beverly Hills: Sage Publications, 1971.

Geisse, Guillermo and Jose Luis Coraggio. "Metropolitan Areas and National Development," pages 45-60. In Guillermo Geisse and Jorge Hardoy, editors, *Latin American Urban Research,* Volume 2, *Regional and Urban Development Policies: A Latin Amercian Perspective.* Beverly Hills: Sage Publications, 1972.

Gilbert, Alan. "Urban and Regional Development Progams in Colombia Since 1951." Wayne A. Cornelius and Felicity M. Trueblood, editors, *Latin Amercian Urban Research,* Volume 5, *Urbanization and Inequality: The Political Economy of Urban and Rural Development in Latin America.* Beverly Hills: Sage Publications, 1975.

Harrigan, John H. "Political Economy and the Management of Urban Development in Brazil," pages 207-220. In Wayne A. Cornelius and Felicity M. Trueblood, editors, *Latin American Urban Research,* Volume 5, *The Political Economy of Urban and Rural Development in Latin America.* Beverly Hills: Sage Publications, 1975.

Lander, Luis and Julio Cesar Junes. "Urbanization and Development," pages 287-337. In Jorge E. Hardoy, editor, *Urbanization in Latin America: Approaches and Issues.* Garden City, NY: Anchor Books, 1975.

Landstreet, Barent. Chapter 7 in Aaron L. Segal, editor, *Population Policies in the Caribbean,* Lexington, Mass.: D. C. Heath and Company, Lexington Books, 1975.

Lozano, Eduardo. "Housing the Urban Poor in Chile: Contrasting Experiences Under 'Christian Democracy' and 'Unidad Popular,' " pages 177-193. In Wayne A. Cornelius and Felicity M. Trueblood, editor, *Latin American Urban Research,* Volume 5, *The Political Economy of Urban and Rural Development in Latin America.* Beverly Hills: Sage Publications, 1975.

————. "The Regional Strategy of 'Unidad Popular' in Chile," pages 301-314. In Wayne A. Cornelius and Felicity M. Trueblood, editors, *Latin American Urban Research,* Volume 5, *The Political Economy of Urban and Rural Development in Latin America.* Beverly Hills: Sage Publications, 1975.

Miller, James C. *Regional Development: A Review of the State-of-the-Art.* Washington, D.C.: AID/DS/UD, 1979.

Pico, Rafael. *Puerto Rico: Planificacion y Accion.* San Juan: Banco Gubernamental de Fomento para Puerto Rico, 1962.

Portes, Alejandro and Harley L. Browning, editors. *Current Perspectives in Latin American Urban Research.* Austin, TX: Institute of Latin American Studies, The University of Texas at Austin, 1976.

Quarterly Economic Review, Nicaragua, Costa Rica, Panama, 1976-1977.

Rhoda, Richard E. "Paraguay: Market Towns—'Bottom-Up' Approach to Integrated Urban-Rural Development." Unpublished paper, Agency for International Development, 1977.

_____. *Guidelines for Urban and Regional Analysis: A Description of Analytical Methods for Development Activities.* Washington: AID/DS/UD., 1978.

_____. *Development Activities and Rural-Urban Migration: Is It Possible to Keep Them Down on the Farm?* Washington: AID/DS/UD, 1979.

Robin, John P. and Frederick C. Terzo. (n.d.) *Urbanization in Peru.* The Ford Foundation: International Urbanization Survey.

Rodwin, Lloyd. "Urban Growth Strategies Reconsidered," pages 1-19. In Niles M. Hansen, editor, *Growth Centers in Regional Economic Development.* New York: The Free Press, 1972.

Stohr, Walter. *Regional Development Experiences and Prospects in Latin America.* The Hague: Mouton and Company, 1975.

United Nations, Department of Economic and Social Affairs. *Selected Experiences in Regional Development.* New York, 1970.

United Nations. *World Population Trends and Policies: Monitoring Report,* Volume II: *Population Policies. Population Studies,* No. 62, 1979.

United States, Agency for International Development. Annual Budget Submission, Costa Rica, 1978, 1979. Annual Budget Submission, Honduras, 1978. Annual Budget Submission, Peru, 1978. Country Development Strategy Statement, Bolivia, 1979. Country Development Strategy Statement, Costa Rica, 1979. Country Development Strategy Statement, Honduras 1979. Country Development Strategy Statement, Panama, 1979.

US/AID Mission to Bolivia. Project Paper: Department Development Corporations, 1979.

US/AID/Panama. Interim Report: Rural Growth and Service Centers, 1977.

_____ . Project Paper: Proposal and Recommendations for the Review of the Bilateral Assistance Subcommittee, Panama: Rural Growth and Service Centers, 1978.

US/AID/Peru, Project Paper: Integrated Regional Development, 1979.

Webb, Richard. "Public Policy and Regional Incomes in Peru," pages 223-238. In Wayne A. Cornelius and Felicity M. Trueblood, editors, *Latin American Urban Research,* Volume 5, *The Political Economy of Urban and Rural Development in Latin America.* Beverly Hills: Sage Publications, 1975.

A.I.D.'S RURAL DEVELOPMENT STRATEGIES IN LATIN AMERICA AND THE CARIBBEAN

Clarence Zuvekas, Jr. *

HISTORICAL OVERVIEW

Rural development programs have become increasingly important parts of A.I.D.'s programming in Latin America and the Caribbean—and elsewhere in the developing world—since the Congress passed the so-called "New Directions" amendments to the Foreign Assistance Act in 1973 (Public Law 93-189). In that legislation, the Congress declared that "United States bilateral development assistance should give highest priority to undertakings submitted by host governments which directly improve the lives of the poorest of their people and their capacity to participate in the development of their countries" (Sec. 102). With respect to food and nutrition (Sec. 103), the legislation states:

> Assistance provided under this section shall be used primarily for activities which are specifically designed to increase the productivity and income of the rural poor, through such means as creation and strengthening of local institutions linked to regional and national levels; organization of a system of financial institutions which

*The views expressed herein are my own and should not be attributed to the Agency for International Development or any other part of the U.S. government. I would like to thank David Lazar and Edward Lijewsky for helpful comments on earlier drafts of this paper. Responsibility for any remaining errors or misinterpretations remains mine alone.

provide both savings and credit services to the poor; stimulation of small, labor-intensive enterprises in rural towns; improvement of marketing facilities and systems; expansion of local or small-scale rural infrastructure and utilities such as farm-to-market roads, land improvement, energy, and storage facilities; establishment of more equitable and more secure land tenure arrangements; and creation and strengthening of systems to provide other services and supplies needed by farmers, such as extension, research, training, fertilizer, water, and improved seed, in ways which assure access to them by small farmers.

Focus on the rural poor in the last half-dozen years is not something new for the U.S. foreign assistance program. Indeed, some of the earliest U.S. assistance to developing countries supported agrarian reform and small-farmer development programs in Japan and Taiwan.[1] And in Latin America, U.S. efforts in agricultural extension from 1942 to the early 1960s were explicitly aimed at providing assistance to small farmers, although as noted below they were not particularly successful. Later, the Alliance for Progress committed the United States to supporting agrarian reform and other programs benefiting the rural poor in the Americas. However, progress toward meeting the reformist goals of the Alliance was disappointing, both because of resistance by vested interests in the Latin American and Caribbean (LAC) countries and because of pressures from within the U.S. government by those concerned about the implication of U.S. support for rapid social change.[2]

Still, many persons within A.I.D., the Congress, and the academic community continued to press for greater attention to foreign assistance that would directly benefit the rural poor and support significant social change.[3] One result of their efforts was the enactment in 1966 of Title IX of the Foreign Assistance Act (FAA), which called for programs "assuring maximum participation in the task of development on the part of the people of developing countries, through the encouragement of democratic private and local government institutions." While Title IX may be regarded fundamentally as an attempt to encourage long-run *political* development (Davidson 1976), it is clear that broader political participation was expected to narrow income inequalities and help relieve poverty.

One objective of Title IX was to further encourage the development of cooperatives, credit unions, and savings and loan associations, as called for in the Humphrey Amendment (1961) to the FAA, and community development, as called for in the Zablocki amendment of 1962. In additon, the backers of Title IX—notably Congressmen Donald Fraser and Bradford Morse—stressed the importance of leadership training that would enable local communities and other groups to more effectively articulate their interests to the national government and to do more to achieve their development aspirations through their own actions (U.S.A.I.D. 1968).

Implementation of Title IX by A.I.D. Missions was mixed. Indeed, a comprehensive analysis of Title IX in the LAC (Latin American and Caribbean) Region, covering the years 1966-71, concluded that it was largely unsuccessful:

> The strategies and programs devised during this period were not undertaken on a wide scale, and the policies and programs that were implemented were not significantly more successful in achieving their stated objective than were previous types of programs—with the exception of some programs in Ecuador and Costa Rica, which did achieve some success in the short term, although their long-term impact remains unclear (Davidson 1976: 463).

The relative success of A.I.D.'s efforts in Ecuador—which included peasant leadership training and agrarian reform— was attributed largely to a highly committed A.I.D. Mission staff that located and secured support from reform elements within a weak, highly fragmented, and permissive host-country bureaucracy. The Mission also successfully resisted opposition to its Title IX programs from within the U.S. government community, probably because the Ecuador program was small, of relatively low priority, and thus largely ignored (Davidson 1976:Ch. 7). In Costa Rica, where A.I.D. Mission personnel were also highly committed, progress toward meeting Title IX objectives was facilitated by the government's strong support for them. Political and economic objectives were integrated to a high degree, and much of the A.I.D. Mission's effort was directed toward small farmers. A legal education program, for example, focused on improvement in land tenure legislation and the clarification of property titles. As in Ecuador, sensitivity training was directed both at peasant leaders and at the extension service and other institutions involved in rural development (Davidson 1976:Ch. 8).

In other LAC countries, Davidson (1976:Ch. 9-10) found implementation of Title IX to be "limited," or, in the majority of cases (including Brazil and Colombia), "minimal." In most countries, he concluded, "the overwhelming thrust of the program [was] entirely traditional in nature and emphasize[d] orthodox strategies of economic stabilization and development which often focus[ed] on high rates of GNP growth" (p. 421). In other words, Davidson argued—with considerable justification—that A.I.D. strategies were strongly influenced by the "trickle-down" theory of development, which assumes that the benefits of economic growth will automatically filter down to almost all segments of the population. The trickle-down theory was widely accepted in the 1960s not just within A.I.D., but also in the international assistance community generally and among Latin American economists, development planners, and policy-makers. In addition, as is well-known, import substitution was widely regarded in the LAC region as the primary engine of growth, and agricultural development tended to receive low priority.

By the early 1970s it had become clear that neither the trickle-down strategy nor import-substitution policies had satisfactorily dealt with problems in employment, income distribution, and poverty.[4] Despite an acceleration of GNP growth rates, unemployment and underemployment rates remained high and often increased, and most evidence pointed to widening income inequalities (Weisskoff and Figueroa 1976; Zuvekas 1975). Recent estimates indicate that the percentage of the LAC region's population living in poverty has declined since 1960, but the absolute number of poor people has remained constant at about 110 million (Molina and Piñera 1979:12-21):[5]

Year	Percentage Below Poverty Line	Millions of Poor People
1960	51	110
1970	40	113
1977	33	112

The incidence of poverty is far greater in rural areas than in urban areas. In 1970, 62% of rural households could be classified as poor, compared with 26% in urban areas (Molin and Piñera 1979:18).

IDENTIFYING THE RURAL POOR AND THEIR CHARACTERISTICS

Since 1973, when the Congress mandated that A.I.D. concentrate on programs that provide direct benefits to the rural poor, A.I.D. has taken steps to obtain more specific socioeconomic data on this target group, its size, and its major development problems. Other development institutions—notably the World Bank (IBRD), the Inter-American Development Bank (IDB), and ECLA—have undertaken similar studies.[6] One thing we are finding is that the economic activities of the rural poor are more diverse and complex than we once thought.

Figures showing 70-90 percent of the economically active population in rural areas to be engaged primarily in farming are very misleading. Household surveys in some countries have revealed that a majority of rural households receive most of their income from off-farm activities. In Ecuador, for example, only one-third of all rural households depend primarily on production from their own farms (Ecuador, MAG; and ORSTOM 1978). In Colombia, off-farm employment is a more important source of income than own-account farming for the very poorest (indigent) families (León 1979:14). In rural Jamaica, sources of income are so diverse that one anthropologist argues that a "peasant culture" does not exist (Comitas 1973). Instead, he maintains, a multi-occupational model is a more appropriate analytical tool for anthropologists studying rural household behavior. This analytical approach can also be usefully adopted by economists.

The distinction between the "farm" or "peasant" household and the multi-occupational household is important for policy purposes. Strategies and policy instruments designed for poor farmers with adequate land are not likely to be appropriate for multi-occupational households with small plots and little or no opportunity to acquire more land. This is why A.I.D. has been sponsoring research on what is being called the "landless and near-landless poor." Although this terminology may be analytically misleading,[7] A.I.D. hopes to gain a better insight into the obstacles facing these households and into the factors affecting their decision-making processes. The best hope for these households may not lie in farming but rather in the provision of non-agricultural employment opportunities, especially in rural areas.

Another of A.I.D.'s research projects is a survey of the literature on rural income distribution and levels of living in twelve Latin American and Caribbean countries. In this exercise, which is expected to be completed in early 1980,[8] A.I.D. is paying particular attention to *micro*-level evidence, including the findings of anthropological and sociological studies. In addition to providing better information to A.I.D. decision-makers on the nature and incidence of poverty and its geographic distribution, these studies will facilitate the identification of obstacles to rural development and suggest the types of strategies and policy instruments that will best respond to the needs of the poor.

One of the discouraging results has been the discovery that most estimates of rural income—in both the macroeconomic and microeconomic studies—are even more seriously deficient than had been expected. Farm-level surveys often fail to account completely for off-farm earnings, particularly of family members other than the head of household. Income from pensions and remittances, especially important in the Caribbean (Zuvekas 1978b:17-20), is likewise excluded. Although imputations are usually made for the value of food produced and consumed on the farm, there is virtually never any imputation for the rental value of housing. Likewise, there is little or no information on the value of services received at subsidized prices or at no direct cost. All of these omissions, of course, result in an underestimation of income—or more appropriately, consumption—both absolutely and relative to urban areas. On the other hand, there are cases where rural incomes are inflated because they are based on gross value of farm production.

Frankly, much of the data on rural incomes is almost worthless. This is why they should be supplemented with other level-of-living indicators and with qualitative judgments about conditions in rural areas and changes in these conditions over time. At the same time, it remains important to seek better measures of rural and urban income and of the purchasing power of this income. Studies being done in this area by UN-ECLA (1979) and by the IDB (Thoumi 1978) are especially promising. There is little doubt that more reliable data will still show the incidence of poverty to be higher in rural areas than in urban areas.

STRATEGIES AND POLICY INSTRUMENTS FOR RURAL DEVELOPMENT

We now turn to some of the specific strategies and policy instruments that A.I.D. has considered in planning its rural development activities in Latin America and the Caribbean.

First, recent experience supports the views of many observers that there are limits on the degree to which rural povery can be eliminated through redistribution of income, assets, and public consumption goods within existing socioeconomic frameworks. Changes in tax policy seem particularly unpromising as redistributive instruments (Adelman and Robinson 1977).

At the same time, there are still ways to move faster within existing frameworks to satisfy basic human needs. The Adelman-Robinson simulation study for South Korea (1977) concludes that the most promising approach is a broad-based rural development strategy centered on agrarian reform but also including complementary measures.

I argue that *comprehensive agrarian reform*—i.e. land redistribution and/or improved tenure security *plus* greater access to productive inputs—is a major requirement for significantly improving the prospects of the rural poor in many parts of Latin America and the Caribbean. In the early 1970s, A.I.D. supported land redistribution efforts through land-sale guaranty mechanisms in Ecuador and Costa Rica. Although these mechanisms were not used as anticipated, land was in fact transferred and the beneficiaries were provided with credit and technical assistance.[9] In other countries, A.I.D. supported progressive government technicians seeking to implement agrarian reform programs, but the necessary commitment from the top leadership was lacking and no such projects were developed. Despite past disappointments, A.I.D. continues to look for opportunities to assist governments in redistributing more land to small farmers, giving them greater tenure security, and providing the supporting services that will enable them to significantly increase their incomes.

In some LAC countries there is also a need for *colonization programs* which enable small farmers to leave overcrowded and badly eroded land—where they would be condemned to be *minifundistas* even after land redistribution—and to settle in previously unexploited or underexploited areas. A decade ago, colonization programs were widely criticized for being poor substitutes for agrarian reform. But it is now clear that hundreds of thousands of small farmers in the LAC region have significantly improved their levels of living by moving to newly-opened lands. While elaborately-planned, directed-colonization programs have had unfavorable benefit-cost relationships (Nelson 1973), spontaneous colonization following road construction is a promising approach, provided that speculative land purchases and threats to the environment can be contained.[10]

I believe that the evidence on colonization in Bolivia, for example, is more favorable than some observers (e.g. León 1979) suggest. While directed colonization programs there have not been very successful (Nelson 1973), spontaneous colonization which accounts for 85 percent of the total (Bolivia, INC, 1976; Calleguillos 1974) has sometimes provided significant benefits to settlers (Nelson 1973; Royden and Wennergren 1973; Wennergren and Whitaker 1976, Zeballos Hurtado 1975). In addition, it has provided important seasonal employment opportunities for underemployed *campesinos* in the highlands. The rate of permanent migration from the Altiplano and Valles to the Oriente—despite difficult adjustments to changes in climate, crops, and way of life— is strong evidence of the attraction of spontaneous colonization for the highland Bolivian campesino.[11]

Nevertheless, one could still argue that some government intervention in the colonization process is desirable, both to guard against environmental deterioration and to ensure that the principal beneficiaries are indeed small farmers. At the same time, experience suggests that basic production decisions should be left to small farmers themselves; bad advice by poorly trained or inexperienced government workers can be worse than no advice at all.[12] Government credit and technical assistance programs to colonists are still desirable, but even more important are favorable price and marketing policies.

A.I.D.'s efforts to help eliminate rural poverty are increasingly focused in *integrated rural development* and *regional development* projects. A significant expansion of rural incomes and rural employment requires direct stimulation of backward and forward linkages between agricultural production and other rural-based activities. Backward linkages that should especially be encouraged are the local manufacture and distribution of simple machinery and equipment and other modern farm inputs. Forward linkages that might be developed include rural processing of agricultural materials and the provision of on-farm and community-level storage facilities. Much of the production in these linkage industries can be carried out efficiently in small firms owned and operated by local residents. To stimulate these firms, industrialization policies in most LAC countries would have to be revised to correct the current bias in favor of large-scale, capital-intensive operations.

A crucial element in strengthening both types of linkages is the construction of an adequate secondary and access road network, which by lowering marketing costs for both outputs and inputs creates new employment-generating activities in production, processing, and distribution. These new activities, created through exploitation of linkage effects, in turn will have multiplier effects that expand rural markets and stimulate the further growth of both agricultural and non-agricultural production.

An integrated rural development strategy focused on these linkages can play a major role in reducing rural unemployment and underemployment. The jobs that can be created directly in agriculture, and through linkage and multiplier effects, may not be glamorous, high-paying factory jobs that quickly convert rural poverty into middle-income levels of living. But they still will be more productive, better-paying jobs than are now available. Among the employment categories for which demand can be expected to increase are skilled and unskilled construction workers, equipment operators and repair specialists; tailors, seamstresses, bakers, and others producing consumer durables and nondurables, extension workers and other agricultural technicians; and a variety of jobs in agricultural marketing and in retail and wholesale trade generally.

One of the more encouraging integrated rural development projects A.I.D. has supported is in Costa Rica, where a number of forward linkages in processing and marketing have been established in *cantones* Hojancha and Nandayure, where levels of living had been deteriorating. One of the linkages is provided through the government's Family Assistance Program, which has allowed nutrition centers and schools to purchase local farm produce. Also, the government has built a sorting and packing plant to provide small farmers another outlet for their products. In addition, that project includes activities in forestry, institutional coordination, local agricultural research, and specialized agricultural training. The government of Costa Rica is now planning similar projects to benefit small farmers in other areas.

Perhaps the most important lesson A.I.D. has learned about rural development projects in general, and integrated projects in particular, is that *much more attention should be paid to the opinions of the rural poor themselves.* Sometimes, it has been discovered too late that the principal problems faced by small farmers are not related to production but rather to prices and marketing. A good example is the case of wheat in Bolivia, where price and marketing policies have tended to favor imported wheat (UN-ECLA 1967; Gomez D. and Gardner 1976; and USAID/Bolivia 1976). *Campesinos* often resist change in production technology *not* because they are ignorant, but because they are very much aware that increased production cannot be marketed profitably. When new marketing opportunities open up, *campesinos* are quite capable of taking advantage of them on their own—even with little credit and technical assistance—as occurred in Bolivia's Cochabamba Valley after the agrarian reform of 1953 (Camacho Saa 1970).

Even when marketing problems are clearly recognized, the appropriate response may require more than a marketing project. A decade ago, A.I.D. was planning to support a project to organize rice marketing cooperatives in Ecuador. Fortunately, the A.I.D. Mission took the time to discuss the project design with the intended *campesino* beneficiaries, who quickly convinced A.I.D. that the project would not succeed unless it also included land tenure reform and technical assistance in production. The comprehensive nature of the final design, insisted upon by the *campesinos* themselves, contributed to the output and income gains under this project.[13]

These and other experiences have led A.I.D. to ask more attitudinal questions in the farm-level surveys it has supported. In a recent survey in Bolivia's Southern Valleys, A.I.D. found that farmers' responses to attitudinal questions confirmed the quantitative evidence regarding major problems revealed by other survey questions, and they provided additional insights as well. A.I.D. is now assisting the Bolivian Government in devising projects that address these problems.

Moving beyond the project design stage, A.I.D. and other development assistance agencies should do more to involve project beneficiaries in the implementation stage. When implementation is unsatisfactory, it is often the rural poor themselves who have the best insights into what is wrong with the strategies and policy instruments being used.

In reexamining the effectiveness of alternative strategies and policy instruments, drawing on the insights of the poor into the problems they face, one of the most important conclusions A.I.D. has reached is that a more direct focus is needed on *the role of women in development.* For some in our Agency, this has been regarded simply as a slogan without much substance. But the studies A.I.D. has sponsored, and considerable evidence from sociological and anthropological studies, suggest that the contribution of women to the rural economy is greater than indicated by labor force data for most LAC countries.[14]

This vast pool of human resources will not be fully utilized until numerous legal and cultural obstacles are overcome. Some countries restrict membership in cooperatives and other organizations to landowners and to persons who are literate. This discriminates against rural women, who have not had equal access to land and education. Wages in agriculture and in other rural occupations are frequently lower for women than for men. Women dominate the marketing of fruits and vegetables in many countries, but they lack the credit that is available for crops marketed primarily by men.

In one country where A.I.D. was asked to support a project designed to increase women's access to productive resources, the principal government bank admitted that it had never made loans to women, not because of regulations but simply because of tradition. Yet a private organization providing small loans in this same country reports that women have a better repayment record than men. In another country where A.I.D. is considering a project, it was found that only men will participate actively in public meetings where loan procedures are explained and credit applications are filled out. But within the privacy of the household in this country, women play an important role in financial decision-making. This suggests that new loan application procedures are needed to ensure that women's views will be better taken into account.

Recently, in collaboration with the Instituto Interamericano de Ciencias Agrícolas (IICA) and local women's organizations, A.I.D. began to support a regional educational media project to provide information to rural women on agricultural production, marketing, credit, and the availability of public and private services. A pilot project is now underway in the Dominican Republic. Another new project, being implemented through the Inter-American Commission of Women, seeks to transfer more productive agricultural and artisan technologies to women in Ecuador, Bolivia, and Peru. In Bolivia, the National Community Development Service, with A.I.D. assistance, is de-emphasizing traditional work in home economics and is facilitating women's involvement in income-generating projects and their participation in cooperatives. Rural health projects in Bolivia and elsewhere have raised the social status of women trained as paramedical technicians. And in its training programs generally, A.I.D. is doing more to ensure that the beneficiaries will include a high proportion of women.

I regard improvements in *health and education* as important components of an integrated rural development strategy. By making the rural population more productive, health and educational programs increase the potential of agricultural and agro-industrial development activities. It is especially important in this respect (1) to place more emphasis on nonformal education, better suited to rural life, and (2) to make greater use of locally-recruited paraprofessionals. Greater reliance on paraprofessionals not only has favorable rural employment effects, but there is also good evidence that the middle-level technicians—including agricultural extension workers—can be more effective than highly-trained outsiders in transmitting new knowledge and technologies to the rural poor.

Another important component of a successful rural development strategy is a *favorable relative price structure.*[15] There is now considerable evidence that the price mechanism is usually a more efficient allocator of resources than alternative institutional arrangements, both for capitalist economies and for socialist economies. Price manipulation is a powerful tool not only for increasing production but also for accomplishing a variety of social objectives, including employment and income redistribution. Some of A.I.D.'s more successful rural development projects in Latin America and the Caribbean—e.g. the Ecuador project discussed above—have included price policy reform. Conversely, some disappointments—e.g. wheat production in Bolivia—can be attributed in large measure to unfavorable price policies.

This emphais on the price mechanism is not a denial of the efficiency of *agricultural planning.* Indeed, effective sectoral planning is one of the most important needs in the LAC region, and during the 1970's A.I.D. supported agricultural planning in many LAC countries. Appropriate use of the price mechanism, rather than being an alternative to planning, is in fact one of its indispensable components. A.I.D's most recently approved agricultural planning project—with the Eastern Caribbean Common Market countries—will pay particular attention to the reform of price policies which have been major disincentives to increased agricultural production by small farmers in these countries (Zuvekas 1978a).

A.I.D. continues to believe that a high priority must be given to *institution building*—the creation or strengthening of national and local organizations which on their own can make wise decisions regarding policies, priorities, projects, and programs. While some of A.I.D.'s efforts have been disappointing—e.g. the agricultural extension programs of the 1940s and 1950s, discussed below—on balance, its experience has been favorable, thus justifying continued emphasis in this area.

A.I.D.'s focus, however, is no longer on individual institutions in isolation. It is now recognized that a more appropriate focus is the entire agricultural sector. Thus A.I.D. has supported a large-scale graduate training program in the Dominican

Republic, covering a wide range of agricultural skills. The beneficiaries of this training program are now moving into key decision-making positions, and the Ministry of Agriculture has increased its capacity to undertake a number of different types of action programs. In Honduras, a recent assessment of the agricultural sector, prepared by the Ministry of Agriculture under an A.I.D.-assisted project, identifies the lack of adequate institutions and training as a major obstacle to progress in agriculture and overall rural development. A.I.D. is responding to this need through a new agricultural sector loan to that country.

Three A.I.D. policy instruments for rural development are agricultural extension, research, and credit. Experience with these instruments has caused the Agency to change significantly its thinking about how they should be used.

Agricultural extension was one of the first agricultural development activities in the LAC region supported by the U.S. Government. A decade ago, A.I.D. conducted a major evaluation of the impact of U.S. assistance in this field from 1942 to the early 1960s (Rice 1974). This study concluded that institution-building efforts in extension had not achieved their desired results for two major reasons. First, the administrative, bureaucratic, and political *ambiente* was not propitious for the establishment of permanent extension institutions. Second, the model that was transferred was too concerned with educational processes and neglected the changes in credit, marketing, and price policies necessary to induce farmers to adopt new technologies.

The study argued that extension activities would have been more effective if provided through development banks, agrarian reform agencies, producers' associations, commercial supply houses, or similar institutions, rather than through the type of independent extension organizations that were traditional in the United States. While many A.I.D. technicians have not accepted this conclusion, there is widespread agreement with the basic argument used to support it, namely, that extension must be closely tied with other development activities. In other words, the role of the extension agent should be not only to transmit knowledge but also to bring farmers into contact with organizations providing new technologies and the means to acquire them, and to assist the farmer in making other linkages.

A.I.D.'s recent activities in extension have taken into account the lessons learned from its earlier experiences. In a number of countries, extension activities have been provided directly by agricultural development banks or have been closely coordinated with them. Extension has also been integrated with other activities in area development programs. Another change in A.I.D.'s approach to extension has been to experiment with the use of paraprofessionals who live in the areas being assisted and have direct experience as small farmers. As noted above, these lesser-trained technicians are often more effective in directly communicating with farmers than university-trained agronomists, many of whom come from urban areas.

Investment in *agricultural research,* recent studies have shown, can have high internal rates of return. There is now widespread agreement that developing countries could profit from increased investment in this activity (Hayami and Ruttan 1971; Evenson and Kislev 1975; Arndt, Dalrymple, and Ruttan 1977). Accordingly, A.I.D. assigns a high priority to adaptive agricultural research. Consistent with its mandate to focus on the rural poor, A.I.D.'s support for agricultural research emphasized multiple cropping systems and other technologies appropriate for small farmers. Some particularly promising activities of this type are now being carried out by two regional research centers, CATIE in Central America and CARDI in the Caribbean.

A.I.D.'s thinking about *agricultural credit* has undergone some radical changes in the last decade. Research sponsored by the Agency and by other organizations has turned the conventional wisdom on its head (Adams 1978; Donald 1976; Lipton 1976). For example, it appears that lack of institutional credit is not as important an obstacle to small-farmer development as was once believed. This does not mean that it should be neglected, only that its relative importance in agricultural development strategies should be less.

A second major conclusion is that low-interest-rate policies on agricultural loans are actually inimical to small-farmer interests. Low interest rates prevent financial institutions from increasing their loanable funds through internal growth and make them dependent on government subsidies, the amounts of which are limited by the serious fiscal problems facing the public sector in many developing countries. The supply of credit, in other words, is restricted. The supply problem is exacerbated because many borrowers regard subsidized public credit simply as another government "service" like extension or research.[16] The result is high delinquency rates, usually 20-30 percent but sometimes as high as 50 percent.[17] The credit rationing implicit in low-interest-rate policies favors medium- and large-scale farmers, with small farmers left standing in the queue after credit resources have been exhausted. Small farmers themselves are less concerned with interest rates than with ease of acquiring credit and flexibility in repayment terms, loan amounts, and credit use. Thus we find that they often reject subsidized credit available to them in favor of credit obtained in the informal market at rates as high as 50 percent or more. When one considers the cost of travel and *trámites* involved in acquiring institutional credit, preference for traditional money-lenders is often a rational choice.

A third important conclusion from the last decade's research on agricultural credit is that greater attention must be given to the mobilization of rural savings as a means of increasing the supply of agricultural credit. The key ingredient here is again interest-rate reform, this time as it applies to interest paid on savings accounts. This can be expected to attract savings from both large and small farmers. Encouragement of local savings institutions—including cooperatives and credit unions—is also important, though A.I.D. has learned that a particular type of savings institution which works well in one country is not necessarily appropriate in another. The most dramatic examples of successful development of rural financial markets, including interest-rate reforms, are Taiwan and South Korea (Adams 1978). In the early 1970s, 95 percent of Taiwan's farmers had access to institutional credit, compared with 1 percent to 20 percent for most developing countries.

Two newer concerns which A.I.D. believes must receive greater attention are environmental protection and energy supply and conservation. In both cases, failure to take action will aggravate rural poverty.

Research conducted during the 1970s (summarized in Eckholm 1976 and Thiesenhusen 1976) demonstrated the need for more investment in *environmental protection.* It is increasingly evident that stagnant or falling incomes for the rural poor are often associated with declining soil fertility attributable to erosion, desertification, salination, and other consequences of poor land-use practices. Environmental destruction occurs not so much because of small farmers' ignorance but because short-term survival takes precedence over long-run productivity considerations. Environmental problems may be traced ultimately to population growth in a socio-economic setting in which farmers are denied access to sufficient land and other production inputs.

What little is known about designing and implementing soil conservation programs in developing countries suggests that they are costly and labor-intensive; that they require close cooperation among all farmers in a watershed area; and that small farmers will not make the necessary investments of their own time and resources unless they have secure land tenure. More pilot projects in soil conservation and other types of environmental protection are needed to provide better guidelines for major investment projects. A.I.D. has supported several such projects in the last few years and expects this to be an important area of project activity during the 1980s.

A.I.D. also intends during the 1980s to increase its support for *rural energy programs*. The rural poor not only face sharply higher prices for petroleum-based fuels, but in many countries they are finding that firewood for cooking and heating is increasingly scarce and expensive. Wood fuel problems are particularly acute in Haiti and in Central America, where wood fuel consumption accounts for about 45 percent of total energy consumption. The high cost or unavailability of rural energy also seriously limits the prospects for irrigation, agricultural processing, and other job-creating industrial activities in the countryside. A.I.D. believes that considerable potential may exist for efficient provision of energy in rural areas through biogas generation, production of electricity from small hydropower plants, rational forest management, and the harnessing of other renewable energy sources such as solar and wind power.

In conclusion, there are no magic keys to accelerating the growth of agricultural output, particularly if employment, income distribution, and nutrition objectives are also considered important. What is needed is a sector-wide outlook and a comprehensive package of policies based on a clear understanding of the interrelationships, complementarities, and conflicts among different policy actions. The most appropriate package will depend upon the specific economic, agronomic, and institutional conditions in each country or region within a country. It is also important to strengthen the linkages between agriculture and other sectors of the economy. Comprehensive rural development programs can make major contributions toward eliminating poverty if governments assign a higher priority to agriculture and commit both the economic and political resources necessary for rural development policies to be carried out effectively.

NOTES

1. For a first-hand account of these efforts, see Ladejinsky (1977).

2. George Lodge (1970:345) has argued that the U.S. commitment to change under the Alliance was contradicted by a simultaneous commitment to political stability, viewed as necessary to prevent "communist takeovers." Revolution, he says, was mistakenly equated with communism by many foreign policy-makers.

3. Interestingly, these supporters of what now would be called basic-human-needs programs also drew on national-security arguments to bolster their position. Specifically, they argued that widening income inequalities and lack of democratic, base-level institutions in Latin American and Caribbean countries would result in growing tensions, the consequences of which might be inimical to U.S. relations with these countries. In other words, they emphasized that "stability" had to be understood in a dynamic context, not a static one.

4. Economic growth seems to have caused similar problems in Western Europe and other presently industrialized countries during the nineteenth century. A recent study (Adelman and Morris 1977) concludes that rapid industrialization and commercialization at that time systematically lowered the *absolute* standard of living of the poorest segments of the population in these countries. The commercialization of agriculture, for example, led to high rents among tenants and dispossession of small landholders burdened by debt and lacking the resources to survive during periods of depressed market prices. In Germany and Belgium, population pressures led to a subdivision of small landholdings, thus decreasing the

average amount of land per family.

5. Similarly, these estimates show that there was virtually no change in the number of people classified as indigent:

Year	Percentage Indigent	Millions of Indigent People
1960	26	56
1970	19	54

Indigence is defined as a situation in which familes have insufficient income to satisfy basic nutritional needs even if all income were spent on food. Poverty is a situation in which nutritional requirements are not met, given the level of income and the percentage of income spent on food.

6. See, for example, IBRD (1978); Thoumi (1978); and Molina and Piñera (1979). The data in these studies are preliminary and should not be interpreted as defining officially-approved poverty lines.

7. Some analysts, for example, interpret "landless" to mean lack of farm land that is owned; for others, it simply means lack of access to farm land under any form of tenure. My own reading of the statistical data and other evidence for LAC countries is that the percentage of the economically active rural population without any land in the latter sense is quite small. On the other hand, it is clear that a high percentage of the rural population has insufficient land (or land plus technology) to support a household without recourse to off-farm employment.

8. Countries (or regions) for which studies have been completed are Bolivia, the Caribbean Region (Eastern Caribbean), Colombia, Costa Rica, Guyana, Haiti, and Honduras. Studies in progress are those for Ecuador, Guatemala, Jamaica, Paraguay, and Peru.

9. The Ecuador project showed "the most impressive income-generating impact" of all the 36 projects reviewed in the 11-country study by Morss et al (1975:Vo. II, p. 1-11). See also Zuvekas (1976). As Tendler (1976: 118-124) points out, however, the project's success was attributable in large measure to a strong subsidy element, including relatively low-cost credit and favorable price policies. Still, though the project later came to be plagued by loan repayment problems and a crumbling of its complex organizational structure, the long-term benefits resulting from land redistribution, as well as the project's demonstration effects, may well be significant. For an internal evaluation of both the Ecuador and Costa Rica projects, see U.S.A.I.D. (1975).

10. Poor land-use practices are not the only potential threat. In Haiti, for example, A.I.D. has found that road construction has sometimes

accelerated deforestation by facilitating the marketing of wood and charcoal.

11. A comparison of the preliminary 1976 census results in Bolivia with the adjusted 1950 census data shows that population in the Department of Santa Cruz, in the eastern lowlands, increased 3.6 percent annually, compared with 1.6 percent for the nation as a whole. Santa Cruz's share of the total population rose from 9 percent to 15 percent. While the 1976 census results showed Bolivia's total population to be substantially less (4.6 million) than projected (5.5-5.8 million), the population of the Oriente exceeded expectation.

12. In reviewing the agricultural development literature for Bolivia, I encountered instances of government technicians recommending crops unsuitable for local soil and climatic conditions or for which marketing costs were too high to justify production for the market.

13. See footnote 9 above. The final design did in fact include land tenure reform.

14. Data for Colombia and Venezuela in 1971-72, cited by León (1979: 12), show that wives of male heads of household accounted for less than 10 percent of the rural labor force in Colombia and less than 5 percent in Venezuela, while male heads of household accounted for 52 percent and 65 percent, respectively. The figures for women are unrealistically low.

15. This was a particularly significant factor in the Adelman-Robinson simulation model for South Korea (1977).

16. Lipton (1976:548) points out that in some South Asian languages the word for "loan from the government" means "assistance" or "grant." Such an attitude contributes to high default rates, and it encourages overinvestment in fertilizers, chemicals, machinery, and equipment at the expense of labor, draft animals, and the use of crop rotations, including green manures.

17. There is growing evidence that default rates are higher for large farmers than for small farmers.

BIBLIOGRAPHY

Adams, Dale W. "Mobilizing Household Savings through Rural Financial Markets," *Economic Development and Cultural Change* 26 (April 1978): 547-560.

Adelman, Irma, and Morris, Cynthia Taft. "A Typology of Poverty in 1850." In *Essays on Economic Development and Cultural Change in*

Honor of Bert F. Hoselitz, ed. Manning Nash. Supplement to *Economic Development and Cultural Change* 25 (1977):313-343.

_____ , and Robinson, Sherman. *Income Distribution Policy in Developing Countries: A Case Study of Korea.* Stanford, Calif.: Stanford University Press, 1977.

Arndt, Thomas W.; Dalrymple, Dana G.; and Ruttan, Vernon W. *Resource Allocation and Productivity in National and International Agricultural Research.* Minneapolis: University of Minnesota Press, 1977.

Bolivia. Instituto Nacional de Colonización (INC). (*Actividades*). La Paz, May 1976.

Camacho Saa, Carlos. *Estudio de caso en el valle bajo de Cochabamba (Caramarca, Parotani, Itapaya).* La Paz: Servicio Nacional De Reforma Agraria, 1970.

Comitas, Lambros. "Occupational Multiplicity in Rural Jamaica." In *Work and Family Life: West Indian Perspectives,* ed. Lambros COMITAS and David Lowenthal. Garden City, N.Y.: Doubleday and Company, Anchor Books, 1973.

Davidson, John Richard. "The Implementation of the Political Development Goals of the Alliance for Progress." Ph.D. Dissertation, University of Wisconsin–Madison, 1976.

Eckholm, Erik P. *Losing Ground: Environmental Stress and World Good Prospects.* Foreword by Maurice F. Strong. New York: W. W. Norton and Company for the Worldwatch Institute, with the Support and Cooperation of the United Nations Environment Program, 1976.

Ecuador. Ministerio de Agricultura y Ganaderia (MAG); and France. Office de la Recherche Scientifique et Technique Outre-Mer (ORSTOM). *Diagnóstico socio-económico del medio rural ecuatoriano: ingresos.* Document No. 7. Quito, November 1978.

Evenson, Robert, and Kislev, Yoav. *Agricultural Research and Productivity.* New Haven: Yale University Press, 1975.

Galleguillos F., Adolfo. *Aspectos sociales de la colonización en Bolivia.* La Paz: Institutio Nacional de Colonización, 1974.

Gomez D. Enrique, and Gardner, B. Delworth. "The Economics of Bolivian Self-Sufficiency in Wheat Production." *Southern Journal of Agricultural Economics* 8 (July 1976):79-84.

Hayami, Yujiro, and Ruttan, Vernon W. *Agricultural Development: An International Perspective.* Baltimore: The Johns Hopkins University Press, 1971.

International Bank for Reconstruction and Development (IBRD). *World Development Report 1978.* Washington, D.C., August 1978.

Ladejinsky, Wolf. *Agrarian Reform as Unfinished Business: The Selected Papers of Wolf Ladejinsky.* Ed. Louis J. Walinsky. New York: Oxford University Press for the World Bank, 1977.

León, Francisco. *Pobreza rural: realidades y perspectivas de política.* Document No. E/CEPAL/PROY.1/14. Santiago, Chile, July 1979.

Lipton, Michael. "Agricultural Finance and Rural Credit in Poor Countries." *World Development* 4 (July 1976):543-553.

Lodge George C. *Engines of Change: United States Interests and Revolution in Latin America.* New York: Alfred A. Knopf, 1970.

Molina, Sergio, and Piñera, Sebastián. *Poverty in Latin America: Situation, Evolution, and Policy Guidelines.* Document No. E/CEPAL/PROY. 1/1. Santiago, Chile: United Nations Economic Commission for Latin America, 20 June 1979.

Morss, Elliot R. et al. *Strategies for Small Farmer Development: An Empirical Study of Rural Development Projects.* 2 vols. Washington, D.C.: Development Alternatives, Inc., May 1975.

Nelson, Michael. *The Development of Tropical Lands.* Baltimore: The Johns Hopkins University Press, 1973.

Rice, Edward B. *Extension in the Andes: An Evaluation of Official U.S. Assistance for Agricultural Extension Services in Central and South America.* Cambridge, Mass.: the MIT Press, 1974.

Royden, Tom, and Wennergren, E. Boyd. *The Impact of Access Roads on Spontaneous Colonization: Chané-Piray, Bolivia.* Utah State University Series 23/73. Logan, Utah, 1973.

Tendler, Judith. *A.I.D. and Small Farmer Organizations: Lessons of the Ecuadorean Experience.* Part of an Inter-Country Evaluation of Small Farmer Organizations prepared for U.S.A.I.D. Washington, D.C., July 1976.

Thiesenhusen, William C. "Hill Land Farming: An International Dimension." LTC Paper No. 109. Madison: Land Tenure Center, University of Wisconsin, December 1976.

Thoumi, Francisco. "Implicaciones de diferentes definiciones de pobreza sobre el tamaño y distribución de las poblaciones, objetivo de préstamos del Banco." Memorandum to Jorge Ruiz Lara, Subgerente, Department of Economic and Social Development, Inter-American Development Bank, 25 October 1978.

United Nations. Economic Commission for Latin America (UN-ECLA). *El desarrollo económico y social y las relaciones económicas externas de América Latina.* Vol. I. Document No. E/CEPAL/1061. Santiago, Chile, 31 January 1979.

_____ . _____ . "The Economic Policy of Bolivia in 1952-64." *Economic Bulletin for Latin America* 12, No. 2 (1967):61-89.

United States Agency for International Development (U.S.A.I.D.). *Intercountry Evaluation of Land Sale Guaranty Programs: Ecuador and Costa Rica.* Washington, D.C., July 1975.

_____ . _____ . *Primer on Title IX of the Foreign Assistance Act.* Washington, D.C., 1968.

_____ . _____ . Mission to Bolivia (USAID/Bolivia). "Toward a Rational Wheat Strategy for Bolivia." La Paz, 1976.

Weisskoff, Richard, and Figueroa, Adolfo. "Traversing the Social Pyramid: A Comparative Review of Income Distribution in Latin America." *Latin American Research Review* 11, No. 2 (1976):71-112.

Wennergren, E. Boyd, and Whitaker, Morris D. "Investment in Access Roads and Spontaneous Colonization: Additional Evidence from Bolivia." *Land Economics* 52 (February 1976):88-95.

Zeballos Hurtado, Hernán. "From the Uplands to the Lowlands: An Economic Analysis of Bolivian Rural-Rural Migration." Ph.D. Dissertation, University of Wisconsin–Madison, 1975.

Zuvekas, Clarence, Jr. "Agrarian Reform in Ecuador's Guayas River Basin." *Land Economics* 52 (August 1976):314-329.

_____ . *Income Distribution in Latin America: A Survey of Recent Research.* Essay Series No. 6. Milwaukee: Center for Latin America, University of Wisconsin–Milwaukee, July 1975.

_____ . "Policies toward Small-Farm Agriculture in the English-Speaking Eastern Caribbean." A paper presented at the October 1978 Meeting of the North Central Council of Latin Americanists. (1978a)

_____ . *A Survey of the Literature on Income Distribution and the Fulfillment of Basic Human Needs in the Caribbean Region.* Caribbean Regional General Working Document Series No. 3. Washington, D.C.: Rural Development Division, Bureau for Latin America and the Caribbean, U.S.A.I.D., September 1978. (1978b)

THE HYDROELECTRIC POTENTIAL
OF THE PARANÁ RIVER AND PROSPECT FOR
REGIONAL ECONOMIC DEVELOPMENT

J. Eliseo Da Rosa

I. INTRODUCTION

The hydroelectric potential of the water of the Paraná River first became evident during the last two decades, first in Brazilian territory where over twenty-two dams, with a potential of 8,000 MW, were already in operation. More recently, the construction and planning of the Itaipú, Yacyretá and Corpus plants resulting from bilateral treaties between Paraguay and its powerful neighbors, Brazil and Argentina,[1] offer an unprecedented opportunity for regional as well as national development. On April 26, 1973, Brazil and Paraguay signed the Itaipú Treaty that will permit the construction of the largest hydroelectric plant in the world (30 percent larger than the U.S. Grand Coulee). The Yacyretá Treaty of December 3, 1973, envisages a new source of energy for both Argentina and Paraguay to meet their critical domestic needs, accelerate economic development, and raise public revenues. Progress is presently being made in negotiating still another treaty between Argentina and Paraguay related to a hydroelectric plant at Corpus, between Itaipú and Yacyretá.

The construction of Itaipú is progressing as planned, and the first generators will be in operation by 1983. When it is completed, 18 generators of 700 megawatts (MW) each, will have a generating capacity of 12.6 kilowatts (KW) with an annual average output of 66,240 gigawatt hours (GWh). Yacyretá will operate with 30 generators of 135 megawatts each, a generating capacity of 4.05 GW and an estimated annual output of 17,000 GWh. The work at Yacyretá is about to start. The potential of Corpus will ultimately depend on the outcome of the negotiations between Argentina, Paraguay and Brazil.

Itaipú and Yacyretá are hydrologically interdependent. The former is being constructed by Brazil and Paraguay and in spite of Argentine claims that present plans will make Corpus economically unfeasible. To obtain the minimum economic output at Corpus, the potential capacity of Itaipú must be reduced. Making Itaipú and Corpus compatible includes other aspects of the operation of the Brazil-Paraguay Project. Argentine claims are based on the principle of the need to recognize the damages arising from a use of the waters of the river that will alter its normal flow and level.[2]

The three plants that are to be completed on the Paraná River by the concerted effort of Argentina, Brazil and Paraguay will have unprecedented effects on the entire River Plate basin. The Paraná River in the first place offers the largest known pool of hydroelectric potential controllable by presently available technology. The generating capacity to be installed will help these countries to meet their estimated demands for energy in their present plans for economic development. To optimize the use of the water of the Paraná River, the conflicting interests among the countries entitled to the use of the water must be harmonized and satisfactory compromises made. For constructing and operating the hydroelectric plants along the lines of current bilateral treaties, adequate bases require development for an effective partnership in production and equitable distribution of the gains. Furthermore, new problems in international jurisprudence arise in the relationships between countries, corporations, and individuals. These must be resolved and incorporated into existing practice.[3]

This paper will discuss some of the theoretical and practical problems arising from the need to attain an efficient use of the commonly owned water of the international section of the Paraná River. It will also deal with the problem of distribution of the benefits and the prospect for economic development that the expected electric power will create. Special attention will be given to the self-interest that Paraguay, the least developed and smallest of the three countries, could develop.

II. THE THEORETICAL FRAMEWORK

The Efficiency Problem

The water flowing in the Paraná River at the sites of Itaipú and Yacyretá and Corpus dams is a specific, fixed, and unsubstitutable factor in the production of hydroelectric power. The property rights on the hydroelectric potential of that water to bordering countries are indivisible under existing technology. Thus, the water constitutes an equal indivisible condominium to be recognized as such according to widely accepted norms of international law. This physical and hydrological reality for these purposes, i.e., the generation of electricity, requires a departure from the conventional treatment of jurisdiction and international borders. Customarily, the national territory of sovereign states is marked by the midpoint of the rivers separating them or the deepest line of the waters.

A conceptually different problem, in addition to the equal and undivided condominium on the water, occurs: the "common pool good" problem that water presents when different users at different dam sites want to maximize the output that can be obtained from the use of that water. The lack of agreement on widely accepted norms to be applied in these cases defining property rights gives to water the characteristic of a fugitive good or *res nullius,* a common pool good in economists' terms.[4]

It is helpful for a better understanding of the efficiency problem as well as the distributional problem to distinguish between the *bilateral* problem concerning the partnerships established in the treaties and the *trilateral* problem arising from the need to allocate the waters among the three projects. The first problem was dealt with rather satisfactorily in the treaties and in their revisions. The second one offers the greater difficulties and yet has to be solved.[5] The conventional optimization solutions (equimarginal principle) for the use of an economic factor of production, e.g., the water flowing in the Paraná River, requires that the last unit of water used in the different applications yield the same increment in output. This applies to the consumptive use of water at Itaipú, Yacyretá and Corpus to the extent that the projects are interdependent, i.e., water used at one site reduces the amount available at the other sites. For all practical purposes, given size and intended operation of the plants, Itaipú and Yacyretá offer no serious problem; but Itaipú and Corpus because of their proximity and heights are clearly interdependent. Water required for one kwh of extra output from Itaipú reduces that available to Yacyretá. If the use of water is unrestricted each of the plants seeking the maximum output of electricity will generate negative externalities to be borne by the other. This is the type of inefficiency characteristic of common pool goods, in this case the water of the Paraná River. The three established solutions to this problem supported by economic analysis are: merging of property into a single regional authority, determining fixed quotas for the use of water, and requiring compensation for the damages produced to other potential users. These must be used separately or in combination if efficient use of the water is desired and a maximization of the production of energy is to be attained. In a broader context, negotiations for reaching a solution to this common pool problem have been underway for many years in international forums at the U.N. or in regional conferences.[6] In the particular case of the dams on the Paraná River, tripartite meetings have been working over the last three years to find an acceptable formula to make compatible the Itaipú and Yacyretá dams.

The Distribution of the Benefits

The distribution of the product obtained with the use of the commonly owned water can be considered equitable when each factor receives the opportunity cost value of its contribution. In the particular case of the use of water for the production of electric power, the specificity and fixed quantity to this factor at the site of each hydroelectric plant make its owner a residual recipient of an economic or pure rent, no matter what arrangement is reached for the operation of the plant; i.e., one-country ownership or some form of shared ownership. Further, the price of the product determines the size of the rent. The compensation to be received for the water is to be divided equally between the co-owners of its indivisible hydroelectric potential. The pricing of raw material and natural resources, especially when they are owned by underdeveloped countries and used by industrialized countries, shows with great clarity how difficult it is to implement the economic criterion of equity in distribution. At present, most Third World countries and exporters of raw materials challenge past practice in search of a more equitable distribution among nations. As part of this philosophy, the Law of the Sea looks for an equal distribution of the wealth in mineral and animal life that the oceans hold.[7] In the Western World, political philosophers have been attempting to clarify some of the old problems of distributive justice along lines not alien to conventional economic theory.[8] In the discussion of the Itaipú and the Yacyretá treaties we shall see to what extent the partners in the hydroelectric plants to be completed on the Paraná receive a fair share of the anticipated benefits.

III. ITAIPÚ, YACYRETÁ AND CORPUS AS BILATERAL BUSINESS OPERATIONS

By the Itaipú and Yacyretá treaties the partners in each enterprise agree to operate a public, binational corporation owned equally by the two countries to be represented by their corresponding electric power authorities (Agua y Energía of Argentina, Electrobras of Brazil and the Administración Nacional de Electricidad of Paraguay, ANDE.) These binational corporations operate with a capital equally owned by the partners.[9] The control and administration is shared by the two countries involved through an administrative council and an executive council composed of an equal number of members from each country. This parity is extended at least in principle to the hiring of the technical and construction personnel as well as to the supply of material and subcontract work. The huge sum of money required to construct the dams is obtained in the domestic markets of Brazil and Argentina and from international financial institutions or foreign banks, at competitive market rates. Guarantee of payment and conversion of currency to the satisfaction of the creditor is also shared to the extent of the credit capability of the countries. Thus, Brazil and Argentina will guarantee larger shares of the loans than Paraguay. The strictly egalitarian nature of the association between two sovereign and independent countries is reflected in the provision in both treaties that the limits and the territory of the partners are not modified or diminished by the treaties, even though some of the territory may be affected by the operation of the binational plants.

To provide an equitable and acceptable distribution of the benefits as a rent that corresponds to the factor water, the treaties confer to each one of the partners the full property rights to the energy purchased by the partners from the binational corporations. That price to be paid includes all the explicit costs of operation, financial services, and administration. The value of the economic rent due to the water is not included but is received by each partner country as it uses that part of the energy to which it is entitled. Otherwise, it is explicitly to be included as royalty or compensation should one country sell its surplus to another.

Brazil and Argentina receive in the Itaipú and Yacyretá treaties the preferential right to buy from Paraguay that part of its share in electric power not absorbed domestically. And the price due to Paraguay is the value of the economic rent of the water contributed by Paraguay. But that price for the transfer of power plus the cost of delivery due to the binational corporation (as compensation) is negotiable and depends on the bargaining position that the two countries have at the conclusion of the agreement. In both treaties the other partner requested and obtained from Paraguay the commitment to honor a price specified in dollars that was to remain constant in real terms for the duration of the treaties.[10] When Paraguay uses energy domestically, the rent due to water is fully recovered. Depending on the pricing policy of Paraguay's Power Authority, the recipient of that rent will be the public electric authority or the consumer of electricity. But when the energy is exported, the rent will be fully recovered only if compensation for the transfer is equal to the difference between the true market value of the power less the explicit costs to be paid to the producing, binational corporation. Agreement to a long-term formula permits the possibility that compensation, even if presently adequate, may not be so in the future. It may fall short of the full rent if new and more expensive sources of energy are required. This requires of Paraguay a decision about the more convenient and profitable way of disposing of that surplus, either by expanding and intensifying domestic consumption or by selling energy to her partners. If Paraguay could sell her surplus to a third country (Bolivia or Argentina from the Itaipú surplus or Brazil from Yacyretá surplus), the price paid by the higher bidder would probably include the whole rent to water. Another possibility is the renegotiation of the treaties. This may be difficult if the position of the two partners is not equal and the stronger is unwilling to bargain.

Renegotiation of the treaties, however, is not impossible depending on the circumstances. Argentina and Paraguay revised the Yacyretá treaty even before construction was begun. A review of this renegotiation episode sheds light on the problem of the distribution of the benefits in the joint undertaking. Argentina and Paraguay had previously agreed to the construction of the hydroelectric plant of Yacyretá at a location with technical and safety characteristics that would have required a flooding of 1690 km^2 of land, a little over 1000 km^2 of Paraguay's territory. The treaty also stipulated that all the land affected by the dam and subject to damages would be expropriated and receive adequate compensation from the binational corporation. In principle, this guaranteed fair compensation to each country arising from the loss in product yield from the land to be flooded. After the Interamerican Development Bank (IDB) and the World Bank (IBRD) had loans approved each for $210 million to start the construction of the dam, Paraguay requested a modification of location and technical characteristics of the dam in order to reduce the area to be flooded in her territory and to divide that area more equally between the two countries. This would have required a delay in construction, the need for the renegotiation of the loans, and as claimed by Argentina, the acceptance of a level of safety for the dam below a minimum reasonable standard. This crisis threatened the whole project. Pressure started to build in Argentina to denounce the treaty. Negotiations were immediately started and finally, on August 31, 1979, a few days before the international credits were to be cancelled, agreement was reached. The agreement involved: (1) the selection of a new location for the dam that will reduce the flooded area on Paraguay's territory to 820 km^2; (2) a more egalitarian formula in the operation of the executive council of the binational corporation; and (3) the adoption of a formula to determine compensation to be paid to each country by the national corporation for the territory to be flooded to be reflected in the price charged to the partners for the energy used.[11] The binational corporation will pay annual compensation for the use of the flooded land rather than a lump-sum as was required by the Itaipú Treaty in its article XVLL.[12] The formula to determine that compensation or rent due to land (which is fixed in real terms), was probably considered by the partners as preferable to the one-time expropriation payment. With the partners sharing in that rent in proportion to the area flooded, it was probably considered fair to both parties. This "compensation for flooded land" now incorporated into the Yacyretá Treaty will increase the price of electricity charged to the partners by the binational corporation. If the payment of a fair price for the expropriated land is also made to the private owners, that compensation payment would then amount to a net addition to the revenues that Paraguay would receive from her partner in addition to the rent for the use of water and in some way in lieu of the rent for the use of land that may not have been included in that compensation. Unofficial estimates made on precarious information put that compensation for the flooded land in the neighborhood of $20 million for 1986 and $30 million for 1990 and subsequent years.[13]

This solution to the flooded area problem, apparently adopted at the request of Paraguay, has been criticized in that country with the argument that since in Itaipú and Corpus Paraguay will suffer a smaller area flooded by the dams, it will be required to pay more as a transfer to the other partner. If Paraguay follows the strategy of selling any surplus, that loss may not be significant; in any case, the country will have a fixed and secure source of revenue accruing to the public sector.

IV. THE TRILATERAL DIMENSION OF ITAIPÚ AND CORPUS

The interdependency in the consumptive use of water raised the common pool goods problem between Itaipú and Corpus. An agreement among the three concerned parties about the overall hydroelectric development in the area becomes necessary if an optimal and equitable solution is desired. But for political and strategic reasons, when the Itaipú treaty was signed, Argentina was left out in spite of her protest that her interests in Corpus were ignored. Brazil and Paraguay are building a plant together at Itaipú—a plant that will maximize the output of electricity at that site. To meet that requirement, the fall of the Itaipú dam (difference between the upper and lower levels of the water) must be 120 meters. As a result of that, Corpus will have to operate with a fall of only 18 meters, which is not sufficient to obtain all the electric power needed to make Corpus an economically viable project. Furthermore, Argentina claimed that under those constraints the two plants taken together would not maximize the output that the Paraná River could yield. The best alternative, in Argentina's view, was to reduce the fall of Itaipú to 90 meters and to increase the fall of Corpus to 48 meters. This alternative will raise the level of water above the Corpus dam to 130 meters above sea level. Negotiations to make Itaipú and Corpus compatible were undertaken three years ago; and although they were interrupted several times, good prospects exist now to have them resumed after the Yacyretá differences between Paraguay and Argentina have been solved. It is believed that both Argentina and Brazil will accept a height of 105 meters above sea level for Corpus.

Other issues under discussion include: whether or not Itaipú will work as a peak, non-peak, or constant-flow dam. This choice will have a significant effect on the level of the waters downstream and the operation of Corpus. Since the construction of Itaipú is progressing at an accelerated pace, the solution of this problem must be reached before construction of the generator facilities begins at the bottom of the dam.

After that time, the possibility of a satisfactory solution will be greatly reduced and engineering modification would at best be very expensive. Paraguay may be able to arbitrate since no great loss in electric power available to her will occur from the transfer of output from one dam to the other. But the results of these negotiations will depend to a large extent on the distribution of bargaining power between Brazil and Argentina.

V. STRATEGIES FOR REGIONAL DEVELOPMENT

A possible annual output of more than 100,000 GWh can be obtained from the waters of the Paraná River from the Itaipú, Yacyretá and Corpus dams,[14] a very substantial pool of electric power for national development as well as for the development of the region adjacent to the hydroelectric plants. Brazil and Argentina can absorb all of their shares as well as the Paraguayan surplus due its small domestic market.

The industrial belt on the Atlantic coast around São Paulo alone could consume all the energy expected to be available to Brazil. In Argentina, the Province of Entre Rios will certainly offer a good market for industrial consumption of the electric power. Depending on national priorities, larger or smaller amounts of power will be channeled into the predominant agricultural zone of the state of Paraná in Brazil and the provinces of Misiones and Corrientes in Argentina. This territory bordering the Paraná River shows a relatively low degree of industrialization. With the new access to cheap energy, new poles of industrial activity will be created and a process of industrialization of locally available raw materials will develop.

Recent events suggest that a large share of the power generated in Itaipú may be used in the Atlantic industrial belt. The Itaipú treaty did not specify the "frequency" of the alternating current to be generated. Brazilian and Paraguayan grids are not compatible since the former utilizes 60 cycles and the latter 50 cycles. And since Brazil was expected to buy Paraguay's surplus, the problem arose as to the proportion of generators to produce 60-cycle and 50-cycle currents. Brazil initially insisted on all generators to produce 60-cycle power with the offer to compensate Paraguay for the costs of conversion. This seemed to increase Paraguayan "dependency," and decision was delayed in the expectation of possibly obtaining greater concessions. The matter was eventually resolved by Brazil informing her partner that generators would be equally divided between the two. The argument for making the two systems compatible lost much of its relevance with the development of promising new technology which permits the transmission of electric power over long distances as direct current. The frequency at origin and at the user's end make little difference. In the immediate region, Brazil will have direct access to 60-cycle power.

For Paraguay, the availability of electric power from Itaipú and Yacyretá alone opens new horizons and great possibilities for attracting electricity-intensive industries with the promise of nearly unlimited energy.

The region directly affected by this "electricity revolution" comprises three departments or political units–Itapúa, Alto Paraná, and Canendiyú–all bordering the Paraná River. Until the early 1960's this was a region with the smallest indexes of population, development, and integration with the rest of Paraguay's eastern region. Although it contains the best agricultural land and the richest forest, its population according to the censuses of 1962 and 1972 was only 1.3 percent and 3.8 percent of the total population, and was 91 percent and 81 percent rural. Roads were non-existent until Route 7 between Asunción and Ciudad President Stroesner (C.P.S.) was completed and linked to the Brazilian highway between Foz de Iguazu and Paranaíba and São Paulo on the Atlantic coast. A few border settlements such as Hernanderias, Pedro Juan Caballero, and Capitán Bads were more in the economic and social sphere of Brazilian life. Currency, products, and public services were Brazilian. Paraguayan families would register their children at the Brazilian Office of Vital Statistics to guarantee them a place to serve in the Army of Brazil which is an effective and free system of education and social assimilation.

The late 1960's and early 1970's saw rapid expansion in western Paraná (Brazil) due to growing world demand for food and especially the increasing price of soybeans. As land became increasingly scarce, Brazilian settlers began to buy land and move to the Paraguayan side of the Paraná River. Paraguay's government did not counter this migration with a significant and larger transfer of Parguayan farmers from the Central Department, who were overcrowded on overworked land. Reports gathered by the World Bank mission in Paraguay and not denied by the government, indicate that in the period between 1960 and 1973, 10,000 Paraguayan familes and an equal number of Brazilian familes settled in the easternmost departments, mostly in the Alto Paraná, and around C.P.S. In 1974-1975 the number of Brazilian familes that officially entered Paraguay as settlers in the Paraná zone was 6,000.[15] These migration figures should be compared with the total population increase in the department of Alto Paraná that went from 24,000 to 90,800 between 1960 and 1973.[16]

This migration into the easternmost departments of Paraguay

preceded the construction of the Itaipú dam and presented interesting geopolitical implications. Most such settlements are now accessible from Route 7 and are linked to the Brazilian highway network via the international bridge at C.P.S. Furthermore, the construction of the Itaipú and the Yacyretá dams is going to stimulate the construction of new coastal highway projects that will go from C.P.S. to Puerto Adela and Salto del Guaira in the North and Puerto Presidente Stroessner-Nacunday-Capitán Meza-Encarnación and finally up to the road over the Yacyretá dam that will be connected to Argentina's highway network. These new lines of coastal communications will help Paraguay integrate all her border lands into the national territory. On the negative side, the agricultural development that is taking place in the region presents some of the problems of dual agriculture with small farmers with incipient technology side-by-side with larger, highly mechanized farms. The small farmers are exclusively Paraguayan settlers; the large farms are cultivated largely by Brazilian immigrants. Serious attention must be given to this problem in the immediate future.

With the increase in farm population and acreage, cultivated agricultural production in Paraguay has already increased and the opportunity is enormous for future growth. So far, most of the increase in production was due to the increase in acreage cultivated.

The urbanization of the easternmost departments of Paraguay will be centered around Encarnación, an old city, and Ciudad Presidente Stroessner. This city, a few miles from the Itaipú dam and on Route 7 with its interconnection with the Brazilian highway network, will be both an administrative and service hub as well as a tourist trade center. Its population of 40,000 in 1978 is expected to double by 1980. It will also absorb the urban area of Hernandarias and the permanent housing settlement built in connection with Itaipú that has a capacity to house 12,000 workers.

The strategies adopted in the middle- and long-term development plans of Paraguay will determine the effects of the Itaipú dam on the department of Alto Paraná and the Yacyretá dam on Itaipú.

Paraguay with a present domestic annual production of 1350

GWh will be entitled to a total output of 42,970 GWh by 1989 without including a share from Corpus. Domestic demand from the national grid is projected to be 1,792 GWh by 1990. This leaves a surplus of about 40,000 GWh. This enviable position of having a practically unlimited supply of electric power may help overcome the disadvantage of location and the lack of mineral resources that has afflicted the country for so many years. The following strategies open to Paraguay for attaining an optimal utilization of her electric power surplus have been summarized by the World Bank mission which reflect the policies endorsed by the government.

a) To expand the national grid in order to supply cheap and abundant electricity to each corner of the country. The electrification of the rural sector, which comprises 60 percent of the country, could help the industrialization of raw materials produced locally and the establishment of light- and middle-sized industries in the area of Asunción.

b) To sell the largest possible amount of the surplus to Argentina and Brazil in order to use the revenue so obtained to strengthen the public sector and to finance badly needed overhead public capital projects.

c) To support and encourage the establishment of energy-intensive industries that would enjoy a guaranteed, unlimited amount of energy.

The World Bank technicians[17] recommend that studies of the possibilities of locating electricity-intensive industries within Paraguay be immediately undertaken. They do not believe, however, that this is the most promising alternative. Some of the difficulties pointed out are the lack of domestic capital and technological know-how to enter into partnership with foreign investors, the lack of mineral resources in the country, and the location far from consumer markets.

The alternative b) is thus considered by the World Bank as the most promising one. Paraguay can anticipate claiming $75 million per year by 1990 from the payment in royalties and compensation for the use of the water at Itaipú and Yacyretá. With the modification of the Yacyretá Treaty discussed above, an additional amount of $20 to $30 million per year has been estimated as the value Paraguay will receive for the land to be flooded by Yacyretá. The World Bank recommends that any domestic project of the conventional or electricity-intensive type be measured against the opportunity foregone by failing to sell that energy to Brazil and Argentina.

A simple comparison between those projects with the revenue received from the transfer of energy does not adequately measure the opportunity cost of the energy that could be used domestically by Paraguay. This is because the royalties and compensation for the use of water paid by Brazil and Argentina do not fully incorporate the economic or pure rent to which Paraguay is entitled. Paraguay could also follow an electricity pricing policy competitive with Brazil, charging a price below the market value for the electric power, determined by the cost of producing energy by the most expensive method. That promotional price could be as low as the price charged by the binational corporations to ANDE plus the cost of transmission. To determine what conventional or electric-intensive industries will be advantageous for Paraguay and which ones should be discouraged is a complicated problem that requires systematic and serious study. Very little has been accomplished so far in that direction.

Although most of the planning is still to be done, the utilization of the hydroelectric potential of the Paraná River by Paraguay opens to this country opportunities that were unforeseen just fifteen years ago.

CONCLUSIONS

The Treaties of Itaipú and Yacyretá, and hopefully the Corpus Treaty to be ratified in the near future, are important and positive moves in the direction of establishing permanent bilateral partnerships between neighboring nations for the use of a commonly owned resource, the water of the Paraná River, for the purpose of producing electric power that will help them to improve the economic and social conditions of their citizens. This is an unprecedented lesson in international cooperation considering the disparity in the economic, technological, and industrial development of the participating countries.

In a broader context, the construction of the three plants will require from all the nations involved an even greater effort to put aside their exclusive national interests in order to look at the interests of all the people in the region. And if they succeed in overcoming the difficulties that still remain, they will have accomplished a great deal toward the creation of a system of real economic integration in a large area of Latin America.

The impact that Itaipú, Yacyretá and Corpus will have in each one of the participating nations will depend on the priorities each one decides to pursue. The alternative open to Paraguay and the strategies to be followed will require serious evaluation of the benefits and costs of each to maximize the returns that the huge amounts of electric power available can provide.

NOTES

1. Itaipú Treaty, Annexes and Letters of Agreement, in República del Paraguay, Honorable Camara de Senadores, *Diario de Sesiones.* Sesión Extraordinaria del 29 de Mayo, 1973. Asunción, 1973, pp. 198-213; Yacyretá Treaty, Annexes, and Letters of Agreement, in Italo A. Luder: *La Argentina y sus claves geopoliticas,* Editorial Universitária de Buenos Aires, 1974, pp. 151-184.

2. For a general discussion of this problem see: Isaac Francisco Rojas: *Intereses Argentinos en la Cuenca del Plata,* Edición Libera. Buenos Aires, 1975; Osny Duarte Pereira: *Itaipú: Pros e Contras.* Paz e Terra. Rio de Janeiro, 1974; and J. Eliseo Da Rosa: *The Optimal Utilization of the Hydroelectric Potential of the River Plate Basin* (mimeograph), paper presented at the International Studies Association Meeting, April 4-6, 1977, St. Louis, Missouri.

3. For a full discussion see: J. Eliseo Da Rosa, *Economic Analysis of the International Law System Regulating the Use of the Water of the Paraná River by Argentina, Brazil, and Paraguay,* (mimeograph), paper presented at the XXI conference of the Inter-American Bar Association, San Juan, Puerto Rico, August 25-31, 1979.

4. A theoretical discussion of the problem can be found in J. Hirshleifer, J. C. de Haven, and J. W. Milliman: *Water Supply,* The University of Chicago Press, 1960, pp. 59-73.

5. J. Eliseo Da Rosa: Economic Analysis of the International Law System . . . . *op. cit.*

6. See Footnote 2.

7. A more extreme position taken by supporters of an equalitarian standard of justice is reflected in the principle of "the nations with lesser

relative development" broadly accepted by third world nations. The "reparation" principle proposed in the U.S. to compensate minorities for past injustices is another example of this position.

8. John Rawls. *A Theory of Justice,* Harvard University Press, Cambridge, Massachusetts, 1971, and Robert Nozick; *Anarchy, State and Utopia.* Basic Books, Inc. Publishers, New York, 1974.

9. Paraguay contributed half of the capital of Itaipú and Yacyretá public corporations. Brazil and Argentina loaned that amount to Paraguay to complete the subscribed capital charging the conventional rate of interest for that type of operation.

10. Paraguay receives from Itaipú US $650 as royalties plus US $300 as "compensation" per GWh sold to Brazil, and US $2,998 for GWh in compensation from Yacyretá (no royalties are included in this treaty). Argentina thus pays 3.2 times more than Brazil per GWh sold as rent due for Paraguay's water contribution. The amounts of royalties and compensation are fixed for the duration of the treaties but are adjustable for the loss in purchasing power of the U.S. dollar.

11. The formula to be used to compute the aggregate compensation for the flooded territory is $T = E \times CE \times .089$, where T is total compensation for flooded territory; CE is cost per unit output (US $/kwh); and .089 is a coefficient purporting to measure the percentage contribution (opportunity cost) of the flooded land needed to produce electric power. $CE = \frac{G + R}{EM}$, where G is annual direct expenses; R is annual amortization cost; and EM is energy produced per year. Once the total value of this compensation is detemined, each country receives a share proportional to the amount of land flooded in its territory. In the Letter of Agreement signed by Argentina and Paraguay on August 30, 1979 to modify the Yacyretá Treaty, reproduced in *A.B.C. Color* (newspaper), Asunción, August 31, 1979, p. 10.

12. Italo A. Luder, *op. cit.*, p. 157.

13. *A.B.C. Color,* Asunción, August 25, 1979, p. 16.

14. The generating capacity of Corpus will be determined by the final agreement that Argentina, Brazil and Paraguay reach concerning the level of water between Itaipú and Corpus. With a fall for Corpus in the range between 53 and 63 meters it may be estimated that around 100,000 GWh per year can be obtained from the three plants.

15. I.B.R.D., A World Bank Country Study; *Paraguay: Regional Development in Eastern Paraguay,* Washington, D.C., August 1978, p. 8.

16. *Op. cit.*, 41, Table 2.

17. *Ibid.* pp. 33-38.

INDUSTRIAL SHIFT AND LABOR STABILITY
ON A GOVERNMENT-ADMINISTERED
EJIDO FARMING DEVELOPMENT PROJECT
IN SOUTHERN YUCATAN, MEXICO

Jacob J. Climo

During the last twenty years, economic planners in Mexico have subscribed to the trickle-down theory of development, which asserts that as the country's output grows, part of the benefits will ultimately reach people in the lower strata of society (Barkin 1971: 1). Implementation of this strategy has resulted in a rapid rate of growth of national income and a steady expansion of the industrial sector. In this strategy, scarcity of capital and technology are regarded as the main obstacles to development. Most Mexican planners assume that problems of underdevelopment such as poverty and rural unemployment will be eliminated as capital and technology are increasingly made available.

The present paper argues that the trickle-down theory has failed, not because it has been judged prematurely, as its defenders claim (Ibid.: 22), but because it has not considered the many non-technical economic factors which also influence development or the lack of development.

One such factor is the organization of labor. This paper examines the structure of a peasant labor force in a southern Yucatan village[1] where national agrarian reform policies replaced a privately-owned sugar cane plantation with a government-administered, mechanized, collective farming development project. The data show that the labor organization remained very stable, despite personnel changes, even though the production base was changed. Even radical technological changes did not result in significant transformations in the life-style of rural working class communities, nor did they change the organization of labor.

The *ejido,* a unique form of land-holding unit encouraged by the Revolution of 1910, constitutes Mexico's principal agrarian reform institution for distributing land resources and labor rights to create a more egalitarian society. Over the last sixty years the government expropriated more than 70 million hectares of land from large private estates and transferred them to close to 3 million peasant beneficiaries.

The vast majority of the collectve ejidos were established in the 1930s when socialist president Lazaro Cárdenas created the program to expropriate the industrialized plantations, land held by the largest private owners.[2] Ejidos are considered "collective" when ejidatarios pool their lands and farm them as a single productive unit (Eckstein 1970:290); a collective labor organization is formed which also functions as a credit association.[3] These differ from "individual" ejidos where the land is divided and parceled among the individual members, who work their plots and market their produce individually.[4]

Recently, the ejido has become the basis of different cooperative farming experiments carried out under government sponsorship and control. The present administration looks favorably on the formation of new collective ejidos and is actively engaged in the economic organization of the ejido sector with strong institutional supports. Within the last three years, five thousand ejidos have become organized along these lines (Stavenhagen 1975). An analysis of specific collective ejidos created in the last fifteen years will enable us to develop an understanding of the problems the ejido must now face.

The Catmis ejido constitutes an example of recent, experimental, government-sponsored projects designed to establish collective ejido credit and labor associations in rural localities deemed appropriate for the development of modern, intensively capitalized, industrialized, commercial agriculture.

In 1967, the federal government established mixed farming and cattle ranching development projects and the collective ejido credit society in the former sugar cane plantation village of Catmis. The main purpose of the project was to raise the local standard of living by alleviating the effects of severe unemployment which the villagers had experienced immediately following the termination of sugar cane production and processing in the area (Pozas 1967, see also Banco Agropecuario del Sureste 1968). In the transition from "plantation" to collective ejido farm, the local peasants officially were transformed from resident workers with no control over the local means of production, into ejidatarios with collective rights to land, loans from the government, and the power to organize their own labor association.

Because a capitalistic mode of production was perpetuated under government controls, however, the project did not achieve its goal of raising the standard of living or eliminating the local unemployment problem. Moreover, the structure of the collective ejido labor organization shows a number of important similarities with the earlier plantation labor organization.

1) First, like the plantation laborers before them, the ejido laborers are divided into unequal statuses with differing privileges.

The most important structural change emerging from the agrarian reform in Catmis was that government technocrats and bureaucrats replaced private owners as the controllers of the local labor force and the decision-makers in the production process. Although a major change took place in labor personnel, the labor organization otherwise remained stable.

In Catmis, the agrarian reform took place in two major phases, the second of which culminated in the complete termination of sugar cane production in the area and the establishment of the collective ejido mixed farming project.

In the first phase, however, beginning in about 1936, the federal government only expropriated the sugar refining factory which was situated in the heart of the village, and a small portion of the sugar-producing lands of the neighboring area. Between 1936 and 1965, private sugar planters continued to grow 75 percent of the sugar cane processed by the factory, and government administrators of the plant and the fields cooperated with private owners to ensure an ample supply of sugar cane.

During this period the labor force was divided into two sets of workers with different privileges; 1) union and free workers, and 2) temporary and permanent workers. Free workers still depended heavily on individual maize cultivation on unclaimed public lands which were not used for sugar cane production. However, they also worked for the private sugar planters in order to supplement their income with cash. Union workers were associated with the National Sugar Workers Union which provided them with a federally guaranteed labor contract specifying their rights and responsibilities as union workers (Diario Oficial 1951, No. 5 Part CLXXXVII; and 1953 No. 24, Part CCI). They worked for government technocrats and bureaucrats who managed the refining factory and the plantings on government lands.

Laborers within the union were further divided into permanent and temporary workers. Permanent laborers were employed under a twelve-month contract. They resided in Catmis and controlled the union organization. Temporary laborers were employed only during the six-month harvest season. During the remaining six months, they either grew maize individually on frontier lands or left the village in search of daily work.

Established in 1967, almost 40 years after Cárdenas' initial agrarian reforms, the collective ejido was formed under optimal loan and farming conditions to ensure economic success. Loans were large, granted over an extended period, and at low interest rates. Moreover, the ejido project consisted of both irrigated crops and cattle ranching, rather than only one of these activities. Finally, crop diversification and rotation were planned to stabilize employment in the village by avoiding the dilemma of limited seasonal employment which had characterized the sugar cane plantation.

Because of the need for technical coordination, one key agency, the National Indigenous Institute (INI) was designated as the principal agency in the region linking the Catmis ejido to the federal government. The Regional Coordinating Center (CCRM) of the Institute, established near Catmis in 1965, accepted the reponsibility of administering the capital and managing the ejido labor credit association.

INI's main goals were to increase employment and earnings

and expand the ejido economy by means of the project. To accomplish these goals, the Institute directs and manages the labor activities of ejido credit association according to a formal management-labor structure (See Figure 1) which includes a technical director, an accountant, and two field technicians. The chief representative is the major elected official of the ejido credit society. He acts as foreman of the work force by assigning jobs to the individual credit society members. He also represents the society to the Institute which pays his salary.

The technical director, an Institute technician, administers the farming and cattle ranching operations with the accountant, markets the produce from the farm, and modifies the projected plans. At the end of each week, he presents the credit society chief representative with a list of work to be done the following week.

Structurally, today's village labor force is similar to the plantation labor force in that it is also divided into two sets of workers with differing privileges: (1) ejido and non-ejido and (2) ejido credit society and non-credit society members.

Non-ejido residents in Catmis included a small number of independent maize farmers and laborers for private cattle ranchers and village merchants. In addition, a small number of ejidatarios cultivate maize and other cash crops or raise goats and cattle on ejido plots which they have fenced off from the rest of the ejido lands.

Such ejidatarios work less for the mixed farming project than the credit society members and are not represented politically within the credit society organization. As a result, the non-credit ejidatarios work and earn less on the development project than the credit society ejidatarios. Of 67 credit society ejidatarios who worked in 1970, 45 (65 percent) earned more than $2,000 pesos whereas of 33 non-credit ejidatarios, who worked on the project that year, only one individual earned more than $2,000 pesos. The average annual project earnings for the non-credit ejidatarios was $851 pesos compared to $3,452 pesos averaged by the credit society members.

2) Secondly, underemployment and unemployment are widespread on the collective ejido development project.

Despite the input of 5 million pesos and the most modern technology available, the federal administration in Catmis

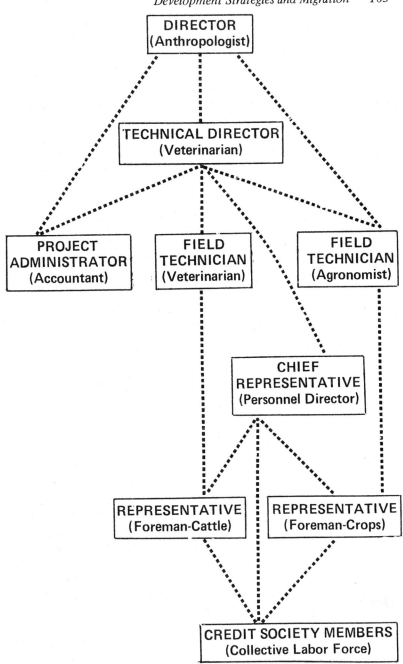

pursued a number of traditional capitalistic business policies that have resulted in job insecurity, low wages, underemployment, and local political conflict.

Administrative restrictions on capital and resources made working conditions highly irregular and insecure for all the ejidatarios. In the first three years of the project, the actual earnings of the credit society members were significantly below the bank's projected earnings (Banco Agropecuario del Sureste, 1968). In 1970, for example, the bank estimated an average earning of $5,700 pesos per member but the actual average earning was only $3,400 pesos. In addition, the amount of money spent for labor fluctuated greatly causing fluctuations in the kinds of tasks performed and the size of the ejido labor force. In 1968, $138,000 pesos were spent for labor, whereas in 1969, only $20,000 pesos were spent for labor. Similar fluctuations characterized the monthly labor expenditures and created conditions of irregular work. Finally, many credit society ejidatarios suffered from underemployment. In 1968, the average number of weeks worked by those who worked the most was 31.5 while in 1970 the average actually fell to 28.

3) Finally, a high rate of seasonal outmigration characterized the plantation system. Although complete data on outmigration are still unavailable for more than a few years after the collective ejido project began, it is believed that outmigration on the project is somewhat less than what it was on the sugar cane plantation but considerably greater on the collective ejido project than what program planners anticipated.

According to the national agrarian code (Código Agrario, 1970), if an ejidatario is found absent from cultivating his lands for two consecutive years, the Ministry of Agriculture may rule that he has abandoned them, and he may be disenfranchised and expelled from the society. His land plot would then be returned to the ejido community which, in turn, may allocate it to a new member. In 1970, five years after the establishment of the ejido, a census from the Ministry of Agriculture revealed that fully 32 percent (55) of the original ejido members were officially disenfranchised and their parcels returned to the ejido community.

The high percentage of outmigration between 1965 and 1970 mainly reflects a temporary problem, i.e. the extreme difficulty of working parcels during the first years of the ejido: the sugar plant had closed but the government-sponsored mixed farming project had not yet begun and, in the absence of capital, irrigation, modern machinery, and wage labor opportunities these ejidatarios abandoned their plots and left the village. In 1970, the ejido added 38 new members, 80 percent of whom were sons of those remaining. Undoubtedly outmigration will continue but probably on a lesser scale than those first few years, now that the project has begun.

In conclusion, let me state that these three similarities: the division of laborers into unequal statuses with different privileges; widespread underemployment and unemployment; and seasonal outmigration are present in the collective ejido labor organization, and show important continuities with the plantation period. The data clearly indicate that even radical technological changes brought about by a fundamental shift in industrial production did not result in significant transformations in the lifestyle of the rural workers nor in the organization of labor. The study should be understood as further evidence of the inadequacy of the trickle-down theory of economic development.

NOTES

1. The field research was conducted in the village of Catmis over an eleven-month period beginning June, 1970. Techniques of data collection included utilization of official government records, closed and openended questionnaires and informal interview with village residents, government bureaucrats and technicians, and participant observation. The author wishes to acknowledge grants from the state of Yucatan and from the Department of Anthropology and the Latin American Studies Center of Michigan State University.

2. Cárdenas then created about 800 collective ejidos in a number of regions where large-scale industrialized agriculture was already highly advanced or where the lands were fertile enough to transform them into highly productive commercial farms. By establishing collective ejidos and credit associations in these regions, Cárdenas sought to maintain modern agricultural methods and to avoid the disadvantages of breaking up the large productive plantations in order to distribute very small parcels of land to rural workers, who lacked both capital and technological skills

(R. Wilkie 1971).

3. The structure of these credit associations which parallels but is not identical to the formal ejido organization includes a general assembly, a vigilance committee, and a delegate or representative (delegado or representante) who represents the credit association members to the bank and distributes work to the members rather than land plots as the ejido president does on the individual ejidos.

4. The size of these individual parcels varies considerably among the ejidos in different regions throughout Mexico depending on the types of crops to be cultivated, the presence or absence of irrigation, and the number of ejido members.

REFERENCES

Banco Agropecuario del Sureste, S.A. Study of the feasibility of a mixed farming project in Catmis, Yucatan. Merida, Yucatan, 1968.

Barkin, David. "The Persistence of Poverty in Mexico: Some Explanatory Hypotheses." Unpublished paper, Dept. of Economics, New York University, 1970.

Código Agrario Y Leyes Complimentaria. Vigesima Edicion, Mexico, D.F., 1970.

Diario oficial organo del gobierno constitucional de Los Estados Unidos Mexicanos, No. 5 (July), Part CLXXXVII. Mexico, D.F.

Diario oficial organo del govierno constitucional de Los Estados Unidos Mexicanos, No. 24 (Nov.), Part CCI, Mexico, D.F.

Eckstein, Sholomo. Collective farming in Mexico. In *Agrarian Problems and peasant movements in Latin America,* Rodolfo Stavenhagen, ed., Garden City, New York: Anchor Books, Doubleday and Company, Inc., 1970.

Pozas, Ricardo (coordinator). "Estudio de los problemas sociales del Ingerio Azucarero de Catmis Yucatan." *Acta Sociologica,* Central de Estudios de Desarollo Serie: Promocion Social I, Universidad Nacional Autonoma de Mexico, Mexico, D.F., 1967.

Stavenhagen, Rodolfo. "Collective agriculture and capitalism in Mexico: A way out of a dead end." In *Latin American Perspectives,* Issue 5, summer, Vol. ii, Number 2, Mexico: The Limits of State Capitalism, 1975.

Wilkie, Ramond. *San Miguel: A Mexican Collective Ejido.* Stanford: Stanford University Press, 1971.

IRRIGATION IN CENTRAL MEXICO AND THE ROLE OF THE STATE: DEPENDENCY RELATIONSHIPS AND MIGRATION PATTERNS[1]

Laura Montgomery

The impact of irrigation upon society is a long-debated issue in the anthropological literature. The debate focuses on one of two levels: either 1) a macroanalysis of the role of irrigation in the development of the state; or 2) a microanalysis of the impact of irrigation upon an isolated community. Unfortunately, the discussion at both levels of analysis is, for the most part, mutually exclusive. As a result, broad generalizations about the relationship of irrigation in peasant communities to the state disregard the range of variation that this relationship takes from one type of irrigation system to the other. Similarly, studies of irrigation at the community level neglect to examine the larger, national context of peasant irrigation agriculture.

A complete understanding of peasant irrigation agriculture in Central Mexico requires analysis at both levels for two reasons. First, the practice of irrigation by peasant farmers in Mexico has been linked historically to economic and political activity at the level of the state. In the Pre-Columbian era, irrigation made possible the production of an agricultural surplus with which to pay tribute to the powerful urban centers such as Teotihuacan. During the colonial period, irrigated agriculture provided the Spanish colonists with food as well as an agricultural surplus for export to Spain. In the modern era, irrigation agriculture provided food for the urban centers as well as a surplus for export to obtain foreign exchange to develop the industrial sector of the Mexican economy. Second, peasant irrigation agriculture encompasses a wide range of irrigation technologies. These various types of irrigation systems in turn influence the nature and the dynamics of the linkages of the peasant community to the Mexican national government. However, the variations are not so disparate as to make generalizations about the impact of irrigation upon peasant societies in Mexico impossible.

Based upon a comparative analysis of traditional peasant irrigation agriculture in Central Mexico, this paper examines the characteristics of the socioeconomic structure of peasant irrigation agriculture in Central Mexico as well as the variations among irrigation types and their linkages to the Mexican national development strategy, dependent capitalism. Furthermore, the paper will discuss the influence of the national development strategy as executed through government irrigation policy upon migration patterns from the rural areas to the cities. The paper will first discuss the national economic and development context of irrigation agriculture in Mexico. Next the paper will discuss those characteristics of peasant irrigation systems which a comparative analysis has shown to be common to all cases of peasant communities that have historically practiced irrigation agriculture in this region. To illustrate the variation between irrigation types, the paper will use examples of peasant irrigation systems which are indicative of the variation of the peasant irrigation systems in Central Mexico. Finally, the paper will focus on the implications for rural-urban migration.

WATER AND MEXICO'S DEVELOPMENT STRATEGY

The practice of irrigation in Central Mexico has a history of several hundred years, but an analysis of the present socioeconomic structure of peasant irrigation in this region must be set within the context of the role of water in Mexico's economy as well as the nation's macrodevelopment strategy. Downing provides a concise description of this strategy:

> Mexico's development strategy has been one of dependent industrial capitalism. Hallmarks of this strategy are (1) exportation of nonrenewable natural resources and agricultural products to industrialized nations; (2) importation of foreign designed, labor-saving technology and capital; and (3) concentration, both in space and among social classes, of vast sums of capital, power, and wealth. This strategy has multiple consequences, including increased

dependence on foreign capital and loans; high susceptibility of the economy to the boom-bust movements in the prices of the world's basic commodities; a rapidly growing, marginally employed population; low wages, high interest rates; and scarce investment capital (1979:160).

As will be discussed further, this strategy has shaped the formation of the national irrigation policy. Moreover, the "multiple consequences" mentioned in the above quote are readily identifiable in those areas involved in irrigation agriculture.

Consistent with this development strategy of dependent capitalism is the government's major commitment to the modernization of the agricultural sector, the purpose of which is to produce a significant agricultural surplus to feed the increasing urban populations and for export to obtain the needed foreign exchange with which to develop the industrial sector. With respect to development in the agricultural sector, water is the most crucial element determining the productivity of Mexican agriculture (Reyes Osorio, *et al.*, 1974). However, water is, perhaps, Mexico's scarcest resource, and the geographical distribution of water resources in relationship to population concentrations further complicates Mexico's water problems:

> About 75 percent of the population lives in the higher altitudes where 70 percent of the industry is also concentrated. In contrast, 85 percent of the water is located on the Pacific and Gulf Coasts below 500 meters in altitude (Sanders, 1974:1).

Thus, the political and economic context of water in Mexico's highly populated areas, which include the areas of traditional irrigation agriculture, is one in which small landholders, large landholders, commercial agriculture, industry, and urban populations compete for access to scarce water resources. Therefore, the regulation of the use and distribution of the nation's water resources has been an important concern of the Mexican government.

In an attempt to exert control over the use of water within the nation, the Mexican constitution declared all water resources to be the property of the state, and since 1917, the Mexican government has created several bureaucratic structures to administer water resources (Reyes Osorio, *et al.*, 1974; Sanders, 1979). To control the use of water specifically within the agricultural sector, the government created the Secretaria de Recursos Hidralicos (now known as the Secretaria de Agricultura y Recursos Hidralicos) in 1946 and organized all areas of irrigated agriculture into national irrigation districts. Within each national irrigation district, the SARH not only controls the access to and distribution of irrigation water but also oversees the development of government irrigation projects. In areas where irrigation agriculture historically has been an important production strategy in the seasonal agricultural cycle, the Mexican government through the SARH tries to obtain control over the use of irrigation water in one of two ways: 1) directly by modernizing traditional irrigation systems with technology too sophisticated to be financed and maintained by peasant communities; 2) indirectly by controlling the access to credit, technology, and other inputs necessary for profitable irrigation agriculture.

The SARH locally administers irrigation water within a federal irrigation district through the formal structure of the Comité Directivo (Reyes Osorio, *et al.*, 1974, 874-876). The Comité Directivo is comprised of a manager (appointed by the SARH), a representative of the Secretaria de Agricultura y Ganaderia, a representative of the ejido association, a representative of the association of private small landholders, and a representative of the Banco Nacional de Credito Agricola and the Banco Nacional de Credito Ejidal.[2] Each member has a vote; however, the majority of the votes represent government interests. Representatives from other government and private agencies concerned with agricultural development participate in the Comité Directivo but have no vote.

The Comité Directivo grants farmers access to water according to the needs of the farmers and the current foreign and domestic market conditions for agricultural products. By law, access to water is to be granted equally among the ejidal sectors and the private sector and within the private sector among small and large landholders. Furthermore, the water itself cannot legally be bought and sold, though the SARH charges a fee for the use of the system. In principle, the only access to irrigation water is through the Comité Directivo and ultimately the SARH;

private irrigation systems, by law, should not exist.[3]

While in principle the administration of irrigation water appears to be highly formalized and tightly regulated, in practice there is a great deal of manipulation of the formal structure. Bribery of SARH officials and other forms of political maneuvering by the larger landholders gives some of these landholders preferential access to water. Since the larger landholdings and agribusinesses are more heavily involved in export cropping and, therefore, more lucrative than ejidal or small private landholdings, they are given priority to water, credit, fertilizer, improved seeds, and agricultural technology—crucial inputs for profitable irrigation agriculture.

Moreover, as demonstrated by the chain well systems in the Tehuacan Valley, the Mexican government in some cases is not able to control the development and maintenance of traditional irrigation systems. As will be further discussed, the degree to which the SARH and, ultimately, the national government both choose to and are able to exert control over the use of irrigation water in the areas where irrigation agriculture is a traditional crop production strategy is dependent upon two variables: 1) the extent to which the crop production resulting from use of irrigation in any given case is consistent with the goals of the national development strategy, dependent capitalism; 2) the technological complexity of the irrigation system.

Throughout the following discussion it is important for one to keep in mind that the Mexican development policy regarding irrigation agriculture is largely to eliminate the small farmer's use of irrigation for subsistence farming and, to a lesser extent, for cash cropping.

SOCIO-ECONOMIC STRUCTURE OF IRRIGATION IN MEXICO

The areas in Mexico where irrigation has been historically a crop production strategy of peasant farmers are the Oaxaca Valley, the Tehuacan Valley, the Teotihuacan Valley, the Valley of Mexico, and the surrounding areas. Irrigation agriculture in this region is an exceedingly complex phenomenon. It encompasses a repertoire of irrigation technologies, some of which result from different historical processes. Some irrigation systems date to the Pre-Columbian period; others were introduced by the Spanish; still, others are recent innovations. The technologies utilized in this region include:

1. Floodwater Irrigation—includes systems with and without canals.
2. Canal Irrigation—ranges from systems of earth dams and canals to systems of concrete dams and canals with sophisticated control systems.
3. Well and Furrow Irrigation—includes systems which utilize hand drawn well water, *pala* and ditch systems which raise water from one level to another, and systems which use power pumps.
4. Pot Irrigation—utilizes wells to handwater intensively cultivated plots.
5. *Galerias Filtrantes*—chain well systems.[4]

Importantly, these different technologies each have different social consequences. For example, floodwater irrigation requires only short-term, informal cooperation, whereas the canal systems require long-term, formal cooperation. On the other hand, pot irrigation requires little or no cooperation between farmers.

One must be aware of not only the technological and historical differences shaping the impact of irrigation agriculture upon communities in Central Mexico, but also one must realize that intra-community socio-economic differentiation is extremely important. The impact of irrigation agriculture has been different upon the ejidal sector, the *pequeños propietarios* (small landholders), the large private landholders, and the agro-businesses. The problem is further complicated, because the membership of each of these groups is not mutually exclusive of the others. The recognition of intra-community differentiation is crucial, because the differences are as much a result of participation or non-participation in irrigation agriculture as the differences and concomitant political economy maintain and stimulate the practice of irrigation. Unfortunately, the literature discussing irrigation in Mexico is not always sensitive to these differences, so any analysis which details all the complexities of irrigation in this region is difficult on the basis of existing research. For this reason, this study focuses on peasant irrigation in the private sector. In this region, irrigated plots, for the most part, are privately owned. The literature suggests that peasants who hold irrigated plots also hold ejidal lands. However, the ejidal holdings tend to be poor, unirrigated land. Thus, this paper does not deal with landless peasants or peasants holding only ejidal lands.

A comparative analysis of traditional peasant irrigation systems in these areas revealed several generally common characteristics. They reflect the socioeconomic structure of peasant irrigation agriculture which is linked to the national development strategy of dependent capitalism.

1. Irrigation is not necessary to practice agriculture *per se,* but it is necessary to produce an agricultural surplus for commercial use.

2. Irrigation agriculture is synonymous with cash cropping for both national and international markets.

3. The complexity of the technology of the physical irrigation system plays a crucial role in determining the locus of control over access to water.

The following discussion focuses on the implications of these characteristics for various peasant irrigation systems and on the way in which these characteristics reflect national development policy.

1. Irrigation is not necessary to practice agriculture per se,
but it is necessary to produce an agricultural surplus
for commercial purposes.

In the areas where historically peasants have utilized irrigation as a crop-production strategy, irrigation is not necessary to produce a crop. However, it is critical in order to produce a marketable surplus. Two elements make it nearly necessary for small farmers to produce such a surplus. First, dry farming produces very little and will not support the populations living in these areas. Climatically, the region has a wet/dry season. Rainfall in the wet season is sporadic and unevenly distributed both temporally and spatially. To make dry farming more reliable, some irrigation is necessary to supplement the natural rainfall. However, the labor and financial inputs required to irrigate make extensive irrigation of subsistence crops unprofitable. Therefore, many farmers irrigate cash crops in the dry season to generate income for food and other needs not provided by dry farming. Second, irrigation of subsistence crops is usually not a viable alternative, since the government controls all or some of the important inputs necessary for irrigation agriculture—water, credit, irrigation technology, etc,—so that subsistence farming on irrigated land is either unprofitable or just not permitted.

This feature provides an interesting theoretical perspective with which to approach irrigation, because it clearly implies that irrigation is more than a response to ecological conditions that make agriculture difficult. More importantly, irrigation is a response to social and economic conditions that demand production of a surplus for commerical purposes if the farmer is to remain economically viable. In fact, those small farmers who cannot obtain access to irrigation water to produce a commercial surplus are forced to diversify their economic strategies. They may seek seasonal usage labor on the large commercial farms or in industry, or sell their lands and migrate to the cities or perhaps the United States.

2. Irrigation agriculture is synonymous with cash cropping for both national and international markets.

In the Valley of Oaxaca, Lees (1974: 1975) describes the situation of peasant farmers who use well water for irrigation. Continual use has lowered the water table so that traditional techniques are no longer effective in raising water. The situation has been exacerbated by the rise in demand for alfalfa, an irrigated crop, resulting from the development of the dairy industry in the area. Thus, peasant farmers must abandon traditional well irrigation techniques for more sophisticated irrigation technology such as power water pumps. Since most farmers purchase their pumps on credit, they are forced to intensify their cash cropping to repay loans. Furthermore, rising costs of fuel, insecticides, and fertilizer combined with fluctuating prices in the markets create an unending cycle of debt. Because government agencies such as the National Agricultural Bank (BNCA) are the sources of credit for small farmers, the government can manipulate the production strategies of these farmers to coincide with national interests. As the traditional source of water fails, the farmer without the capital to meet the rising costs of fuel and other inputs can no longer participate in irrigated agriculture.

A further incentive for increased cash cropping is the rapidly expanding markets for agricultural products. In the Oaxaca Valley, the growing dairy industry has increased demand for alfalfa. In the Tehuacan Valley, Whiteford and Henao (1980) describe the development of the *galeria filtrante* (chain well) systems by peasant irrigation associations to provide irrigation water. A chain well is a tunnel system which taps veins of water which run between layers of rock (Whiteford and Henao, 1980: 1). Much of the impetus for the development of these operations was growing demand in Mexico City for elote (sweet corn), garlic, tomatoes, and other produce. The systems are financed, constructed, and maintained by peasant irrigation associations. Peasant farmers gain access to the water from chain wells by purchasing water shares in an irrigation association. Thus, access to water is limited to those farmers that have the ready capital to make the necessary investment. This excludes the poorer peasants from cash cropping to supplement falling yields from subsistence production, especially with rising prices of water shares.

3. The complexity of the technology of the physical irrigation system plays a crucial role in determining the locus of control over access to water.

One of the striking results of the comparative analysis of peasant irrigation systems was the consistency with which the complexity of the irrigation technology determined the locus of control over water, the means of production. In this context, the means of production is largely access to water, although access to land is also important. More specifically, the greater the amount of technology and labor required to develop and maintain the physical irrigation system, the more restricted will be the access to the use of the system. Furthermore, the locus of control over the access to water seems to explain much of the variation among irrigation types in terms of the strength and rigidity of the linkage of the peasant farmer or community to the national development strategy, dependent capitalism. Examples from the comparative analysis clarify this point.

Floodwater irrigation is technologically the simplest irrigation one finds in Mexico, and it is probably the oldest means of irrigation practiced in this area. Kirkby defines floodwater irrigation as "the growing of crops by attempting to control temporary, natural water flows (1973: 36)." Cases of flood-water irrigation are reported in the Oaxaca Valley, the Tehuacan Valley, and the Teotihucan Valley.[5] In the Valley of Oaxaca, floodwater irrigation can involve the use of canals, though not always (Kirkby, 1973). Walls, depressions, and low terraces are sometimes built by farmers to slow down and divert the floodwater. The construction of these devices is within the means of most any peasant farmer. But the benefits are unpredictable, since the water flow depends upon infrequent and non-periodic rain storms. The practice of floodwater irrigation is spontaneous, though it does require some cooperation.

As Kirkby comments on the Oaxaca Valley, "participation in a floodwater scheme does not secure water for a cultivator's fields unless he actually directs the flow onto his land during the period of flooding (1973: 38-40). If flooding occurs in an area which also practices canal irrigation, participation in the use of floodwater is restricted to those cultivators who have helped in the cost and maintenance of the canals. Thus as the technology of floodwater becomes more complex, the locus of control over access to water shifts away from the individual farmer to the group of farmers which shared in the investment of time and labor.[6]

In cases of traditional pot irrigation and well and furrow irrigation, the development and maintenance of the technology is within the means of individuals. The technology is unmechanized and labor intensive.[7] Since the practice of these techniques is in small scale operations that do not require cooperative effort from others in the community, the locus of control over access to water rests with the peasant farmer. But not every peasant farmer does or can participate in this production strategy. Participation is limited to those who not only have cultivatable land but also have a water source on their land.

A significant shift in the locus of control over access to water for farmers who practice either pot irrigation or well and furrow irrigation has occurred in the Valley of Oaxaca. Because of the falling water table, farmers must seek more sophisticated, mechanized technology to extract the water. For many farmers, this has involved increasing indebtedness to their creditors, the Mexican government. The repair and maintenance of the new technology, is beyond the expertise of many peasant farmers, and they become dependent upon government technicians to assist them. By controlling the necessary credit to obtain the new technology and the information to repair and maintain the technology, the government effectively controls access to water as well as cropping patterns, etc. The means of production, water, is out of the hands of the individual farmer and is controlled by an outside force, the SARH.

Moreover, irrigation becomes more and more concentrated among those farmers who either have water resources on their land or have sufficient capital to make production with the new technology profitable. And small farmers can no longer participate in irrigation agriculture. Since dry farming is not profitable, many sell their lands to larger farmers who can make the necessary investment. Thus land ownership also becomes more highly concentrated in the hands of a few.

A similar shift in access to water has occurred in those communities where the Mexican government is modernizing the traditional canal irrigation systems with sophisticated dams and concrete canals. These communities are located throughout the areas of traditional canal irrigation systems: the Teotihuacan Valley, the Tehuacan Valley, the Oaxaca Valley, the Valley of Mexico, and the surrounding areas of central Mexico.[8] Until the governments's introduction of the more sophisticated technology, the maintenance, operation, and construction of the canal technology was within the capabilities of each community. Likewise, the community controlled the distribution of water to the various cultivators. All cultivators had equal access to water and had only to request it from the *síndico,* a member of the civil-religious hierarchy who organized the various requests. A cultivator who used water was expected by the community to contribute to the repair and maintenance of the canal system. Failure to do so resulted in temporary loss of water rights.

The replacement of the traditional canal systems with concrete dams and canals radically shifted the control of the means of production away from the community and into the hands of the SARH. Not only does the community have to rely on highly trained engineers to operate the irrigation systems, but the SARH controls the allocation of water. Furthermore, even though under Mexican law water can not be sold, the government requires users to pay for the use of the system. Thus, again irrigation agriculture is an activity for those farmers with the necessary financial resources. Also, as previously discussed, the government manipulates access to water, credit, improved seed, fertilizer, and other technological inputs to the advantage of the larger, more commercial landholdings.

A final example which illustrates how the technological complexity of an irrigation system affects the access to water is the chain well systems in the Tehuacan Valley described by Whiteford and Henao (1980). They argue that because the technology and financial resources to build and maintain these systems are within the means of peasant irrigation associations, the peasant associations have been able to maintain control over the systems despite government attempts to gain control. Whiteford and Henao comment,

> The decentralized irrigation system of chain wells has provided many peasants of the Tehuacan Valley with a viable means for developing water resources. The construction process has been labor intensive, generating employment for valley residents, and has maintained technical expertise within the valley, thus avoiding dependence on government agencies for technology, loans, and other services. Peasants who particpate in the associations avoid the debts which are often necessary to establish other types of irrigation systems. Without government technology or credit the wells have contributed to the expansion of agricultural production in the valley (n.d.) 13).

Even though the water and the technology of these systems are controlled by the producers, the irrigation associations, the construction of the systems require financial investments which not all peasant farmers are in a position to make. Participation in the irrigation systems is restricted to those peasant farmers who have the necessary finances available.

Since the control of the means of production varies with the complexity of the technology of the irrigation systems, one can argue that even though all peasant irrigation agriculture is tied to the national development strategy, the nature of the linkage is not the same for all cases. Reciprocally, the technological complexity of the irrigation system affects the ability of the

SARH to control the usage of irrigation water. In those instances where the government has installed irrigation works or modernized existing systems, the linkage of the community and the individual peasant farmer with the national economy is the strongest. The SARH controls through direct and indirect means, cropping patterns and production strategies to be the most beneficial to the state. In these cases, government policy governing water is most strongly evoked. In areas such as the Oaxaca Valley where peasant farmers are becoming more dependent upon government sources of credit and technology to practice well irrigation successfully, the linkage to the national economy and government control is becoming stronger and stronger. The increasing commitment of these farmers to cash cropping to pay back loans for technology, fertilizer, seeds, insecticides, etc., reduces the flexibility of the farmer to change his production strategy if market prices for the crops fluctuate. Peasant farmers using the chain wells in the Tehuacan Valley are not as tightly linked to government policy. Because they control the technology and access to the water, they also control the type of crops they produce and the amount of land they commit to any given crop. These farmers have much more flexibility to adjust their production in response to changes in market prices and demand. Moreover, since these farmers are also providing needed produce for urban markets, the governmental system "allows" a private irrigation system; government controls are not invoked.

IMPLICATIONS FOR MIGRATION PATTERNS

The discussion thus far has focused upon certain characteristics of the socioeconomic structure of irrigation in Mexico as a reflection of the national development strategy to modernize and control irrigation agriculture. The impact of the government's irrigation policy in the areas of traditional irrigation practices has been to make irrigation agriculture unprofitable for peasant farmers with small landholdings. On the other handn, irrigation agriculture has become very profitable for the wealthier peasants with large landholdings and for large commercial farms. The resulting socioeconomic conditions are factors which influence migration patterns from these areas. Whiteford and Henao (1979) and Corbett (1979) are the only investigators who have examined this problem.

Whiteford and Henao found that one of the influences of the expansion of commercial irrigation in the Tehuacan Valley was that it reduced the volume of seasonal migration from the valley to areas of sugar production (1979: 29). However, this reduction was among those peasants who were able to secure access to water to benefit from the growing demand for agricultural products in the cities. Poorer peasant farmers, who were forced out of irrigation agriculture because of the rising costs of water shares in irrigation associations and fluctuating prices in the markets, continued to migrate for seasonal labor. On the other hand, Whiteford and Henao observe that among the wealthier peasant families with significant access to land and water the unmarried sons would migrate to the U.S. to participate in the bracero program (1979: 30).

With the similar disintegration of peasant agriculture occurring elsewhere, we would expect effects on migration to be similar to those found in the Tehuacan Valley. However, Corbett (1979) argues that the mechanization of irrigated agriculture on commerical operations has significantly reduced the labor requirements for these operations, forcing many seasonal workers out of employment. Thus, those small holders forced out of irrigation agriculture may find themselves unable to fill the ensuing economic gap with seasonal labor on commercial farms. For some this means migration to the urban areas or even the U.S. (Corbett, 1979). The peasants who can afford to participate in irrigation agriculture migrate less to seek supplemental employment. The issue warrants further research. Nonetheless, the government's development policy to modernize and commercialize irrigation agriculture creates a socioeconomic structure which tends to destroy the small peasant farmer in the areas of traditional irrigation agriculture.

CONCLUSION

Based upon a comparative analysis, this paper has attempted to argue that to fully understand the dynamics and significance of irrigation in Central Mexico, one must understand that the very practice of irrigation agriculture at the local level is intricately linked to political and economic activity at the national level. Thus one cannot abstract local irrigation practices from their macro context and examine them as discrete entities. However, this does not negate the value of micro-level analyses; the discussion has shown that while local practices of irrigation are linked with the national political and economic context, the impact of the linkages upon either individuals or communities is not uniform. In the case of irrigation, the degree to which the linkages control and change those communities or individuals engaged in irrigation agriculture is dependent upon the technological complexity of the physical irrigation system and the degree to which the crop production strategies of local farmers are consistent with the short term and long term goals of the Mexican government's development policies.

The arguments presented in this paper have important implications for Mexico's future in terms of migration, employment, production, and distribution of wealth if the nation continues its current policies in regard to irrigation agriculture. The migration that is stimulated by the structural constraints which make irrigation agriculture unprofitable for small farmers, illustrates how a development strategy of dependent capitalism creates labor pools among peasants for industry and commercial agriculture. However, the continued adoption of capital intensive production strategies by both commercial agriculture and industry will not absorb this newly created labor pool. Mexico's problems of unemployment and underemployment will only persist and worsen. Thus, with the modernization of irrigation agriculture, the small farmer finds his pool of economic strategies for survival shrinking. Furthermore, the modernization of irrigation agriculture continues to skew the distribution of wealth not only by affecting the employment rates but also by contributing to the concentration of land and technological and financial resources in the hands of those that are wealthy enough to participate in irrigation. Also, intensive use of irrigation, as in the Oaxaca Valley, creates ecological imbalances—falling water tables, salinization of soil, water logging of soil, etc.—which threaten the productive capacity of Mexico's scarce arable land resource. As food prices continue to inflate rapidly, Mexico's continued commitment of a large proportion of its agricultural production to cash crops for exports at the expense of food production for domestic markets only imperils the survival of the poor.

NOTES

1. The author would like to express her appreciation to Dr. Scott White-ford for his encouragement and helpful comments during the preparation of this paper.

2. It is important to note that the ejidal associations and the associations of small private landholders do not represent groups of peasants which are mutually exclusive. In the Oaxaca Valley (Kirkby, 1974), for example, many farmers hold both small private irrigated plots and ejidal lands. Others may hold only ejidal land. Therefore, the political structure of the Comité Directivo does not necessarily represent the actual distribution of land and power.

3. There is an exception to this law. A water source which is contained within the boundaries of private property is considered as such unless it transverses another private landholding in which case the water source is considered to be in the public domain (Reyes Osoria, *et al*, 1974: 865).

4. Kirkby (1973) provides a thorough description of these various irrigation technologies. Though her discussion focuses specifically upon the Oaxaca Valley, it is applicable to similar systems in other areas. White-ford and Henao (n.d.) provide a more complete description of the *galerias filtrantes.*

5. These are noted by Kirkby, 1973; Whiteford, 1979, personal communication; and Price, 1971.

6. Interestingly, floodwater irrigation is one of the only irrigation strategies used to irrigate subsistence crops exclusively. The data suggest that this method is more to replenish soil because of the high silt content of the flood water rather than to supply additional moisture for crops.

7. Kirkby, 1973, provides a thorough discussion on these technologies.

8. These cases are described by Million, *et al*, 1962; Whiteford, 1979, personal communication; and Lees, 1973, 1974, and 1975, and Hunt and Hunt, 1974, respectively.

BIBLIOGRAPHY

Corbett, John G. "Agriculture Modernization and Rural Employment in Mexico, 1980-1985: Implications for Mexican Migration to the United States." Paper presented at the II Symposium Sobre Relacione Econo-micas—Estados Unidos, XLIII Meetings, International Congress of Americanists, 1979.

de Alcantara, Cynthia Hewitt. *Modernizing Mexican Agriculture: Socio-economic Implications of Technological Change* 1940-1970. Geneva:

UNRISD, 1976.

Downing, Theodore E. "Explaining Migration." In Camara and Van Kemper, eds. *Migration Across Frontiers: Mexico and the United States.* Contributions of the Latin American Anthropology Group (AAA), Vol. III, 1979.

Hunt, Eva and Robert C. Hunt. "Irrigation, Conflict and Politics: A Mexican Case." In Downing and Gibson, eds. *Irrigation's Impact on Society.* Tucson: University of Arizona Press, 1973.

Kirkby, Anne V. T. *The Use of Land and Water Resources in the Past and Present Valley of Oaxaca, Mexico.* Memoirs of the Museum of Anthropology, No. 5. Ann Arbor: University of Michigan Press, 1973.

Lees, Susan. *Sociopolitical Aspects to Canal Irrigation in the Valley of Oaxaca.* Memoirs of the Museum of Anthropology, No. 6. Ann Arbor: University of Michigan Press, 1973.

_____ . "The State's Use of Irrigation in Changing Peasant Society." In Downing and Gibson, eds. *Irrigation's Impact on Society.* Tucson: University of Arizona Press, 1974.

_____ . "Oaxaca's Spiraling Role for Water." *Natural History* LXXXIV: 4, 1975.

Million, Rene F. and Clara Hall and May Diaz. "Conflict in the Modern Teotihuacan Irrigation System." *Comparative Studies in Society and History* 4(6): 494-524, 1962.

Price Barbara. "Prehispanic Irrigation Agriculture in Nuclear America." *Latin American Research Review.* 6(3): 3-60, 1971.

Reyes, Osorio, Sergio, *et al. Estructura Agraria y Desarrollo Agricola en Mexico.* Mexico: Fondo de Cultura Economica, 1974.

Sanders, Thomas G. "Population Growth and Resource Management: Planning Mexico's Water Supply." *American Universities Field Staff Reports* 11(3), 1974.

Whiteford, Scott. Personal Communication, 1979.

Whiteford, Scott and Luis Emilio Henao. "Commercial Agriculture, Irrigation Control, and Selective Labor Migration: The Case of the Tehuacan Valley." In Camara and Van Kemper, eds, *Migration Across Frontiers: Mexico and the United States.* Contributions of the Latin American Anthropology Groups (AAA), Vol. III.

_____ . "Decentralized Irrigation, Development, and Social Change: A Case of Mexican Peasant Organization and Division." *América Indigena* XL:1, 1980.

CHARACTERISTICS OF MANUFACTURING ENTERPRISES BY LOCALITY SIZE IN FOUR REGIONS OF HONDURAS: IMPLICATIONS FOR RURAL DEVELOPMENT*

Judith I. Stallmann and James W. Pease

INTRODUCTION

Honduras has a land area of 112,088 square kilometers and a population of 2,752,541 (1974 census) and thus, a population density of 24.6 persons per square kilometer. Population is increasing annually at approximately 3.6 percent—2.5 percent in rural areas, and about 5.5 percent in urban. GNP per capita is approximately $340 U.S., distributed so that eighty percent of the population has an average income per capita of less than $80 U.S. Most of the poor live in the rural areas which have 70 percent of the population. Seasonal unemployment in these areas is estimated as high as 70 percent (Mejia, 1978).

Because of poverty, high rates of rural unemployment, and the high rates of urban growth, the government of Honduras began considering alternative employment opportunities in the rural areas. One such alternative is rural industry, especially small-scale firms located in rural areas which produce inputs and simple consumer goods for the local population. Unfortunately, little was known about the characteristics of rural

*This paper was prepared as part of Michigan State University's Off-Farm Employment Project, which is financed by the Office of Rural Development and Development Administration, Development Support Bureau, U.S. Agency for International Development (AID/ta-CA-2). Funding for the survey and analysis was provided by this project as well as USAID/Honduras.

industries or their potential for increasing employment and output.

This paper discusses the preliminary results of a survey of rural industries carried out in four priority regions[1] in January and February, 1979, by the Honduran Center for Industrial Development, the United States Agency for International Development, and Michigan State University. The survey results were used to design a program of assistance to small industries in the regions.

Within each of the four regions, the localities were divided into five strata according to population size, and random sampling was done from each stratum (see Table 1). When fieldwork in the first region demonstrated that very few industries existed in the stratum with 1-49 inhabitants, this stratum was dropped from further study.

The enumerators went street by street in the communities thus selected, listing and interviewing all manufacturing and repair enterprises. It should be pointed out that persons who provide services, other than repair and trading enterprises were not interviewed. The set of questionnaires included a census form concentrating on employment and physical plant characteristics; a stock form listing machines and tools, raw materials, and finished items; and a socioeconomic questionnaire which was administered to every third industry of a kind. The findings reported in this paper utilize data from the census questionnaire only.

This paper discusses the magnitude of firms, the compositions of industries, labor intensity, and ownership by sex to test the hypothesis that firm characteristics change as community size changes. The final section summarizes the major findings and discusses some policy implications of those findings.

II. PRINCIPAL CHARACTERISTICS OF INDUSTRIES

A. Magnitude

From the survey, we estimate[2] there are 3,820 firms employing 8,657 people in localities with more than 50 inhabitants.[3] When these findings are compared with official government

TABLE 1
COMMUNITIES AND POPULATION BY LOCALITY SIZE

Locality Size	Number of Localities	Population	% of Total Population
Stratum 1 1-49 inhabitants	1,805	35,361	14.09
Stratum 2 50-499 inhabitants	930	131,155	52.24
Stratum 3 500-1999 inhabitants	48	40,057	15.96
Stratum 4 2000-4999 inhabitants	5	14,427	5.75
Stratum 5 5000+ inhabitants	3	30,034	11.96
Total	2,791	251,034	

TABLE 2
NUMBER OF INDUSTRIAL ESTABLISHMENTS AND EMPLOYMENT
BY INDUSTRY SIZE IN FOUR REGIONS

	Census		Survey[c]	
	No. of Firms	Employment	No. of Firms	Employment
Artisan Industry	2,709[a]	4,078	822	1,364
Small Industry			2,850	6,162
Medium Industry	39[b]	*	23	548
Large Industry			3	583
Repair Services			(122)	
TOTAL	2,748	*	3,820**	8,567**

*Data not available.
**These totals underestimate the actual number of firms and employment, given that communities of less than 50 people are not included. Based on information from the region of Ocotepeque, there are approximately 100 firms in that stratum. This would indicate an under counting of 500-600 firms and 600-750 workers.
[a]Industria Artesanal: Censo de Población y Vivienda, 1974.
[b]Censo Industrial, 1974.
[c]Honduras Rural Industry Survey, 1979.

statistics, there is some indication of undercounting of industrial establishments in the governmental data (see Table 2); and consequently, the contribution of rural industries to Gross National Product and employment is probably larger than estimated.

B. Composition

The survey found fifty-nine types of industries and repair services in the regions surveyed. They were grouped into categories following the International Standard Industrial Classification. As shown in Table 3, the most important broad category of industries is textiles and apparel, followed in order of importance by the food, beverage, and tobacco industries, nonmetallic mineral production, wood and wood products, and repair services. In terms of individual industries, the garment industry (tailors and seamstresses) accounts for 36.3 percent of total firms; bakers, 13.9 percent; carpenters and cabinetmakers,[4] 10.2 percent; and potters, 8.9 percent.

C. Firm Size

Categories of firm size are based on the following definitions from the Honduran government:

Artisan Industry:	1-5 workers and no machinery.
Small Industry:	6-19 workers or fixed assets less than $25,000.
Medium Industry:	20-100 workers or fixed assets between $25,000 and $375,000.
Large Industry:	More than 100 workers or fixed assets greater than $375,000.[5]

The average firm is small, as 77 percent of firms are classified as small and 22 percent are classified as artisan. Medium and large-scale firms are less than 1 percent of the total.

This industrial size classification, using a definition which combines employment and assets, obscures a very important feature of firm size. In absolute numbers, 2,251 firms (58.8 percent) in the four regions are one-person firms; and 94.3 percent of the total have five or less workers.

III. FIRM CHARACTERISTICS BY COMMUNITY SIZE

Although not directly addressing the hypothesis, some previous

TABLE 3
NUMBER OF FIRMS BY BROAD INUSTRIAL CATEGORY
AND BY SPECIFIC INDUSTRY TYPE[a]

Industrial Classification	*Number of Firms*[b]	*% of Total Firms*[b]
31 Food, Beverages, and Tobacco	857	22.4
3111 Packing Plant	1	
3111 Sausage Making	2	
3112 Milk Processing	37	
3113 Food Preservation	9	
3117 Tortilla Maker	69	
3117 Corn Bread	59	
3117 Baker	532	
3119 Candy Makers	38	
3121 Salt	2	
3131 Alcohol Distillation	1	
3134 Water Purification	5	
3134 Popsicles, etc.	3	
3140 Cigar Making	6	
3118 Sugar Cane Mill	92	
32 Textiles, Apparel, Leather	1,673	43.8
3213 Knitting and Crocheting	6	
3214 Straw Mats	34	
3215 Articles of Plastic Twine	21	
3215 Macramé	1	
3215 Rope and Rope Products	103	
3220 Tailor	262	
3220 Seamstress	1,126	
3231 Tanning	7	
3233 Animal Pack Saddles	1	
3233 Leather Worker	27	
3240 Shoemaker	84	
33 Wood and Wood Products	440	11.5
3311 Sawmill	17	
3312 Basket Weaver	23	
3319 Woodcarver	1	
3320 Carpenter	382	
3320 Cabinet Maker	8	
3320 Upholstery	7	
3320 Mattress Maker	1	
34 Paper and Paper Products	6	
3412 Paper Bags	3	
3420 Printer	2	

TABLE 3 Con't

Industrial Classification	Number of Firms[b]	% of Total Firms[b]
35 Manufacture of Chemicals	2	
3529 Fireworks	2	
36 Nonmetallic Mineral Products	537	14.1
3610 Potter	339	
3691 Clay Brick and Tile	115	
3691 Adobe Blocks	49	
3692 Lime Kiln	14	
3699 Tombstone Carver	1	
3699 Cement Tile	13	
3699 Cement Blocks	2	
3699 Cement Blocks and Culverts	2	
3699 Stone Mason	1	
38 Fabricated Metal, Machinery and Equipment	103	2.7
3811 Blacksmith	84	
3812 Ironmonger	6	
3819 Tinsmith	8	
3819 Welder	2	
3821 Metal Industry	2	
3829 Firearms Repair	1	
39 Other Manufacturing Industries	81	2.1
3909 Broom Maker	10	
3909 Flower Maker	71	
94 Recreational and Cultural Services	2	.05
9415 Sculptor	2	
95 Personal and Household Services	120	3.2
9512 Radio Repair	36	
9512 Electronics Workshop	6	
9512 Refrigeration Repair	2	
9513 Motor and Auto Repair	56	
9514 Watch Repair/Jewelry Maker	17	
9519 Bicycle Repair	3	
TOTAL	3,820[b]	

[a]Honduras Rural Industry Survey, 1979.
[b]Totals are not exact due to rounding errors in the extrapolation.

studies of small-scale industry have documented variation in firm characteristics in localities of different sizes..

In Haiti, larger localities have a larger variety of industries which have a higher average number of workers and also a higher capital intensity than firms in smaller localities (Haggblade *et al.*, 1979). A survey of small industries in Jamaica found a larger average number of workers in larger communities (Davies *et al.*, 1979). In Sierra Leone the composition of industries varies by locality size and the mean annual value added increased with locality size (Liedholm and Chuta, 1976). The average number of workers per firm also increased in the larger localities (Chuta and Liedholm 1975).

All of the findings cited above concentrate on small-scale industries. In Ghana, Steel (1977) found that the different scales of industry, defined by the size and composition of the labor force, varied in importance by locality size. In Honduras, industry of all sizes was surveyed. Thus, we expect that changes in magnitude, composition of industry, firm size, and labor intensity may be more pronounced than those documented in research which concentrates only on small-scale industry.

A. Number of Firms by Locality Size

Steel (1977) suggests that one test of the changing magnitude of firms by locality size is to compare the number of firms to the total corresponding population. Table 4 shows that the number of firms is a small percent of total population, ranging from 1.05 percent to 2.5 percent. This figure tends to increase slightly as community size increases, although there is some variation from a direct, straight-line relationship.

In general, the percent of firms in each stratum of a region corresponds closely with the percent of regional population in the stratum. This suggests that numbers of firms are more closely associated with absolute numbers of population than with community size. It may also be possible that our range of community sizes, 50-11,000 inhabitants, was simply too small to demonstrate the variation which has been found in other countries where the localities surveyed had a much larger size variation.

TABLE 4
FIRMS AS A PERCENTAGE OF STRATUM POPULATION BY REGION[a]

| Locality Size | Firms as a % of Stratum Population | | | | Stratum Mean |
	Ocotepeque	Marcala-Guascoran	Jamistran	Guayape	
Stratum 2 50-499	1.9	1.4	1.05	1.6	1.5
Stratum 3 500-1999	2.5	2.4	2.3	1.9	2.2
Stratum 4 2000-4999	1.9	2.5		2.4	2.3
Stratum 5 5000+			2.1	2.1	2.1
Regional Mean	1.7	1.4	1.3	1.6	1.5

[a]Honduras Rural Industry Survey, 1979.

TABLE 5
INDUSTRIAL CATEGORIES BY COMMUNITY SIZE
AS A PERCENTAGE OF REGIONAL TOTALS[a]

| Industrial Category | % of Firms in Region | | | |
	Stratum 2 50-499	Stratum 3 500-1999	Stratum 4 2000-4999	Stratum 5 5000+
31 Food	23.6	24.4	26.7	13.9
32 Textiles and Apparel	42.5	43.1	44.7	48.2
33 Wood	11.5	11.4	10.3	12.2
34 Paper				1.0
35 Chemicals		.2		
36 Mineral Products	19.8	10.3	4.0	6.4
38 Metal Products	1.8	3.1	5.2	3.8
39 Other Mfg.	.6	4.8	4.0	2.4
94 Cultural		.2		.2
95 Repair Services	.25	2.4	5.5	12.0
Total	100.0	100.0	100.0	100.0

[a]Honduras Rural Industry Survey, 1979.

B. Types of Industries

Having found that the number of firms seems to be more closely related to the population than to community size, we now turn to a discussion of the variation in types of industries by locality size.

As seen in Table 5, the major industrial categories do not vary substantially between the different community strata. There are some exceptions. Food industries, for example, account for 23-25 percent of all firms in each stratum, except for the largest localities in which they account for only 13.9 percent. It is possible that a few larger firms in this stratum may have displaced many of the smaller firms such as bakeries.

The importance of repair services increases as community size increases. This is not surprising, given that car and electrical equipment repair firms predominate and the demand for these activities is more highly concentrated in the larger towns.

Within the mineral products category, the importance of potters increases with community size. These changes might also be traced to demand factors. In the case of clay tiles, the high growth rates of the towns necessitate more construction materials than the lower growth rates of the rural areas. The demand for pottery is reversed; rural areas have a higher demand than the larger communities where more durable, metal substitutes are available.

Shoemakers increase in importance in urban areas, while in rural areas, demand is low because people go barefoot, make their own sandals from tires, or purchase molded plastic shoes and sandals. Ironmongers who make iron grillwork and balcony irons exist only in the large towns where the use of glass windows necessitates protection. Rural houses have few windows and these are shuttered from the inside at night with wooden shutters.

There is also some variation of industrial composition by region, often due to the availability of raw materials in the region. In the Marcala-Guascoran region there are large numbers of ropemakers and potters, both of which require raw materials native to the region. The garment industry is more important in Ocotepeque than in any other region (42.7 percent of regional firms), perhaps due to the availability of cheap textiles from neighboring Guatemala and El Salvador. Overall, the region of Marcala-Guascoran varies most from other regions in its composition of industries.

C. Firm Size

Table 6 indicates that artisan and small firms are numerically more important in the smallest communities, although once again their numerical importance varies directly with absolute population. Surprisingly, the two smallest community strata also account for ten of the twenty-three medium-sized firms. A closer look at these particular firms reveals that seven of them are sawmills which employ substantial amounts of labor and capital, although located in rural areas for their raw materials. Of the remaining three, two may be food processing cooperatives, and one is engaged in metalworking. It is also interesting to note that only one medium-sized industry is located in the five towns in the stratum of 2,000-4,999, the other eleven medium-sized industries are found in the three towns above 5,000 people.

The regional figures show medium-sized industries to be distributed somewhat unevenly among the four regions, while large-scale industries exist only in the Jamistran region and are located in Danli, municipal seat of the region and the largest town in the survey. The region of Olancho has few medium-

TABLE 6
NUMBER OF FIRMS IN EACH COMMUNITY STRATUM BY FIRM SIZE[a]

| | Locality Size | | | | | |
Industry Size	Stratum 2 50-499	Stratum 3 500-1999	Stratum 4 2000-5000	Stratum 5 5000+	Total	% of Firms
Artisan	441	231	84	92	850	22.2
Small	1,540	644	244	516	2,944	77.1
Medium	5	5	1	11	23	.6
Large				3	3	.1
Total	1,987	881	329	624	3,820	
% of Firms	52.0	23.1	8.6	16.3		

[a]Honduras Rural Industry Survey, 1979.

sized firms and no large firms even though it has a population of 19,000 in its larger towns. The relative importance of artisan and small industry does not seem to vary significantly by region. This is expected if they produce primarily simple consumer goods and processed food for local demand.

Employment and assets, the two variables defining firm size, will now be discussed individually because variation in these two explains differences in firm size.

D. Employment

A total of 8,657 persons is employed in 3,820 firms in the four regions, with an average of 2.17 persons per firm (including proprietor).[6] There is a clear tendency for average employment per firm to increase as community size increases, although the average does not fit this pattern well for localities with 500-1,999 inhabitants.

The dramatic increase in average employment in the food industries as locality size increases is attributed mainly to several large- and medium-scale meat processing firms and a tobacco firm located in the larger towns. The wood industry and repair services also demonstrate fairly large increases in average employment as locality size increases.

Although the general tendency within an industry is for average employment per firm to increase as community size increases, there are exceptions. Once again, potters show a decline as community size increases, most likely for the reasons discussed earlier. The category of other manufacturers, which is composed of makers of brooms and flowers made from dried, natural materials, also shows a decline in average employment as community size increases. Both of these industries use agricultural and forestal materials which are not readily available in larger towns.

E. Assets

Fixed capital, in defining industry size, includes buildings (when not part of the home), tools, and machines, but excludes land values. Once again, the size classification obscures the distribution of fixed assets among firms. A total of 54.7 percent of all firms have fixed assets of $100 or less. Over half of such firms were located in the smallest community stratum.

Nearly 81 percent of all firms have fixed assets of less than $250 and 92 percent of all firms have fixed assets of less than $500.

Some care must be taken in interpreting these figures since, as mentioned above, buildings were not assigned a value when the shop was in the family living quarters. This was the case for 76 percent of all firms, and not assigning a value to such space clearly understates the value of fixed assets. Of the shops located within the home, 54 percent are in communities of 50-499 inhabitants.[7]

Of the firms with $100 or less in fixed assets, over half are located in communities of 50-199 inhabitants. Of all firms in this stratum, 62.4 percent have fixed assets of under $100. There is a tendency for fixed assets to increase as community size increases.

Likewise, fixed assets per firm in all industrial categories increase as community size increase. Firms described as "other manufacturers" have the smallest average fixed assets (approximately $10) and also have the smallest spread of fixed assets between strata—from $5.75 to $16. Tilemakers have the highest average fixed assets at $4,100 and, at the same time, demonstrate the largest spread of average fixed assets, ranging from $27 in the smallest localities to $18,500 in the largest. Mechanics are second in average value of fixed assets with $2,750.

F. Capital-Labor Ratio

The ratio of fixed capital to labor is important with respect to employment generation to indicate which industries are using relatively less of scarce capital and relatively more of abundant labor. It is generally expected that larger firms are more capital-intensive and smaller firms are more labor-intensive.

The following chart, which lists average fixed capital per worker, shows that Honduran firms deviate somewhat from the expected pattern as medium-scale firms are more capital-intensive than large-scale firms:

Artisan Industry:	$40 per worker
Small Industry:	150 per worker
Medium Industry:	630 per worker
Large Industry:	200 per worker

The capital-labor ratio varies both by firm size and by industry. Mechanics average $693 of fixed capital per worker, while potters average less than $10 per worker. The garment industry (the largest industry) averages $160 of fixed capital per worker, approximately the price of a sewing machine.

Within an industry, the amount of fixed capital per worker increases as locality size increases, indicating that a range of production techniques are being employed. This range of ratios and production techniques indicates that it might be possible to increase employment by using specific techniques of production. Further study could define those production techniques which employ relatively more labor and less capital.

G. Ownership by Sex

Country surveys have documented varying levels of importance of women in industrial ownership and employment. In Ghana, women are 54 percent of the industrial work force (Steel, 1977). Liedholm and Chuta (1976) found that employment of women in small-scale industries was important only in the gara-dyeing industry. Women in selected areas of Bangladesh are only .1 percent of proprietors, but 34 percent of the work force in rural industries (Bangladesh Institute, 1979). In Haitian small industry, women are 20 percent of the entrepreneurs and 16 percent of the labor force (Haggblade *et al.*, 1979). The Honduras data show a much larger role for women, who own 60.7 percent of all firms and are nearly 50 percent of workers. A similar role exists for women in other Central American countries.

According to the Nicaraguan Office of Census (1974), 22 percent of all employers in industry and manufacturing are women. Women are 46 percent of employers in hotels, restaurants, and commerce (Diebold de Cruz *et al.*, 1975). The same report goes on to say ". . . most rural women engage in some kind of small business activity to supplement the family income . . ." (Diebold de Cruz *et al.*, 1975).

In Guatemalan rural enterprise, women are 8 percent of the work force for wood products; 50 percent for textiles; 17 percent for leather; 47 percent for food processing and baking; and 65 percent for commercial services (Daines, 1978).

Of the Honduran firms owned by women, 58 percent are located in localities with 50-499 inhabitants. In that stratum women own twice as many firms as men own. The number and percent of firms owned by women declines as community size increases. In the largest communities, men own 56 percent of all firms. Across strata, female ownership is concentrated in bakeries, the garment industry, and pottery. Men own all carpentry firms and nearly all tilemaking firms and mechanics shops.

Although men and women account for approximately 50 percent each of total employment, there is a definite sex-typing by industry. This pattern is so strong that no pattern or trend by community size can be discerned. The food, textiles and apparel, and other manufacturing categories are heavily female. The mineral products category is almost evenly divided between male and female employment. However, within this industrial category, the pottery industry is almost exclusively female and the clay tile industry is nearly all male. Within the textiles and apparel category, which is heavily female, the shoemakers are almost all male. Wood industries, metal products, and repairs services are nearly exclusively male. Firms with female owners tend to employ almost exclusively female workers and male owners have nearly all male workers.

IV. SUMMARY AND IMPLICATIONS OF MAJOR FINDINGS

Survey results show 3,820 firms in the four regions employing 8,657 workers.[8] This indicates an undercounting by government statistics of small-scale industries in rural communities so that industrial employment and output are probably higher than current statistics indicate.

Of the 3,820 firms, 22 percent are classfied as artisan industries and 7 percent as small-scale industries. More specifically, 94 percent of firms employ five or fewer people and 59 percent are one-person firms. Average fixed assets per firm are also low with 81 percent of all firms reporting fixed assets of less than $250. Composition of firms varies by community size and region. The number of firms seems more closely related to absolute population than to locality size. Average employment, average value of fixed assets, and capital intensity do vary directly with locality size. Family living quarters also double as the workshop for 76 percent of the firms.

Because of the undercounting of small firms in rural areas,

government policy has not taken advantage of the potential of these firms to create employment with low capital investment.

The number of firms is a fairly consistent percentage of stratum population which may indicate that these firms respond directly to local demand. Programs to promote the expansion of local industry, besides removing supply or financial constraints, may also need to include programs for increasing effective demand of rural consumers through increased income from agricultural or other employment.

Perhaps the most interesting results of the survey are the findings concerning ownership and employment by sex. The number of firms owned by females is inversely related to community size. A total of 60.7 percent of the firms have female owners. The female owners are concentrated in bakeries, the garment industry, and pottery, and employ almost exclusively female workers. Owners of carpenter shops, mechanic shops, and tilemaking firms are almost exclusively male and predominantly employ male workers. Female firms hold 9 percent of the fixed assets and employ 42 percent of all workers.

Government industrial programs must consider their impact on women engaged in small industry. Boserup (1970) points out that programs which encourage large industries gradually drive the home industries out of business and women from their jobs because (1) they cannot compete with factory production, or (2) they are displaced by men as industries become more mechanized.

NOTES

1. The four regions selected by the government as priority regions were: the Department of Ocotepeque in the west, bordering on El Salvador and Guatemala; the Marcala-Guascoran region in the southwest, bordering on El Salvador and located within the Departments of Valle and LaPaz; the Jamistran Valley in the southeast, a rich agricultural region; and the Guaype Valley in the east central, a rich agricultural region which has large forest reserves.

2. Estimations were made by weighting survey results by the inverse of sample percentage for each stratum in each region.

3. Although industries were found in all strata, fieldwork in the region

of Ocotepeque showed that very few industries existed in localities with less than 50 inhabitants. This stratum was dropped from further study in the other regions. For this reason, the figures presented probably under-represent actual numbers of firms and employment. Based on the data collected in the Ocotepeque region, there are approximately 100 firms in the smallest localities of that region. Over the four regions, this would indicate an undercounting of 500-600 firms and 600-750 workers.

4. Carpenters produce unfinished wood products and furniture in a workshop while a cabinetmaker produces the same types of products, but with finishing work. Carpenters who work only in the construction industry (i.e., do not have a workshop) are not included.

5. If the firm fits one of the two conditions, it is classified into the higher of the two categories.

6. Totals and means are calculated with total firms, including three firms with 100 or more employees.

7. The longitudinal follow-up study hopes to assign a value to the space within the home used by the industry.

8. It should be remembered that these figures themselves are a under-counting as communities of less than 50 people were not included in the survey.

BIBLIOGRAPHY

Bangladesh Institute of Development Studies. "Rural Industries Study Project: Phase I Report." Dacca: Bangladesh Institute of Development Studies, 1979.

Boserup, Ester. *Women's Role in Economic Development.* New York: St. Martins Press, 1970.

Chuta, Enyinna and Carl Liedholm. "The Role of Small Scale Industry in Employment Generation and Rural Development: Initial Research Results from Sierra Leon." *African Rural Employment Paper* No. 11. East Lansing, Michigan: Department of Agricultural Economics, Michigan State University, 1975.

Daines, Samuel and G. Smith. *1978 Rural Enterprise Survey.* Guatemala: Ministry of Agriculture and BANDESA, 1978.

Davies, Omar, Yacob Fisseha, Annette Francis and Claremont Kirton. "A Preliminary Analysis of the Small-Scale Non-Farm Sector in Jamaica." Research, University of the West Indies, 1979.

Diebold de Cruz, Paula and Mayra Pasos de Rappacioli. "Report on the

Role of Women in the Economic Development of Nicaragua." Managua, Nicaragua: USAID, 1975.

Dirección General de Estadística y Censos. Censo Industrial, 1974. Tegucigalpa, Honduras: Dirección General de Estadística y Censos, 1975.

Dirección General de Estadística y Censos. Industria Artesanal: Censo de Poblacion y Vivienda, 1974. Tegucigalpa, Honduras: Dirección General de Estadística y Censos, 1977.

Haggblade, Steve, Jacques Defay and Bob Pitman. "Small Manufacturing and Repair Enterprises in Haiti: Survey Results." *MSU Rural Development Series Working Paper* No. 14. East Lansing, Michigan: Department of Agricultural Economics, Michigan State University, 1979.

Liedholm, Carl and Enyinna Chuta. "The Economics of Rural and Urban Small-Scale Industries in Sierra Leon." *African Rural Economy Paper* No. 14. East Lansing, Michigan; Department of Agricultural Economics, Michigan State University, 1976.

Mejia A., Concepción. "Honduras: Status of the Five Categories of Section 102 (D) of the Foreign Assistance Act." USAID/Honduras. AID-522-390, 1978.

Stell, William F. *Small-Scale Employment and Production in Developing Countries: Evidence from Ghana.* New York: Praeger Publishers, 1977.

III
Urbanization: The Rural-Urban Interface

FROM SQUATTERS TO SKYSCRAPERS: NEW DIRECTIONS IN LATIN AMERICAN URBANIZATION RESEARCH

Robert V. Kemper

The 1970's saw a revolution in the study of Latin American urbanization. This revolution was both theoretical and method-ological. Theoretically, a fundamental shift occurred from the modernization framework to the dependency perspective; methodologically, there was a concomitant reorientation away from isolated case studies of cities (or their segments) toward vertically integrated analyses of the urban system broadly defined. This revolution—a shift in focus from squatters to skyscrapers—has been the object of considerable recent comment (Abu-Lughod and Hay 1977; Castells 1975; Levine 1979; Portes and Browning 1976; Walton 1979; and Chance *in press*). The new directions in Latin American urbanization research may have profound consequences for both Latin American studies and comparative urban studies.

I shall first review some of the major features of research on Latin American urbanization since the 1950's and then examine some of the implications for the new urban research for Latin American studies in general. In the euphoria of the revolution, the domains of theory and methodology have dominated scholarly discussions. It is time to consider the impact of the revolution on the training of specialists in urban and Latin American studies, and its possible consequences for the integrity of this regional focus in the social sciences. Moreover, we must ask what the new approach to urban Latin America will mean for the prevailing organizaton of the social sciences and the disciplinary "cultures" which currently dominate these fields. And, finally, moving beyond the realm of the social sciences themselves, it is necessary to question the potential utility of theoretical and methodological innovations in the domains of urban planning and governmental policy-making in Latin America.

CENTRAL PROBLEMS OF LATIN AMERICAN URBANIZATION RESEARCH

To answer the questions just posed, it is necessary to discuss the central problems of Latin American urbanization research and to examine the revolutionary innovations of the 1970's.

Definitions of Urbanization

One of the central problems has been the plethora of definitions used for basic terms such as "urbanization," "urban and rural," "city and hinterland," and "urban development." I will not dwell on definitional problems, but it is worthwhile to recall the linkages between definitions and research foci.

For instance, demographic-ecological approaches have focused on population growth and population redistribution in regional, national, and continental contexts. Economic approaches have emphasized the rationality of decision-making by individuals, corporations, and governments vis-à-vis the temporal-spatial allocation of resources. And socio-cultural approaches have concentrated on the modern behavior and values of the urban setting and their diffusion to the countryside. There are others, but these three illustrate the problem of seeking concensus when so many disciplines have given competing, and often conflicting, definitions.

Contexts of Urbanization Research

The variety of disciplinary approaches is also manifest in the *contexts* in which research has been conducted. It falls into three main categories: that based in urban areas, that conducted in the hinterlands, and that concerned with the urban system.

First, we may distinguish two general types of *city-based* research. Many studies, for example, examine some aspect of life in which the city is merely the location of some activity rather than the focus of the research. Such studies, in effect, take the city for granted. Such studies *in* cities so concentrate on specific problems such as education, housing, crime, or public health that they reveal little of the coherent urbanization process.

On the other hand, studies *of* cities ask questions about the character of the urban setting and focus on the ways in which the city influences behavior and beliefs. Scholars following this approach treat the urban setting as a kind of independent variable, often with city-hinterland comparisons in mind. Thus, studies *of* cities come closer to dealing with the urbanization process than do studies *in* cities (Eames and Goode 1977, Rollwagen 1972).

The second major category of urban research focuses on the countryside. On the one hand, numerous scholars have investigated city influences on the hinterlands. These diffusionist studies often treat topics like mass communication, transportation networks, market penetration, and changes in rural lifestyles. Unfortunately, few give attention to the counter-flow of goods, services, and ideologies from countryside to city.

Then, there are the ubiquitous studies of rural-urban migration. With the high rates of population movement toward Latin American cities, so much attention to the study of cityward migrants and migration streams is not surprising. The single-mindedness of social science thinking about migration to urbanization is reflected in the paucity of studies on return migration.

The third main category of research concerns *urban systems.* Such systems may range from narrowly-defined regions to entire nations to all of Latin America. Unfortunately, mere expansion of the geographical limits of such studies may not result in a better understanding of the linkages between the demographic, ecological, economic, political, and socio-cultural aspects of the urbanization process.

Units of Analysis in Urbanization Research

Context is closely linked to the problem of *units of analysis.* Within the three contexts (and their sub-types) sketched above, it is possible to distinguish five categories of analytical units, each of which reflects theoretical and methodological assumptions about Latin American urbanization.

First, there is a tradition of research on *individuals or families* caught up in the urbanization process. This ethnographic, life-history approach was made famous by Oscar Lewis' writing on Tepoztecan migrants and slum dwellers in Mexico City (Lewis 1959, 1961).

Second, many studies emphasize the analysis of *residential* units, ranging from central-city slums to peripheral squatter settlements. The focus on the "community" dimensions of such environments is clear in William Mangin's research on the barriadas of Lima (1967).

Third, some scholars deal with *socio-economic groups* living in Latin American cities, especially the poorest, so-called "marginal" groups. The study of such groups has ranged from the small-scale studies which lead to the idea of the "culture of poverty" (Lewis 1959) to extensive survey research exemplified by the Monterrey Mobility Project (Balan, Browning, and Jelin 1973). In both cases, poverty and the possibility for vertical mobility have been important themes related to Latin American Urbanization.

Fourth, some analysts emphasize specific *populations* instead of individuals, residential areas, or socio-economic groups. These population-oriented urban studies often focus on ethnic groups, particularly in the context of rural-urban migration. Such research is well represented by Douglas Butterworth's studies of Mixtec migrants from Tilantongo, Oaxaca, who have moved to Mexico City (1962).

A fifth and final approach to the analysis of Latin American urbanization focuses on *political-administrative units.* These can include whole cities (or their sub-units), regions (e.g., *municipios, estados*), or even entire nations. This "macro" approach is heavily dependent on census and survey data keyed to such units and thus tends to focus on the character of the urban system rather than the behavior and beliefs of individuals. The work of the Inter-American Development Bank on the interrelationship of urbanization and population growth in Latin America is a well-known example of this category of research (Fox 1975).

Case Studies versus Comparative Research

Our knowledge of Latin American urbanization has generally been pieced together from *case studies* of a variety of analytical units examined in a wide rage of urban contexts. Comparative research has tended to emphasize secondary data analysis, either of the results of small-scale ethnographic field studies or of the products of higher-level demographic-economic surveys or censuses. Only rarely has a series of field studies been conducted with an explicitly comparative framework. In these circumstances, the ability of social scientists to link the peculiarities of specific cases to the general phenomenon of Latin American urbanization has not been awe-inspiring.

To make matters worse, most case studies have been one-shot affairs, with relatively little attention to the historical dimensions. As a result, social scientists have been placed in the position of having to use a series of unrelated, cross-sectional studies to comprehend spatial and temporal phenomena. And where attention has been given to the historical aspects of urbanization, the focus often has been on the comparison of the Latin American urban experience to that of the United States and of Western Europe.

Let me summarize the discussion to this point. From the early 1950's into the early 1970's, research on Latin American urbanization was beset by a series of theoretical and methodological difficulties. These included: finding appropriate definitions of key concepts, diversity of contexts for research, the wide range of units analyzed, and emphasis on one-shot case studies at the expense of systematic comparative research. These problems are more apparent in retrospect than they were a decade ago. More importantly, many of these problems appear to stem from the general framework of modernization within which most Latin American urban research was then conducted.

FROM MODERNIZATION TO DEPENDENCY

During the 1950's and the early 1960's, the modernization perspective dominated social scientific research on urban Latin America. Its impact is amply demonstrated by the published results of the 1959 U.N.-sponsored conference on Urbanization in Latin America (1965). By the late 1960's, however, a number of social scientists—especially Latin Americans with interests in economics—were beginning to question the role of urban development implicit in the modernization perspective. As the First U.N. Development Decade was coming to a close, economists and other social scientists realized that the gap between developing and developed regions was not closing as predicted. The resulting re-examination and critique of modernization theory shifted away from the internal problems of Latin American countries and toward the international economic-political environment and its consequences for Latin American underdevelopment.

At that point, the focus of criticism was the broader setting of modernization in which urban development was only one of several interrelated components. Of course, the magnitude of urban problems in Latin America and the ready availability of an arena for research meant that the generalized attack on modernization theory was quickly joined by a more specific critique of prevailing ideas about urbanization.

Major criticisms of the theory and methodology of Latin American urban research emerged as a consequence of the broader shift from modernization to dependency perspectives in Latin American social science in the late 1960's and 1970's. (For an excellent review, see Valenzuela and Valenzuela 1978). As we shall see, the triumph of the dependency perspective over the modernization framework had significant implications for the definitions of key terms, for the contexts of research, for the selection of units of analysis, and for the role of case studies.

First, the effect of the dependency perspective has been to create a consensus among social scientists that urbanization is a multi-dimensional process which includes demographic, ecological, economic, political, and socio-cultural aspects. Even more significant, however, is the growing awareness that urbanization is a process which itself is only one component of the overall transformation of society, a transformation with unique historical and structural characteristics (Quijano 1967).

This redefinition of urbanization also overturned the traditional view of the relationship between city and countryside. Rather than being the motor for societal modernization, the city now came to be seen as a center of domination over a dependent periphery while serving as an extension of the external metropoles—i.e., the United States and Western Europe—into Latin America. Thus, the city has the role of intermediary in the process of surplus capital extraction and cultural exploitation.

As a corollary of the broader definition of urbanization, the contexts of research have been reinterpreted. No longer is it considered appropriate to limit investigations to the city or to the countryside. Instead, emphasis is now placed on understanding the societal context in which urban processes occur. The old dualism inherent in the folk-urban continuum model and the tradition-modernity model has been replaced by a unitary approach that explicitly bridges local, regional, national, and even international boundaries. This approach, exemplified by the research of Anthony Leeds (1976) in Brazil, Peru, and elsewhere, diminishes the traditional emphasis on geographical places and focuses on the differential allocation of specializations (e.g., economic, political, social, cultural) in and beyond Latin American nations.

Another way to look at this fundamental transformation in the study of urbanization involves the demise of "culturalism" and the rise of "historical-structuralism" (Kemper 1979). Whereas the modernization perspective stressed the key role of culture and community in the development process, the dependency perspective emphasizes an ecological-societal (Schwartz 1978) or political-economic (Walton 1979) approach to urbanization. As a result, neither the city nor the countryside—nor even a narrowly defined segment of the urban system—provides a necessary and sufficient context for research. As Portes and Browning have commented, "It is perhaps ironic that the proper course for future urban research be defined as laying beyond the city itself" (1976:4).

This redefinition of the contexts for urbanization research is also reflected in reconsiderations of appropriate units of analysis. Whereas urban studies conducted under the banner of modernization tended to be highly empiricist and oriented to specific disciplinary problem-sets, the new urban research of the 1970's has acquired a multidisciplinary structural character. As a result, investigations of "individuals or aggregates of individuals, their values, attitudes, and beliefs" have tended to be replaced by a focus on "the mode of production, patterns of international trade, political and economic linkages between elites in peripheral and central countries, group and class alliances and conflicts, and so on" (Valenzuela and Valenzuela 1978:550).

As John Walton has pointed out, what is "beginning to emerge in recent urban research . . . is a new unit of analysis based on distinctive *vertically integrated processes* passing through a network from the international level to the urban hinterland" (1979:164). This systems approach does not require that studies of individuals and families, residential areas, socioeconomic groups, populations, and political-administrative units be abandoned. What it does demand is the examination of all these units in a broader context. To cite just one example, the continuing studies of Leeds in the *favelas* of Rio de Janeiro have shown convincingly that these peripheral squatter settlements are manifestations of a hierarchy of variables ranging from the form of the national economy to the development of a specific city and its labor markets to the structure of family units (Leeds 1974).

IMPLICATIONS OF THE REVOLUTION IN LATIN AMERICAN URBAN STUDIES

Before discussing the research implications of the revolution in Latin American urban studies, two related transformations require comment.

First, whereas modernization theory stressed a consensual view of society, the dependency perspective emphasizes conflict and relationships of inequality within and beyond Latin American societies. This shift in social science worldview reflects a general trend away from the exportation of U.S. democratic ideals and the resurgence of Marxist or neo-Marxist notions of the class struggle and revolution. The generation of social scientists trained in the framework of modernization theory was ill-prepared to explain the continuing series of conflicts in Latin America during the 1960's and 1970's. In contrast, scholars trained in the wake of Project Camelot and the Vietnam protests are much more attuned to the utility of a conflict approach to understanding Latin American urbanization.

Second, the general optimism inherent in the modernization writings has been controverted by the experiences of the 1970's. The presumed positive interaction of urbanization and industrialization which was supposed to improve the conditions of life in both city and countryside is being reinterpreted in terms of dependent urban development. The optimism that extended even to social scientists' views of squatter settlements and migrant adaptation has been balanced by a preoccupation with the inequalities built into the structure of Latin American societies. As urbanization has become more pervasive, equity has not increased and perhaps the gap between poor and wealthy is growing within these societies as it appears to be growing among nations in Latin America and beyond. In sum, the new directions in urbanization research suggest that the optimism of the 1960's was a passing fancy unwarranted by recent events. As Cornelius has remarked in introducing a collection of papers devoted to metropolitan problems,

> The sheer magnitude of the problems confronting most of the metropolitan areas . . . , whose populations are expected to double within the next 15 to 20 years, combined with the record of governmental performance in dealing with these problems thus far, give little cause for optimism that the Latin American primate cities of the year 2000 will be "manageable" in any conventional sense of the term (1978:22).

Implications for Training and Teaching

In such an atmosphere of realism and conflict, what are the implications of the revolution in Latin American urbanization research for the training of the next generation of specialists and for the teaching of Latin American studies?

At the broadest level, the new directions in Latin American urban studies are having the effect of blurring academic boundaries, although, as Portes and Browning have argued, ". . . this seems a small price to pay for a growing understanding of the realities faced by urban and rural populations in Latin America and the lines along which their present situation is likely to evolve" (1976:14). This is especially ironic, since the post-1960's period saw both the increasing importance of the dependency perspective and conscious efforts to create a separate identity for the study of Latin American urbanization. The continuing series of symposia at the International Congress of Americanists since 1966, the publications of the Latin Amercian Urban Research series by Sage Publications between 1971 and 1978, the activities of the Inter-American

Planning Society (SIAP), and the work of the Latin American Socal Science Council (CLASCO) have all contributed to the remarkable growth of urban-related scholarly research in recent years. The multidisciplinary character of these efforts has been reinforced by works in journals such as *Latin American Research Review* and *Latin American Perspectives*, primarily for Latin Americanists, and such as *Comparative Urban Research* and the *International Journal of Regional and Urban Studies*, principally for urbanists.

This multidisciplinarity runs counter to the traditional graduate training and undergraduate teaching programs in most U.S. colleges and universities. Thus, Latin Americanist-urbanists are usually found in discipline-specific departments with a Latin American studies program and/or urban studies program. Given the current crisis in U.S. higher education, stabilization and retrenchment are more widespread than expansion and innovation. In such a climate, those programs with regional or topical foci crossing various disciplines face hard times. So, at a time when Latin American urban research has moved firmly in the direction of multidisciplinary studies based on the dependency perspective, the academic environment is inimical to such innovations.

This multidisciplinary orientation, characterized by Walton as the "new political economy" (1979:166), faces a number of practical problems. For instance, the coming generation of specialists needs to be trained in a much broader range of topics than was previously thought necessary. The "world system" and comparative Latin American, African, and Asian urbanization must be woven into the fabric of disciplinary programs within which Ph.D. degrees are granted. Students in Latin American or urban studies programs need to master a wider range of theory and methodology if they are to make effective contributions to the new research. And, of course, scholars already active in the field face the prospect of re-tooling or up-dating their skills.

Implications for Professional Social Science

Funding for research tends to follow traditional directions. Commitment to a broad multidisciplinary perspective goes far beyond the imposed boundaries of many grant managers.

Applicants for funding and peer reviewers thus face the challenge of educating funding agencies.

The reward structure of contemporary social science still stresses individual scholarly achievements over the work of research teams. The new directions of Latin American urban research suggest that teamwork in a multidisciplinary framework is likely to replace or supplement individual discipline-bound investigations. This team orientation goes beyond national boundaries as well, and this may be one of the most important implications of the new directions in Latin American urbanization studies. Whereas the bulk of key studies conducted under the banner of modernization were done by U.S.-based scholars, the most recent advances have been mainly the work of Latin American-based (or exiled) social scientists. These new "exemplars" (Kuhn 1977:306) of urban research based on the dependency perspective have given new meaning to the interaction of foreign (mainly, U.S. and Western European) and Latin American scholars. The days of "borrowed theory" (Cornelius 1971) are over; the era of cooperative research in which Latin American scholars take a dominant or at least equal role is now well established. The social organization of Latin American-based scholars facilitated their movement to a dependency perspective not subject to the disciplinary boundaries that still encumber U.S.-based social sciences.

To those of you familiar with the provocative writings of Thomas Kuhn on the character of scientific revolutions, as well as his remarks on the "pre-paradigmatic" aspects of the social sciences, you may be pondering the question: does the revolution in Latin American urbanization research stand as a full-fledged "scientific revolution" or is it merely the predictable change from one school of thought to another in the meandering ways of the social sciences?

In my view, the revolution has been so self-conscious, so clearly a break from the theory and methodology of modernization, and so polemical—both at the level of social sciences and social movement—that we can only fully appreciate the transformation in worldview if we treat it as revolution. Moreover, the evidence is clear that a new set of "exemplars"—a scientific community's standard examples—have arisen in the 1970's and that these are operating within a new "disciplinary matrix"

(Kuhn 1977:318-19). This matrix reflects and accounts for a scientific group's "unproblematic conduct of research" (Kuhn 1977:318) and embraces "all shared group commitments" (Kuhn 1977:319). In the case of Latin American urbanization research carried out within the dependency perspective, there is little doubt that the collaborators in this research have forged a sense of solidarity as an international scientific community.

Implications for Urban Planning and Policy-Making

The new leaders of Latin American urbanization research have an evident political commitment to the transformation of Latin American societies. It is unfortunate and hardly surprising that this commitment is felt more strongly by urban researchers than by politicians. The new orientation is highly critical of most governmental efforts to improve the urban situation; the dependency perspective stresses that the continuing intervention of the multinational corporation and international agencies perpetuate and increase monopolistic tendencies in Latin American development.

CONCLUSION

The decade of the 1970's sired a revolution in the study of Latin American urbanization. After examination of some of its major theoretical and methodological features and after consideration of the implications of this revolution for Latin Americanist and urban studies, what conclusions appear?

First, the shift from modernization to dependency has ushered in a new era in Latin American urban studies. As Chance has argued, this new approach rests on three premises:

1) urbanization must be regarded as a social formation within the world system;

2) in Latin America, it cannot be understood apart from the historical evolution of dependent structures of capitalism; and,

3) the appropriate units of analysis are not geographical entities such as rural or urban areas, but *processes* which link together a hierarchy of core-periphery relationships stretching from the international level down to the hinterland of a specific city (*in press*:4).

Second, although the revolution has been underway in some places for more than a decade, relatively few studies have been carried out which demonstrate the full range of dependency relationships in urban life.

Third, the emphasis on process rather than place opens new horizons in Latin American urbanization research. The city and countryside cease to be seen as places arbitrarily distinguished by population size criteria and come to be seen as integrated social processes (Leeds 1976). Moreover, the shift from horizontal to vertical modes of analyses promises a better balance between the study of so-called "marginal" populations and elite groups. The expansion of analyses of processes from local environments to international settings brings a new dimension to urban studies. This new dimension may, eventually, blur the contours of Latin American urban research and blend these fields into investigations of national-regional development in the context of the world system.

Finally, the revolution in Latin American urban research has important implications for the disciplinary, academic and professional aspects of Latin American studies and urban studies. If the decade of the 1980's replicates only a portion of the transformation and confrontations that we witnessed in the 1970's, then we can look forward to continuing progress in our understanding of Latin American urbanization, even if under another, broader perspective.

REFERENCES

Abu-Lughod, Janet and Richard Hay, Jr. (eds). *Third World Urbanization.* Chicago: Maaroufa Press, Inc., 1977.

Balan, Jorge, Harley L. Browning, and Elizabeth Jelin. *Men in a Developing Society: Geographic and Social Mobility in Monterrey, Mexico.* Austin: University of Texas Press, 1973.

Butterworth, Douglas S. "A Study of the Urbanization Process Among Mixtec Migrants from Tilantongo in Mexico City." *America Indigena* 22(3):257-274, 1962.

Castells, Manuel. *La Cuestión urbana.* Mexico, D.F.: Siglo Veintiuno, 1975.

Chance, John K. "Recent Trends in Latin American Urban Studies." *Latin American Research Review* 15, in press.

Cornelius, Wayne, A., Jr. "The Political Sociology of Cityward Migration in Latin America: Toward Empirical Theory." *Latin American Urban Research* 1:95-147, 1971.

————. "Introduction." *Latin American Urban Research* 6:7-24, 1978.

Crane, Diane. *Invisible Colleges.* Chicago: University of Chicago Press, 1972.

Eames, Edwin and Judith G. Goode. *Anthropology of the City.* Englewood Cliffs, N.J.: Prentice-Hall, 1977.

Fox, Robert W. *Urban Population Growth Trends in Latin America.* Washington, D.C.: Inter-American Development Bank, 1975.

Hauser, Philip (ed.). *Urbanization in Latin America.* Paris: UNESCO, 1961.

Kemper, Robert V. "Frontiers in Migration: Culturalism to Historical Structuralism in the Study of Mexico-U.S. Migration," pp. 9-21. In Fernando Camara and Robert V. Kemper (eds.), *Migration across Frontiers: Mexico and the United States.* Albany, N.Y.: Institute for Mesoamerican Studies, SUNY, 1979.

Kuhn, Thomas S. *The Essential Tension: Selected Studies in Scientific Tradition and Change.* Chicago: University of Chicago Press, 1977.

Leeds, Anthony E. "Political, Economic and Social Effects of Producer and Consumer Orientations Toward Housing in Brazil and Peru: A Systems Analysis." *Latin American Urban Research* 3:181-215, 1973.

————. "Housing-Settlement Types, Arrangements for Living, Proletarianization, and the Social Structure of the City." *Latin American Urban Research* 4:67-99, 1974.

————. "Urban Society Subsumes Rural: Specialties, Nucleations, Countryside, and Networks–Metatheory, Theory, and Method." *Atti XL Congresso Internazionale degli Americanisti* 4:171-182, 1976.

Levine, Daniel H. "Urbanization in Latin America: Changing Perspectives." *Latin American Research Review* 14(1):170-183, 1979.

Lewis, Oscar. *Five Families.* New York: Basic Books, 1959.

————. *The Children of Sanchez.* New York: Random House, 1961.

Mangin, William P. "Latin American Squatter Settlements: A Problem and a Solution." *Latin American Research Review* 2(3):65-98, 1967.

Morse, Richard M. "Recent Research on Latin American Urbanization: A Selective Survey with Commentary." *Latin American Research Review* 1(1):35-74, 1965.

Nader, Laura. "Up the Anthropologist–Perspectives Gained from Studying Up." In Dell Hymes (ed.), *Reinventing Anthropology,* pp. 284-311, New York: Random House, 1973.

Portes, Alejandro and Harley L. Browning (eds.). *Current Perspectives in Latin American Urban Research.* Austin: University of Texas, Institute of Latin American Studies, 1976.

Quijano, Anibal. "La urbanización de la sociedad en Latinoamerica." *Revista Mexicana de Sociologia* 29(4):669-703, 1967.

Rollwagen, Jack. "A Comparative Framework for the Investigation of the City-as-Context: A Discussion of the Mexican Case." *Urban Anthropology* 1(1):68-86, 1972.

Schwartz, Norman B. "Community Development and Cultural Change in Latin America," *Annual Review of Anthropology* 7:235-262, 1976.

Valenzuela, J. Samuel and Arturo Valenzuela. "Modernization and Dependency: Alternative Perspectives in the Study of Latin American Underdevelopment." *Comparative Politics* 10(4):535-557, 1978.

Walton, John. "From Cities to Systems: Recent Research on Latin American Urbanization." *Latin American Research Review* 14(1): 159-169, 1979.

URBAN HOUSING AND COMPETITION: RESPONSES TO RURAL-URBAN MIGRATION

James F. Hopgood

Eric Wolf (1956) called attention over twenty years ago to the importance of levels of social organization and their inter-relations in complex societies. Wolf argues that throughout the history of post-Conquest Mexico, government and the private entrepreneural sectors have vied for political power and control of the poor and of labor, whether Indian or mestizo (1956: 1067-1073). During the era of dominance by the *hacienda* system, for example, "Indian peasant groups became satellites of the entrepreneurial complex" (1956: 1073). Following the Revolution, power moved back in the direction of a centralized government, where it had been during the colonial period.

The struggle for control of urban poor continues between central government and private entrepreneurs. Conflicts and tensions are found today in many arenas. One such arena is the competition between public and private control of the populations of urban poor in Mexico's largest cities, particularly in the area of housing.

My purpose is to make a preliminary assessment of the recent state of public and private housing policy and action for the poorest sectors of Monterrey. Monterrey provides an especially good test case for Wolf's thesis. It is Mexico's second most industrialized center; and since the beginning of the 20th century, and especially since the Revolution, Monterrey's industrial elites have struggled to maintain economic and political autonomy from the central government (cf. Portes and Walton 1976: 128-129). This has been expressed in nearly every possible area of public life: control over local and state government, labor relations and unionization, education, communications, housing, and others.

The urban poor, the concern here, are largely migrants. Together with the native-born poor, they constitute a labor pool of "subproletariat"; the unskilled and semiskilled.

POPULATION AND MIGRATION

The population of the Monterrey metropolitan area[1] increased by 67.3 percent between 1960 and 1970 from 708,400 to 1,185,349 (Dirección General de Estadística 1970). These figures do not include two other nearby communities which have been pulled into the metropolitan area since 1970. Including those (Apodaca and General Escobedo) the 1970 metropolitan population was 1,242,622. That represents a 5.66 percent annual increase from 1960 to 1970. At that rate the Monterrey metropolitan population will exceed 2,150,000 by 1980 and by the year 2000, a population of almost 6.5 million can be expected.

Since 1950 most of the growth has shifted to the six *municipios* surrounding Monterrey. For example, between 1960 and 1970, those *municipios* grew 233.21 percent from 115,397 to 384,515.

In-migration has contributed substantially to population growth. Between 1940 and 1950, 60 percent of the growth of Monterrey (*only*) was due to in-migration and between 1950 and 1960, 51 percent of the growth can be accounted for by in-migration (Unikel 1971: 258-259, Tables 7 and 8). A 1965 representative sample of Monterrey men indicated that about 70 percent were born outside the Monterrey metropolitan area (Balán, Browning, and Jelin 1973: Table 3-1). Most migrants to Monterrey are of rural or small town origin (Balán, Browning, and Jelin 1973: 62 ff.), and rural migrants tend to be over-represented among the urban poor and those living in squatter settlements (Hopgood n.d.; 1976: 100-105). In any consideration of the problems of housing the urban poor the previous and continuing influx of migrants must be given a substantial role.

HOUSING AND HOUSING POLICY

The impact of rural-urban migration on Monterrey's housing

problems has not been adequately studied or measured. It is, of course, only part of the larger problem of housing the urban poor. In 1977, it was estimated that 18,820 new housing units were needed just to satisfy *new demand* that year (Cadena R. and Cadena C. 1977: 1). Seventy percent of that demand came from those earning incomes from averages of U.S. $68 to $240 monthly (or from about one-half to one and three-fourths of the minimum wage).[2] Sixty-two percent of the demand came from those earning from U.S. $68 to $172 monthly. Only 4 percent of the demand came from those earning from U.S. $687 and above (Cadena R. and Cadena C. 1977: 3).

More recently it was reported that the Monterrey area is deficient in housing to the tune of 90-100,000 units, with another 150,000 units not being fit for habitation (*El Diario de Monterrey,* June 6 and July 13, 1979). The report determined the deficiency was greater than that in 1973 and also indicated that land prices had gone up by 58.37 percent in recent years.

Clearly, in housing and housing policy and action, Monterrey has lagged far behind its spectacular development in other areas. Public and private sectors have been slow to respond to the mounting problems of housing the urban poor. The housing industry remains largely involved with supplying single family units for salaried workers and the middle and upper income groups.

Before the creation of the public housing program (FOMERREY) in 1973, there was no clear-cut centralized public policy regarding the increasing instances of invasions of public and private lands by the urban poor. Nor were there clear-cut policies for providing basic urban services for an estimated 250,000 squatters (in 1972). During the 1960's, and especially from the mid-60's on, organized squatting in certain areas was encouraged by governmental and party leaders. Additionally, squatters were encouraged to organize into settlers' unions (*uniones de colonos*). Once organized, they affiliated with one or another of various governmental agencies and party groups in their efforts to acquire land titles, basic urban services, and to gain political patronage.[3]

These affiliations also benefited the politicians by providing for mobilization of support for any number of politically oriented occasions. There have also been several efforts to organize squatters into larger, city-wide organizations.

Although land invasions continue and squatter settlements grow, the late 1960's and the 1970's have seen several additional responses to the housing dilemma of the urban poor. A public housing program (FOMERREY), a program for housing cooperatives (PROSECO), and a Marxist political movement oriented towards the acquisition of land ("Tierra y Libertad") are among the most visible.

I will examine only two of these: PROSECO and FOMERREY, since they are private *and* public sector responses to housing the poor. PROSECO represents the private entrepreneural response of Monterry's industrial elite.

PROSECO

The "Monterrey Group" (*el grupo Monterrey*) is a label widely applied throughout Mexico to the city's industrial, entrepreneural elite.[4] Frequently it is described as a number of inter-marrying and inter-locked families descended from a handful of early 20th century factory founders. Their involvement in housing has traditionally been in providing housing for their own employees, typically only the salaried, contracted workers.[5] This dates back to 1911 when the Fundidora started colonia Acero across the street from the factory. The Cervecería Cuauhtémoc followed with a program to assist its workers with housing in 1918.

Other involvement by the industrialists has been the organizing of the Instituto Promotor de Habitaciones Populares (IPHP) in the 1960's to channel Alliance for Progress funds into housing for workers in the larger enterprises. The IPHP was organized via the local Centro Patronal, a "union" of employers and arm of the industrialists.

Previously, the industrialists had shown little interest in housing problems of the urban poor. Their current involvement in such housing with the Promotora Socioeconómia de la Comunidad, A.C. (PROSECO) is of considerable interest.[6]

PROSECO was reconstituted in 1972 from an earlier organization, Cultura y Difusión, A.C. Cultura y Difusión began in 1962 with funds donated by a group of German bishops and was oriented towards the stimulation and creation of rural cooperatives. Later, its work was continued through funds provided by local industrial and business leaders.

Its first experience with urban housing cooperatives for low income people came with Colonia Tampiquito in the late 1960's. Cultura y Difusión's entry and involvement with that project was facilitated by the project's informal leader who was a local industrialist (Rosenfeldt 1975: 30 ff.). The industrialists facilitated contacts as well with other professionals in and out of Cultura y Difusión.

In 1972, due to internal disputes, Cultura y Difusión was reorganized as PROSECO by its board of directors. PROSECO's purposes are to promote, organize, and provide technical assistance and credit guarantees to urban cooperatives, and to foster economic self-sufficiency. This can take the form of self-help construction of housing, or as production, consumption, and savings and loan cooperatives. But, to date, PROSECO's major focus has been on self-help housing cooperatives, with some successes in the area of production cooperatives. By the end of June, 1978, six housing cooperatives were in operation and two others were just getting started. These are to provide housing for 2700 families.

The PROSECO director's board is made up of representatives from some of Monterrey's largest industrial groups, including the Cervecería Cuauhtémoc, ALFA, Ladrillera Monterrey, and others. These industries pay the salaries of the PROSECO staff and contribute to and control a fund to guarantee bank loans for PROSECO projects. They may have other funds committed to its operations, but their extent is unclear at this time. Assistance has also been given by the Fundación Mexicano para el Desarrollo (FMD) and the Inter-American Foundation has granted funds for certain cooperative production projects, but control is in the hands of the board of directors.

FOMERREY[7]

The Fomento Metropolitan de Monterrey (FOMERREY) was created in 1973 by the state government of Nuevo León in conjunction with various federal agencies to deal with the problems created by the constant stream of in-migration and uncontrolled squatter settlements. FOMERREY employs a triple approach for dealing with squatters and others in need of housing: the establishment of new settlements, and, in some cases, relocating residents of existing settlements to newly created ones.

Between the inauguration of activities (May, 1974) and March, 1978, FOMERREY established 13,370 families (88,000 people) in its first twenty-three settlements. By mid-1979, FOMERREY claimed to have incorporated 250,000 people into its programs. This included a total from residents of thirty-one new settlements, residents of seventy-four regularized old squatter settlements, and the residents of twenty-six other settlements who were relocated (*El Nacional,* 26 May 1979).

FOMERREY's program for the "social integration" of the urban poor is comprehensive. It includes not only providing areas for settlement, but financing for the purchase of house lots, credits towards purchase of building material, basic urban services, schools, medical facilities, CONSASUPO stores, sports and cultural facilities and programs, churches, adult education programs, community betterment associations, and so on. The comprehensiveness of FOMERREY's program for the urban poor is reminiscent of the social service programs organized by the factory groups for their employees.

The involvement of Monterrey's industrialists in FOMERREY is difficult to establish. Significant, however, is the fact that four Monterrey "proprietors" and their assistants sit on the Comité Técnico y de Distribución de Fondos. This is the group with maximum authority within FOMERREY's operations. Additionally, much of the land acquired by FOMERREY for its new settlements must come from private land owners.

DISCUSSION

The critical lack of sufficient housing for the urban poor provides the circumstances for an inquiry into public and private sector competition. Conclusions, to repeat the caveat, at this point remain provisional.

The possibility, if not probability, of cooperation exists in both PROSECO and FOMERREY. PROSECO's goals of assisting the urban poor to achieve economic self-sufficiency can be subverted at any time by its board of directors. To the extent that the industrialists on the board pay the salaries of the

PROSECO staff, the potential of cooptation is great. They could, or course, just as easily expand their financial involvement and use PROSECO-supported cooperatives as a basis for political mobilization.

The degree of influence and impact of the industrialists on FOMERREY cannot be clearly ascertained at this time. To the extent that the private sector can influence FOMERREY in its policies and operations through their positions in its structure, a more direct involvement in housing for the urban poor will not be needed.

The incorporation of more and more of the urban poor into FOMERREY's programs, with FOMERREY becoming the sole *patrón*, possibly signals an end to most of the local level initiatives by squatters as have occurred in the past and an end to the competition between party groups and government agencies for their support. In the past, at least, settlers had some options regarding whether to affiliate with party organizations, state or city agencies; or to remain independent. They, of course, still have the option of joining the "Tierra y Libertad" movement rather than FOMERREY, but, politically, settlers tend to be realistically conservative. Through FOMERREY the control that could not be universally achieved in previous years, may now be much easier to gain. Support will come more readily from the urban poor to the party and government.

One of the problems with my thesis is making a clear case for the proposition that both the public and private sectors are competing for the support and control of the urban poor via the housing problem. The connection is to be found here: The urban poor provide easily obtainable, cheap, and temporary (*eventual*) industrial labor, *and* the urban poor are a major source of support for politicians. From this perspective, the urban poor are to be won over by favors and exist in a patron-client relationship with government and/or the industrial and business sector. Control is the objective of both.

Recalling the many years of struggle by Monterrey's industrialists against federalism and control from Mexico City in nearly every area of public life, an important extension of that struggle is seen in program options with repect to housing the urban poor.

NOTES

1. Usually defined as including the *municipios* of Monterrey, Villa de Guadalupe, San Nicolás de los Garza, Garza García, and Santa Catarina.
2. The 1977 minimum wage in Monterrey was $100.40 pesos per day (U.S. $4.52 @ $.045 per peso).
3. Among others these include the Confederación Nacional de Organizaciones Populares (CNOP), the Confederación de Trabajadores Mexicanos (CTM), and the Confederación Revolucionaria de Obreros y Campesinos (CROC). See Hopgood (n.d.; 1976: 238 ff.) for a discussion of settlers unions or *juntas* in one Monterrey squatter settlement.
4. The "Monterrey Group" are conglomerates consisting of several groups and sub-groups. The major two are Cervecería Cuauhtémoc group and the Fundidora group. Each has its own extractive and manufacturing industries and financial and commercial sectors. They are sometimes at odds with one another, but more commonly the major groups cooperate.
5. For a study of a factory sponsored *colonia* in Monterrey see Stillwell (1969).
6. For information and data on PROSECO I am indebted to its director for his assistance in 1978 and to Sally W. Yudelman of the Inter-American Foundation.
7. Data on FOMERREY were collected during trips to Monterrey in 1976 and 1978. I am indebted to several FOMERREY officials for consenting to interviews and for providing published and unpublished material. For an earlier statement of FOMERREY see Hopgood (1977).

REFERENCES

Balán, Jorge, Harley L. Browning, and Elizabeth Jelin. *Men in a Developing Society: Geographic and Social Mobility in Monterrey, Mexico.* Austin: The University of Texas Press, 1973.

Cadena R., Raul and Javier Cadena C. *Apuntes sobre el problema de la vivienda en Monterrey, N.L.* Memoria presentada al Congreso del Insituto Mexicano de Valuación, Guanajuato, Nov. 1-3, 1977.

Dirección General de Estadística. *Estado de Nuevo León; IX Censo de Población y Vivienda,* 1970, Datos Preliminares, Enero, 1970. Secretaría de Industria y Comercio, 1970.

El Diario de Monterrey. Monterrey, N.L., Mexico.

El Nacional. Mexico, D.F., Mexico.

Hopgood, James F. *Settlers of Bajavista: Urban Adaptation in a Mexican Squatter Settlement. Latin American Series, Papers in International Studies.* Athens: The Ohio University. (in press)

_____ . "In the Mountain's Shadow: Social and Economic Adaptation in a Monterrey, Mexico, Squatter Settlement." Ph.D. Dissertation, University of Kansas. Ann Arbor: University Microfilms International, 1976.

_____ . "FOMERREY: An Urbanization Program for Squatters in Monterrey, Mexico" Paper presented at the 53rd Annual Meeting of the Central States Anthropological Society, April 1, Cincinnati, Ohio, 1977.

Portes, Alejandro and John Walton. *Urban Latin America: The Political Condition from Above and Below.* Austin: The University of Texas Press, 1976.

Rosenfeldt, Martin H.E. "Cooperative Housing Aided Self-Help: Selected Managerial and Behavioral Concepts in Two Examples in Monterrey, N.L., Mexico." Ph.D. Dissertation, University of Texas-Austin. Ann Arbor: University Microfilms International, 1975.

Stillwell, William D. "House of Glass: The Study of a Mexican Urban Marriage Relationship." Ph.D. Dissertation, University of Pittsburgh. Ann Arbor: University Microfilms International, 1969.

Unikel, Luis. "The Process of Urbanization in Mexico: Distribution and Growth of Urban Populations." In *Latin American Urban Research,* Vol. 1. Beverly Hills, CA: Sage Publications, 1971.

Wolf, Eric. "Aspects of Group Relations in a Complex Society: Mexico." *American Anthropologist* 58: 1065-1078, 1956.

THE LEBANESE ARAB COMMUNITY IN CALI, COLOMBIA*

Leila Bradfield

Early Lebanese migrants to the New World were truly immigrants. They intended to stay and to become citizens of their new homelands—Mexico, Colombia, Ecuador, Brazil. They were not just visitors intent on mining the resources of the host country and then repatriating themselves and hoped-for riches. This paper deals with one such group—in Cali, Colombia, a nation which received few Lebanese because of discouraging legislation.

Lebanese migrants to Colombia in the 1880's went mainly to Bogotá. The earliest records in Cali indicate that the majority arrived around 1908 from the Lebanese mountain village of Bhamana to be followed by others from the same village. One responded that after his father and uncle arrived in Bogotá and lived there for a while they headed towards Cali in the Cauca Valley, which was a far more open society than the rigid one of Bogotá. Later, and prior to World War I, they sent for one of their sisters to join them; and after the war, they sent for their wives and their children. These stages of migration were typical of the Lebanese in Cali. Many of them landed first in Quayaquil, or Barranquilla and were later attracted to Cali to join relations.

The *first generation* of immigrants typically arrived in Cali in their second stage of migration. They started out by "selling"

*The author wishes to acknowledge the critical comments and aid of Stillman Bradfield and Louis Walker.

and forming small "negocios" (small businesses) and by pooling their joint resources. Many of these early pioneers were living in 1974 and were interviewed in the exploratory study. The single men in this group sent to the home country for wives. These arranged marriages were mostly May-December marriages with the husband 15-20 years older than the wife. Many of the women were eventually widowed, and some of these widows also took part in this study.

The *second generation,* mostly born in Lebanon and emmigrated to Cali, engaged in "commercio y industria" types of occupations. Three of the largest factories in Cali are today owned by members of this group. Several of these managers were respondents in this study. They play a variety of key roles in the society.

The *third generation,* born in Colombia, is included in the well-educated, professional class. It includes a world-renowned cancer researcher, highly regarded physicians, a congressman, writer-poets, architects, engineers and government officials besides industrialists and key businessmen, such as bank presidents.

"La Colonia Libanesa", as it is referred to by the Christian Lebanese and Colombians, was made up of approximately 600 adult men and women. This is the group of Lebanese discussed in the paper. The Jewish segment is excluded from the colonia because social relations between the Jewish and Christian segments of the Lebanese population are cordial but distantly formal. The events in the Arab world between Israel and its Arab neighbors had definite repercussions in Cali.

The main focus of this paper is on the characteristics that the Lebanese immigrants possessed which aided them in their integration into and acculturation to Colombian society. Moreover, factors that made the transition from immigrant status to citizenship possible will be discussed. More specifically, the variables are those that directly relate to successful integration: (a) conditions in the homeland and in Cali, (b) presence or absence of hostility in the host culture, (c) socioeconomic position (education, occupation, consumption patterns, social mobility), (d) patterns of the immigrants' value compatibility and (e) boundary maintenance mechanisms.

METHODOLOGY AND SAMPLE

The population in Cali in 1974 was approximately one million, and the Lebanese community of adults was around 600 persons. The writer conducted fourteen unstructured interviews with eight men and six women from all three generations and social classes, whose ages varied from the early twenties to the late seventies. Also four Colombian laborers and five Colombian upper-class men and women were interviewed in a non-systematic sample regarding their views of the Lebanese in Cali. The interviews with the Lebanese varied from forty-five minutes to three hours in length. Participant observation techniques were also used to supplement the data gathered through the interviews.

A WORD ON FIELD WORK

After reading about the Lebanese community in the Cali daily newspapers and hearing about it, I started this study by trying to enter through the formal structure of the Lebanese-Colombian society. I was unable to make contact, but I gradually made individual contacts through informal channels and found acceptance. The informal approach to locating key leaders and interviewing them was far more acceptable. Needless to say, the entrée to these respondents had to be via a person known to them, *i.e.,* the old Arab tradition of a "wasta" or go between.

A. CONDITIONS IN THE HOMELAND AND IN CALI: A HISTORICAL VIEW

Lebanon under the Ottoman Empire was economically depressed as was most of the Middle East. After World War I and the participation of the Arab world, Lebanon and Syria were separated from the rest of the Arab world and came under the French mandate. At this time out-migration to Central and South America increased. That part of the area under British mandate did not experience the same magnitude of out-migration as did Lebanon. The Lebanese even today profess that their most successful "export" items are people: migrants help their native villages and kin by sending financial aid and by representing Lebanon in the New World. Such remittances have not been a source of conflict between the Lebanese and the Colombians as they have been with many minority groups for several reasons: The Lebanese who helped maintain their villages and relatives back home regarded these economic contributions as charity, rather than as investments in their own futures, unlike many overseas Chinese. The Colombians, on the other hand, did not view this behavior as indicative of dual loyalties, but rather as a positive attribute of an ethnic group. The group had succeeded economically and still retained sufficient affective kinship ties to support those kin who had not been able to "make it." Furthermore, as the Lebanese prospered and settled in Cali, they were quick to change their citizenship from Lebanese to Colombian. In the words of one respondent, "We are Colombians first and Lebanese second . . . we have no split loyalties and no split identities."

According to another respondent, "Our children who went to study abroad in Europe and the U.S. have returned to Cali; they did not migrate anywhere else; in contrast to the European immigrants whose children go to the U.S. and stay there." It was evident to the writer that the vast majority of these Lebanese regarded their stay in Cali as a permanent residence and invested of themselves as well as their resources to improve their society.

Cali at the turn of the century was a small town with great potential for development and an ideal climate. The Lebanese who came to Cali from Buenaventura, Quayaquil and Bogotá found an open society with little emphasis on inherited wealth. In Colonial Popayán or Bogotá, on the other hand, migrants encountered relatively closed societies which offered little chance of upward mobility to migrants. According to one respondent, "Even though my father and his brothers came from a village in Lebanon, when they came to Cali, they taught the people here to wear shoes, lent them money to start their businesses and we both prospered." Another young industrialist told me, "If you build an outstanding building and surround it with six others, then it is no longer outstanding, but if you build it alone then it stands out." Thus the Lebanese Christians found not only a land of opportunity but a society where their contributions were meaningful and rewarded both economically, socially and personally. Again the same young industralist said, "When I went back to Lebanon for a visit after I finished university work in the States, I found that the part I would play in Lebanon is very small, whereas the part I play here is very important to the community and I feel I am doing something. I also like the pace here better—it is slower."

B. PRESENCE OR ABSENCE OF HOSTILITY IN THE HOST CULTURE

The first Lebanese generation in Cali stayed, baptized its children there, and educated them abroad. Later these children returned as professionals to Cali. An only son in a family told me, "When my father and his brothers first came to Cali they were called "Turcos," but that didn't last. You see, I married a Colombian and I've brought up all my children here. This is my home and the Colombians know it. The Lebanese men make very good husbands and the Lebanese women make very good wives; they are strong and able." Another young Lebanese said, "We have built up industries and created jobs for others. Like my father before me, we created businesses and we brought with us our skills. Since my father's generation, many of us have gone into politics, medicine, science, the fine arts, and so on. From the beginning we were accepted because of hard work and honesty in our relationships." These observations were prevalent among most of the people interviewed.

One government official said, "When I was a young child I was called 'Turco,' and I was insulted and a fight ensued. But fighting for integration was greatly facilitated through education, that is, as the Lebanese people studied the many disciplines of medicine, law, textiles, music, and practiced them in Cali, they became assets and spokesmen for the Colombian community rather than 'Turcos' who were there to take advantage."

One older lady told me that while there was little hostility directed towards them as "Turcos," there was; nonetheless, a great deal of loss due to "envidia" or envy. They lost several properties through bombing, but she quickly added that this was during the epoca of "La Violencia." Another time when she and her sons were in the finca while her husband worked in a less desirable climate, there was some reaction by the villagers against her. But she quickly added, "It isn't because I am Lebanese but because we owned so much and the finca mansion was unique, being built for my taste. When we left for town we gave the house and finca to the Municipio."

In general, there was a remarkable absence of discrimination towards the Lebanese. In fact, they were regarded as a great asset in the community as evidenced by the high rate of inter-marriage, positive regard for them by all classes. The poor and laborers said, "They have brought us jobs in a time of high unemployment," and the upper classes recognized their contri-bution in medicine, politics, business, industry, and the arts. In fact, they view themselves as blessed by a climate of toler-ance and acceptance; they have been accepted as role models. In the words of a physician, "We have been a modernizing force and an example to others."

Hence the opportunities for upward mobility were infinitely more attractive in the New World than in their homeland of Lebanon. They arrived in Colombia with the intent to settle and succeed in the host culture. It is this orientation that greatly facilitated their integration into Colombian society and reduced the hostility and antagonism frequently directed at successful minority groups.

C. SOCIO-ECONOMIC POSITION

The Lebanese did not enter the Cali society on the bottom rung of the social class ladder. Rather, they came in somewhere in the lower middle and worked their way upward. How did they accomplish this? A combination of factors were responsible for this upward mobility.

1. Education

Without exception all the respondents placed an extremely high value on education. As one physician stated, "No matter how poor we are, a very good education is a must, preferably a professional education. We go through extreme sacrifices to provide an education for our children. Less than 2 percent of all enrollees, (students enrolled in colleges) ever finish college in Colombia! With us it is almost a pathological need to succeed; it isn't just an economic failure."

As testimony to this avowed value, the Colonia Libanese has

produced some outstanding members. For example, there are physicians (a psychiatrist among them), architects, economists, senators, government officials, a chief of the liberal party, presidential candidate, and writers. "The best schools are usually the most expensive like Bolívar and San Sylvestre, but if that is where they can best be educated, then we will cut back drastically in our life style to educate them," said one respondent who lived simply while his children studied at the British school. The American and British elementary and high schools are very expensive, therefore only the local elite could afford to send their children there along with children of the diplomatic corps and those of families employed by foreign corporations that abound in Cali. The benefits of this formal education are evident by the fact that youngsters who attend these schools are highly successful in later life, especially in their occupational pursuits.

Parenthetically, the Colonia Libanesa did organize to establish a Lebanese school situated not too far away from the prestigious Colegio Bolívar and San Sylvestre. It was hoped that this school would not only teach the children Arabic heritage and language, but would replace the need for the other good schools. As of 1974 the Lebanese school was still struggling and had not achieved the academic standing of the other two schools. But it did enroll both Lebanese and Colombian students and was supported by donations from the Colonia Libanesa.

The first generation of Lebanese that arrived in Cali had had limited education opportunities but had developed great entrepreneurial skills and a blind determination to succeed. Early migrants were "hardy" pioneering people with a single-mindedness of purpose and perseverance.

In describing the various occupations of the Lebanese, one lady told me, "So and so's son is an economist, this one's son is a gynecologist, this one is an architect; they are all 'tehja.' " "Tehja" is roughly translated from Arabic to mean admirable . . . a jewel, a precious being!

2. Occupation

"Ascendants of the Lebanese are over represented in entrepreneurial, public service and professional fields relative to the total population. Look at the President of the Senate, Chamber of Deputies, and Governors and you find Lebanese surnames," said one of the respondents.

The Lebanese have representatives in every social institution except formal religion. "Some were even in guerrilla warfare in the llanos," said Jorge. "There are certain types of business that we don't find any of our people attracted to; for instance we don't run bars or night clubs." In terms of conflict with the law and antisocial occupations, one had this to say, "There are a few illegal occupations such as smuggling or small commercial crimes, but they quickly run into bankruptcy." In 1974, the newspapers reported only one case of a Lebanese who had to be deported because he got into trouble with the law. The only occupation where the Lebanese are not represented are in the "obrero" class—unskilled blue collar work. One person put this very nicely in Arabic, "Natsna Kebera!" (Our egos are too big for this kind of work!) Unlike the Latin American who disdains manual labor, the Lebanese will do even that to get ahead. The reason no Lebanese stay in the obrero class is that they either worked their way out of it quickly or never started at the bottom of the ladder. Even the early villagers that migrated to Colombia established small businesses rather than be hired at lower occupational levels.

Furthermore, nepotism is prevalent, and the likelihood of working for kinsmen or those from one's own village in Lebanon is also high. Those with few skills were given "overseer" positions in the businesses because they were trusted. So "confianza" plays an important role along with that of the "wasta," or a go-between, in the social and occupational upward climb.

What about social relations among the various occupational groups? One person summed it up by saying, "Those that I socialize with are honest, hardworking people no matter what class they are in; not crooked people, such as gangsters or amoral or unethical people. Then they are unacceptable." The older generation's social life is mainly with other Lebanese, whereas the younger generation has intermarried with Colombians and feels at ease in both groups.

They attribute their business acumen to their Phoenician heritage which enables them to establish a business, work hard, expect and overcome hardships. One large factory owner attributes his success to "honesty in money." While all the respondents agreed that hard work and perseverance are the backbone to success, one respondent put it this way, "We are like the Armenians back home; show us an opportunity and we know how to work. We are good people."

The Lebanese women of the first generation were in general assertive, fearless women who had to contend with difficult living conditions in coastal cities, a foreign language and long separations from spouses while they cared for their children. Even so, their adjustments and contributions were remarkable. Doña Maria says, "I went to Buenaventura where my husband, 30 years my senior, owned fifteen buildings. There was no light, running water or sewer services, and lots of yellow fever. But I worked right along with him. I remember once we had a shipment of merchandise that we couldn't sell; they were shoes (all for the right foot), sugar bowls without tops, and umbrellas for the rain, etc. This turned out to be merchandise left over from World War I. My husband, dismayed, didn't know what to do, but I organized a 'gran baratillo,' a large-scale sale and sold them all for 1 peso, 2 pesos, etc. and unloaded the merchandise and the people were happy to get them so cheaply."

Doña Maria was 20 years younger than her husband. She was, therefore, considered less experienced and knowledgeable. It is even more remarkable that her husband would listen to her advice and act upon it, as is illustrated in the following account:

"Another time I told my husband that he needed to insure his fifteen buildings and place of his business, and I dreamt that they were burning. In fact, I dreamt all Buenaventura was going up in flames. He said it would cost a fortune to do so; but I told him it is better than losing *all* your fortune. His partner did not agree to investing money in insurance so they had to split the business by flipping a coin. The ex-partner got the buildings, while my husband got the business. A month later the buildings went up in flames and the ex-partner lost his shirt."

The strategies used by the women varied. Not all the women used the direct intervention approach as did Doña Maria. Samia was more devious. For instance, Samia said, "The men would go on business trips for a long time; sometimes it would

be months before they came back. We all missed our Arab
bread that we made in the villages back home and were tired of
the tortillas. So I got a bricklayer to build us an oven. I
remembered that we needed broken glass to put in the construction of the different layers of this beehive shaped oven.
We got the oven built and the excitement of firing it the first
time was so great everyone came to see if it would work. When
we saw the first smoke go up the chimney we started getting
ready for baking. When my husband got home, I had Arab
bread ready for him and he was very pleased but couldn't
understand where we got it from. I kept telling him eat, don't
ask questions. You see I know he didn't want me to build an
oven, but now presented it to him as done. In the end, he was
pleased and amazed that I remembered the construction of such
a complicated oven."

The wives of today's Lebanese participate in their husbands'
occupations in varying degrees depending on the nature of the
occupation. Some women are gainfully employed outside the
home but the majority of them are not, but they take an active
interest in the "business." Finally, one of my informants
said, "Wherever you find Coca Cola, you will find a Lebanese,"
meaning that Coca Cola is the symbol of modernization and
prosperity and the Lebanese have been instrumental in making
this abundance a reality.

3. Consumption Patterns

The Lebanese made use of banking systems, saving and investing
their incomes; they also made use of insurance policies. That is
to say, they participated in the bureaucratic structure more so
than the average Colombian. When they could afford it they
built themselves elaborate houses in the countryside or in town.
But their most valued investment was in the education of their
children. Those of the first generation who started out in small
business selling machetes, fishing equipment, machinery or
wood, found during their lifetime that they could acquire
property and that the invested incomes permitted the third
generation the best in education at Boston University, London
School of Economics, Johns Hopkins University, or the Julliard
School of Music. The rich and their children travel to their

homeland to visit relatives in parental villages to maintain ties with the homeland and kin.

4. Personality Characteristics

When the Lebanese were asked what personality traits helped them to be successful, there was a fairly wide agreement about the role of work in its various facets. All agreed that hard work is the most essential ingredient, but in addition they said, "We know how to work, but in order to do business we have to locate near our customers and learn his customs and understand him." Therefore, astuteness and understanding were also essential to their success. Another person said, "It is not so hard to be outstanding. If you are willing to work hard, you don't have to fear competition." Interpersonal relations related to business arrangements and which led to success were based on "honesty in money matters and competent management." When I asked about any poor Lebanese in the community, I was informed that they had mismanaged their businesses.

Another aspect of personality is "goal orientation" and its manifestations. For instance, I was told of the first pioneering generation that "they persevered, with a phenomenal single-mindedness of purpose." As for the third generation, they described themselves as "determined to succeed . . . we have a commitment to succeed." This kind of dedication has other consequences. For instance, there is little introspection of the "who am I sort?" as identity issues are resolved. The men described Lebanese women as "resourceful, self-confident, fearless, and self-sufficient." The women said of Lebanese men that "they are great enterpreneurs and outstanding managers."

From my observation, close-knit family ties provide a great sense of security as well as a system of social welfare and internal aid. These close-knit bonds, especially between mother and son, and family reponsibility, even after marriage, have enabled many to survive in a very austere environment.

D. NUCLEAR FAMILY VALUES

Most of the respondents agreed that more Lebanese men married Colombians than did the Lebanese women. The reasons given for this exogamous marriage pattern were, "We are more strict with our women than we are with our boys, more than the Colombians are, so the women don't have as much opportunity to get to know other Colombians" or "Lebanese families are more possessive of their daughters and shield them from reponsibility more so than Colombian families." One man told me that "Lebanese women who marry Colombian men lose their identity as they enter the kin circle of the Colombian family." Therefore, one of the greatest means in integration has been the pattern of intermarriage. The prevailing custom of intermarriage, especially between Lebanese men and Colombian women, is the culminating point in the integration process.

The whole family life cycle is Colombian, as Farid put it, "My people didn't make money and go back home. They intermarried here, so some are half Lebanese. I've married Maria who is Colombian and orthodox while I am a Maronite. People baptized us here and they died here."

Summary of family and kinship organization and practices:

a. Age and sex segregation. The young people are polite and obedient to their elders and their older siblings. Daughters are treated differently from sons in Lebanese families since daughters are supervised more and permitted less freedom than their brothers.

b. Close knit and nuclear families with extended kinship networks. They socialize among themselves and support each other. A man's loyalty is to his family of origin first, and to his wife and children second. This was more true of the first generation. As one lady told me of her husband, "He was ten when his father died and he had to take care of all his brothers and sisters. So even after he had his own children his brothers and sisters still came first." Among the third generation, this did not seem to be the pattern, and loyalty seemed to center around the conjugal couple but with strong, respectful ties to the parents.

c. A high fertility rate and a love of children. Children are loved and showered with attention by all members of the family. "It is important to marry and bear children," one respondent said.

d. A very low divorce rate. Most conflicts are resolved within the family network, so families are stable.

e. Parental domination. Parental influence lingers on into adulthood. Parents control their adult children and feel it their duty to reprimand them when they find it necessary.

f. Patriarchal patterns. Ideally, the male head of the household sets the norms of behavior.

All of these family practices are compatible with those of the Colombians. Hence couples who inter-marry undergo fewer conflicts and adjust rather easily.

E. BOUNDARY MAINTENANCE MECHANISMS

Many of these mechanisms are more symbolic than functional and serve to rekindle ties to others in the community. For instance:

a. Two or three times annually there is a fiesta with cocktails, and all the Lebanese come dressed in their Arab clothes and jewelry. Colombian friends are included for the social occasion. "Dia de Libanon," November 22, is the main social event of the Lebanese community in Cali.

b. Arabic foods are served at important functions, such as births and weddings. There is a Lebanese-Beirut Restaurant and a coffee shop in the main plaza that serve Turkish coffee and sweets and are frequented by Colombians and Lebanese. Colombians are very fond of traditional dishes such as Kibbeh, etc.

c. Many Lebanese purchase Arabic records for the music even though they no longer understand the words.

d. Arabic is rarely spoken at home as the children speak Spanish, but Arabic words are interspersed with the Spanish. Many Arabic sayings and expressions persist.

e. Once a month a mimeographed sheet is sent to all members of the community telling them of events in Lebanon. This is produced by a Lebanese in Ibagué and distributed by the Lebanese consulate. The purpose of this newsletter is to inform and maintain ties to the home country.

f. Wealthy Lebanese still send their children on pilgrimages to see their father's village for a year. But they never stay, as they prefer living and working in Cali.

g. The Lebanese school in Cali is still something of a controversy as it has not drawn the student body expected from the Lebanese community.

SUMMARY AND CONCLUSIONS

By 1974 the Lebanese community in Cali had largely integrated into the Colombian society. We find their residences dispersed all over town, except in squatter settlement areas. There is no Lebanese ghetto area like some other minority groups settling in a host society, such as the early Italian and Irish-American ghettos on the Northeastern seaboard in the U.S. Therefore their integration is evidenced by a marked absence of self-segregation.

Second, attraction to Colombian marital partners is indicative of a close social affinity between the minority group and host members. Contrast this with the stigma and resistance Jewish minority groups in the U.S. had towards exogamous marriages. The literature also indicates that Jews in Latin America are very resistant to out-marriage patterns.

Third, the Lebanese have sought the best education for their children yet did not establish an Arabic school for their children until fairly recently. The establishment of the Lebanese school aimed at keeping the language alive since it was no longer spoken at home. The Lebanese were seeking academic excellence and while many in the community contributed financially to it, they did not send their children to the new school.

Again, many distinctive cultural patterns of other ethnic groups such as the role of religion among the Mexican-American groups, are not features of the Lebanese community in Cali. They belong to various Christian sects. The majority is Maronite Catholic, but one also finds Presbyterians and Methodists. In fact, formal religion appears to be the only social institution in which the Lebanese do not take leadership roles. I heard of no Lebanese priests or ministers.

Finally, their active participation in both local and national politics is one of the most remarkable features of this group. The literature clearly shows that minority groups do not participate in politics in the host society except where it directly relates to their business affairs or their group. But the

Lebanese in Cali *have participated* in guerrilla movements, and have been senators, governors, deputies to various ministries, union leaders, and mayors. This indicates a genuine interest and concern in their community and nation. They are very proud of these accomplishments that have brought a "good name" to the Lebanese community besides serving as role-models to others.

Thus the Lebanese group in Cali was well integrated into the larger society although it had not altogether lost its identity. For instance, surnames and Christian names are still Arabic Lebanese. Men are called Khalil, Samir, Salim, Mulhem, Jamil, Kamil and so on. Women have names like Sumaya, Zowaya, Farida and so on. Some had Christian names easily "Hispanicized" such as George became Jorge, Antoine became Antonio, Leila became Lily and so on. One friend told me, "We did not change our names, because we never found being Lebanese a handicap."

Physically, the Lebanese look very much like their Latin American hosts, so there is no distinguishable feature that has set them apart as the case with the Brazilian-Japanese or Peruvian-Chinese ethnic groups.

The fact that they still have Arabic expressions and feel at home with Arabic sayings is a form of boundary maintenance mechanism. Lebanese foods which they cook often and serve at ceremonial gatherings also serve as a boundary maintenance mechanism. Births are always greeted with "Mughly" a boiled cereal with almonds, raisins and sweets. Weddings call for Arabic music and Baalbeck dancing and possibly the wearing of some Arabic fabrics or jewelry. Baptisms bring the family and friends, both Colombian and Lebanese, together for the festivities as do first communion and school graduation parties. At graduation functions, parents socialize with their cohorts, while the younger generation has its dance downstairs or apart from the older group. A death in the community brings the whole "colony" together as individuals share in the bereavement. There is no Lebanese cemetery in Cali, so as they lived in dispersed residential pattern, in death they are buried in the various cemeteries.

In conclusion, the Lebanese have assimilated into Caleño society while maintaining a few symbolic characteristics that are culturally pluralistic. This cultural pluralism is evidenced in their Arabic sounding names, and in certain ceremonial behavior, such as those associated with rite-de-passage. Other culturally pluralistic characteristics are Arabic newspapers, monthly newsletters about Lebanon and the region, and visits to the homeland as well as financial aid to the father's village in the Lebanese mountains.

Hence, while the Lebanese community is assimilating into Colombian society it has far from lost its identity and disappeared. The community is growing as a result of both a high birthrate and in-migration but it is not growing as a distinct unit due to the widely accepted inter-marriage pattern in Cali. Some boundary maintenance mechanisms are maintained by both the Lebanese and the Colombians, but the edges of these boundaries do not produce obstacles for the minority group nor the host group since mobility between the two groups is fluid and smooth.

REFERENCES

Barth, Frederick. "Introduction." *Ethnic Groups and Boundaries: The Social Organization of Culture Differences.* Edited by Frederick Barth: Boston, Little Brown & Company, 1969.

Blalock, Herbert M. Jr., *Toward a Theory of Minority-Group Relations.* New York, John Wiley & Sons, Inc., 1967.

Bonacich, Edna. "A Theory of Middleman Minorities. A Theory of Minorities." *American Sociological Review.* Oct., 1973, Vol. 38, pp. 583-594.

THE SUBURBANIZATION OF CAMPESINOS AND THE METROPOLITAN CRISIS IN MEXICO CITY

William Collins

Rural-urban migration and the modernization/urbanization process is one of the most interesting and frequently researched topics in Latin American studies; an historical phenomenon which is central to understanding social change in Latin America. However, many studies are somewhat myopic in scope, and some lack substantial empirical support. Most veiw the first visible evidence of social dynamics to be migrant resettlement from rural areas to urban centers. They view the migrant as settled in and undergoing the variable trauma of adjusting to his new environment. More current studies superficially treat a secondary, center-periphery migration. But the migration/urbanization process is a continuous, stepwise social movement. It involves ongoing locational changes, socio-economic adjustments and deductive decisions that proceed to higher stages of adaptation to metropolitan conditions.

This research carries campesino-urban integration forward to the second and third stages in the process, those being the center-periphery relocation and the migrant readjustment to the social and environmental repercussions of suburbanization. It will look at the spatial outcomes of decision behavior that searches among many locational variables. It will review government policy to reverse the problems created by unchecked metropolitan growth, and; finally will evaluate the prospects of the success of these policies.

MIGRATION RESEARCH IN MEXICO CITY

New dimension was added to research in the urbanizaton

phenomenon in Mexico City by work undertaken by John Turner. The Turner hypothesis included a simple intra-urban migrational component or secondary stage to the migration process. The Turner model was not substantially tested in Mexico City by Turner himself, and the decision and spatial parameters which underlie the theory's assumptions were not appropriately measured.

The Turner model states that migrants initially settle in the metropolitan core and after a period of adaptation move to the periphery. Turner hypothesizes that the first concern for the migrant is with the location of housing, second with security of land tenure and third with amenities of the location. Much of the intra-urban migration process is intuitive, generalized from the Lima experience of the barriadas in the 1960's, and may or may not be fairly extended to Mexico City.

The shortcomings of the Turner model include the narrow range of factors used to explain the decision-making process. The process for decision and relocation is not spatially or chronologically articulated by his model.

Research by Brown (1972) and this author (1974) have treated the spatial relocation patterns that are the best explanation of the sum of decision-making factors. This study reviews and substantiates those factors.

THE STUDY BASE

In a field study of the *colonias proleterias* of eastern Mexico City a random areal sample was taken and interviews conducted with 201 colonist families. They were questioned about their previous residences, their reasons for leaving them, the choices available for relocation, the factors influencing the relocation decision; they were asked about their experiences in the suburbanization process. All of the families originated outside the Federal District. Ninety-one percent of the families migrated to the colonias from the center city as Turner's theory would predict. Only 30 percent of these lived with relatives in the central city. Thus, the social contact appears to be much less important for this sample than Turner would have us expect. Nine percent of the sample moved directly from outside the capital to the metropolitan periphery.

The process of suburbanization on poor quality lands of the

ancient Texcoco lake bed began about 1930. Colonias Agricola and Moctezuma were among the first established, and almost 10 percent of the respondent families moved to the peripheral location during that time. The study includes migration examples and the expression of growth in eastern Mexico City in a time series to 1970 so that trends in factor importance could be measured. These explain the process and ultimately the form of Mexico City's growth. (See Figure 1)

CENTRAL CITY-PERIPHERY MIGRATION FACTORS

The center-periphery migration process in Mexico City has been caused by the poor conditions of the central city *tugurios, vecindades* or *cuidades perdidas.* The process is stimulated by the opportunity for independence and a new start in the suburbs and an increased level of expectations of the recent rural-urban migrant for better housing.

The decision to relocate in a particular place cannot be made without an increased level of awareness of the range of alternatives available. The amount of information came from a number of sources, the most common of which were personal contacts. Rossi (1955) finds the same factor in a Philadelphia study. In the 40-year study period in Mexico City information was given by friends and relatives in 45 percent of the cases. Information about housing alternatives received from radio, newspaper or notices accounted for 43 percent of the migrants' sources, rumors for 8 percent and other sources for 4 percent.

The selection of a particular colonia and site was based upon a much wider range of variables. Some of these were clear to the migrant family while others were confusing and were included intuitively in the relocation decision.

The factors found in the research to have been most important in influencing selection of colonia and residential lot on which to build were the location of relatives or friends, economic factors, physical land use factors, employment factors, government policy factors and accessibility factors. (See Table 1)

1) Social Factors

Social contact was critical in the first step of migration to the city and somewhat less so in the second step of household

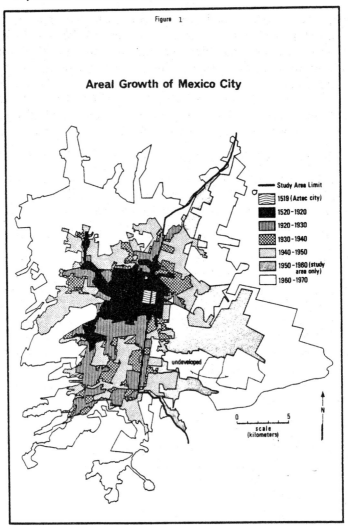

Figure 1

Areal Growth of Mexico City

Study Area Limit
1519 (Aztec city)
1520 - 1920
1920 - 1930
1930 - 1940
1940 - 1950
1950 - 1960 (study area only)
1960 - 1970

undeveloped

0   5
scale
(kilometers)

N

Sources: *Plano de la Ciudad de Mexico en el que se senalan diversas fases de su crecimiento de 1524 a 1960,* by Departamento del Distrito Federal for the 8th Mexican Book Fair, (Mexico, 1967); Hector Sanchez Campero, "Desarrollo de la Ciudad de Mexico 1524-1960," in *Demografia de la Cuenca Mexico,* IGU, Latin American Conference, (Mexico, 1965); Study area limits of growth for 1960 and 1970 taken from aerial photographs.

relocation. The residential location of each family's closest relative or friend was plotted and compared to the locational choice made by the family. The data for the period 1930-1960 show a high correlation between selection of new residential site and the nearness to kin. In the first decade 78 percent of the families located a residence within 5 kilometers of a relative with a mean distance of 1.5 km. In the second decade, 1940-1950, 70 percent of the families moved within 5 km. of a relative with a mean of less than 1.4 km. From 1950 on, this proportion began to drop substantially. Forty-four percent settled within that range after 1950 and only 31 percent after 1960.

Early in the suburbanization process there is a high level of uncertainty associated with the purchase of land and a home. When there has been little experience with settlement on lands of questionable title and the family is adapting to a wholly new lifestyle, the need to be nearer family contacts is apparently great. As time passes and the dynamics and security of large scale subdivision increases, being near family remains important, but other factors gain ascendancy, especially economic ones.

2) Economic Factors

Once the decision to relocate has been made, information is gathered about alternative settlement locations. The consideration of costs of the alternatives becomes a major factor.

The cost of a residential lot and the migrant's ability to pay are variables which were used to explain the colonia selection/decision process. To determine the probability that a migrant might select one area or another, cost curves were drawn through the suburbanized western zone of Mexico City. Land cost data were taken from the Federal District Cadastral and Tax office and were verified by colonists' statements of price paid per lot. Final curves were then studied for conformity to land use and published sales prices for land in the suburbanizing fringe. The distribution of lot sizes was also studied and mapped to determine the expected price per residential lot by outlying region.

The resultant surface for each period was compared to colonists' mean monthly incomes for the periods and the amount of disposable income that was expended in installments for land cost. This was found to be from 16 to 38 percent of gross monthly income (a mean of 29 percent). This distinguished a migrant's ability to compete for alternative sites. Then, given a particular household income for any particular period, the range of alternative sites available to it was estimated. All this was performed in the migrant's head in a sort of trial and error search behavior. The result is that in this decision and growth model migrants were distributed among areas of affordable land. Confidence is high for this factor since colonists rated it most important (29%). (See Table 1)

TABLE 1
REASON GIVEN FOR LOCATIONAL (*COLONIA*) CHOICE OF AN
AREA TO WHICH THE HOUSEHOLD MIGRATED

	1931- 1940	1941- 1950	1951 1960	1961 1970	Total	Percent
Cheaper	2	9	19	29	59	29.3
Close to work	2	2	8	8	20	9.9
Near transportation	1	1	2	4	8	3.9
Near relative	0	2	0	9	11	5.5
Better environment	1	5	2	4	12	5.9
Better services	1	1	1	11	14	6.9
Secure title	1	1	1	0	3	1.5
Nearest to CBD	3	2	16	8	29	14.4
Other*	5	10	10	20	45	22.4

Source: field interviews.
*The category, "other," includes the very common answer "*Me gusto*" (I like it). No elaboration was generally given.
The category, "better services," was considered by most respondents to mean schools, police protection, and government health and organizational services. Services such as water, sewer, and drainage were seldom if ever available on purchase or even as much as five or ten years after occupation of the area.

3) Physical Land Use Factors

The eastern periphery of Mexico City is characterized by the completely flat lakebed lands of the Lake Texcoco basin. Historically, the land was not used because of infertility caused by high alkalinity, frequent flooding of the lake bed during the rainy season, and poor bearing capacity and tractability of the impermeable clay surface. Most of the land had been innundated, and no private or communal ownership patterns existed. Only a few small ejido tracts surrounded the early margins of the lake in the northeast sector of the study areas. (See Figure 2) As metropolitan demand for water increased, greater amounts were pumped from groundwater reserves which, along with other factors, caused the lowering of the watertable. The lake has receded to a few impondments and has given up thousands of hectares of flat land. The question of ownership was not resolved by the government; and the scramble by speculators and developers led to illegal sales, unclear titles, and government expropriations.

The land that was opened up was of poor quality. Vegetation would not grow; soil corrosiveness and instability made very poor bases for infrastructure and heavy stone building. There was no drainage away from the surface, the land was frequently inundated to one or two foot depths. Dry season dust storms were unhealthful and destructive. All these negative environmental conditions made the land very cheap and therefore more attractive to the colonist. Throughout the study area, in fact, inconvenience, poor quality, and hazardous nature were associated with attractiveness for settlement by central city migrants. Land and home ownership was a dynamic and socially prestigious step upward for the traditionally landless peasant. Poor physical land conditions were in no sense a deterrent to the ownership opportunity. Colonists often made light of the bad conditions and likened their situation to a pioneering environment. The colonists attempted to minimize the problems but did not consider them a negative factor in the resettlement decision.

In the southeast region, non-flooded and good quality agricultural land was an ideal area for settlement. The limitation on land supply, large lot sizes and higher cost made the purchase decision feasible only to a smaller, better-off group of migrants.

Land use factors important to the suburbanization process here include land already committed to urban use. These uses exert externalities on the attractiveness of nearby undeveloped land. The pattern of manufacturing, public, agricultural, and

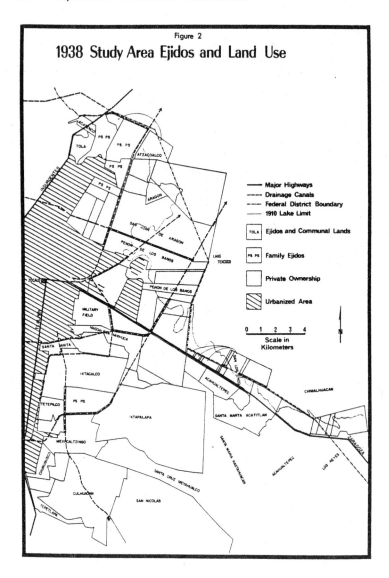

Figure 2

1938 Study Area Ejidos and Land Use

Source: *Carta Ejidal del Distrito Federal,* Departamento Agrario, (Mexico, 1938)

vacant land each helped to structure the location decision made by the migrant.

The chief effect of these uses is to block or channel suburban expansion. For example, there are very large tracts of ejido land near Ixtacalco, Ixtapalapa, the airport, and at San Juan de Aragon. (See Figure 2) These have blocked settlement due to inaccessibility of areas beyond. More distant ejidos ranging west to east from Culhuacan to Chimalhuacan have continued to hold major tracts of land from the development market which has deflected development to more distant points north and east into the Lake Texcoco basin. By limiting supply, the land market is artificially inflated. This then stimulates further subdivision at more distant locations.

"Leap-frogging" subdivision is also caused by the position of these tracts of land. This occurs in speculative settlement or through channeling or deflection of settlement.

There are no major industrial or commerical areas which preceded residential expansion into the eastern periphery of Mexico City. Major employment centers are on the north end of the area and in and around the central city. These factors did not structure the pattern of suburbanization as much as may be expected by transportation analysts.

4) Employment Factors

Data were collected from migrant families on journey-to-work patterns made before the relocation and afterwards. The purpose was to evaluate the importance of employment centers on the location decision.

Journey-to-work before relocation to the *colonias proleterias* was of relatively short distance. Before families moved to the suburbs their average distance to place of employment was 2.8 km for the 1930 group of migrants and 3.1, 3.3 and 5.2 km for successive periods of study. (See Figure 3) After the relocation average travel distance increased. The move to the suburbs increased the average distance to employment by .5 km for the 1930's group, 2.3 km for the 1940's group, 5.4 km for the 1950's group and 4.2 km for the 1960-70 group. (For each group between 42 and 50 percent of the migrants worked in the same job after the move.) Increasing distance to employment was correlated with data collected on mean round-

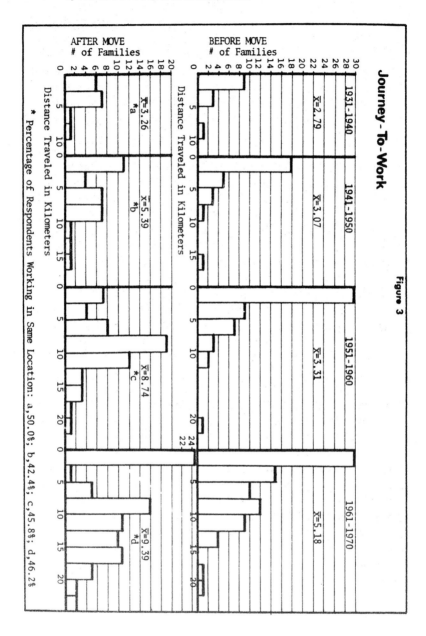

Figure 3

trip travel time. The four period responses reported average round trip travel times of 52 minutes, 82 minutes, 95 minutes and 110 minutes. The implications of these data are that nearness to place of work was not a significant factor in the household relocation decision process. Travel time to work was not considered important against the social and economic gains of home and land ownership.

5) Government Policy Factors

Until the 1950's there was no official public policy with regard to popular urbanization on the east side of the metropolitan core. The tradition had been to discourage *paracaidistas* and land seizures and to drive colonists from such land. A great number of unplanned and poorly serviced subdivisions were laid out and sold legally on private land. The growth in demand for land and popular housing grew critically large. In the absence of a policy or plan, the Mexico City government in 1954 placed a ban on all further development. It hoped to curb the peripheral sprawl of what appeared to be undesirable growth. Existing colonias were allowed to "topout" but no subdivisions would be approved for fourteen years.

With a steady influx of rural-urban migrants to the central city, the pressures for housing mounted in the limited market. The resourcefulness of developer, speculators, and migrant organizations soon found an alternative. Four to five kilometers out from the leading edge of development lay the boundary of the Federal District and the State of Mexico. Migrants began organizing invasions of the open land as yet unclaimed by private or public sectors. Just as quickly, developers were printing up deeds to unclaimed land and selling inexpensive lots. The availability of free or cheap land, albeit of questionable title, triggered wholesale movements of families who considered no factor other than opportunity. Equilibrium was quickly established and suburbanization of the state of Mexico portion of the metropolitan area began in earnest. There were no further näive attempts at growth control by the city, state, or federal governments.

The chief problem with many subdivisions has been the questionable validity of deeds held by colonists. The federal government established the legal basis of *colonias proletarias* in 1943 but did not intercede to correct problems until the late 1950's. A series of planning laws was passed requiring subdivision design standards, plan approval, land taxes, provision of services and title guarantee (Avalos, 1962). Colonists felt secure in the passage of the law they had long sought. Unfortunately, developers complied with all provisions except service installation. They would capitalize on their land investment and default the agreement. Colonists, past and present, have fallen prey to the unscrupulous developer. They are eager for the land and their pride of ownership and are usually ignorant of government planning law. Ultimately, however, faced with the developers' unfulfilled promises and no recourse to severe service problems, the colonists have called for federal land expropriation.

The state of Mexico, under siege with the bulk of migrant resettlement in areas like Netzahualcoyolt, Ecatepec and Naucalpan, established a planning control law only in 1967. The establishment of its planning authority, AURIS, was done concurrently.

One recent federal policy affecting migrant suburbanization gives the federal government the power to expropriate the large tracts of ejido lands in the public interest. The Federal Agrarian Law Reform (1972) allows use of urban area ejidos for government sponsored housing (*unidades habitacionales*). The examples of government-sponsored, low density housing at San Juan de Aragon, Acahualtepec and Chimalhuacan in the eastern periphery are laudable efforts, but they offer few units and require rental agreements. But they are poor substitutes for family-owned land and a private home.

THE IMPACTS OF SUBURBANIZATION

The suburbanization of campesinos in Mexico City has been, for them, a social opportunity and solution to economic problems, but the cost to the migrants, the city, and the nation has been high, as discussed below.

The drain on rural resources development is severe. The most ambitious persons leave behind a human energy vacuum and accelerate rural regional decline and regional income and employment inequalities.

The negative impacts on the migrants and their faimlies are also great. These have been studied in terms of family relations, psychological problems, and coping issues. Other impacts include those which are created by the environment of the *colonias proleterias.* The colonists fall victim to a hostile living environment composed of natural conditions, service inadequacy, and a type of colonist predation.

1) Natural Conditions which Impact on Suburbanization

The natural conditions of the *colonias proleterias* of the northeast area of the city are the most severe of all the outlying suburbs. One major problem is the threat of perennial flooding of land and homes. During the rainy season it is not uncommon for a foot or two of water to stand in the streets and yards. This increases the incidence of water-borne disease, contamination, property damage, and inconvenience. Movement is severely inhibited on muddy streets, and the use of power is curtailed for extended periods.

Soil alkalinity is very high in areas along the northern reaches of Netzahualcoyotl, the airport zone, and south and eastern Ecatepec. It is problem enough in other areas in that little vegetation will prosper, but in the heavily saline soils the problems include corrosion of exposed metal, deterioration of wooden materials and composition stoneworks. Building walls and exposed metal surfaces last only about 10 years.

Soil instability affects building foundations and use of the surface during wet periods. Foundations improperly laid in the plastic soils settle differentially and crack in a few years. Many buildings in the frequently flooded areas lean to one side and pose safety hazards. When the surface is wet, throughout the six-month rainy season, vehicular movement on unpaved streets is extremely difficult. The soils will not bear moving weights. The impermeability of the soils and small gradients cause extended retention of surface moisture.

Natural conditions are accepted by the colonists as a given condition of their colonia. They "accept" these conditions only in a relative sense because there are other undesirable conditions which they consider to be subject to alleviation by the government.

2) Public Services

Public services in the *colonias proleterias* are wholly inadequate.

Systems of drainage, water supply, waste disposal, road improvements, decent markets, and open spaces are rare amenities of colonia life. The Texcoco basin colonias are at the lowest elevation in the region. They are a sink for runoff from all the surrounding region. The Gran Canal de Desague along the region's western margin operates at virtually no gradient and creates an offensive condition for all inhabitants along its route. A newly inaugurated deep drainage system is not yet a proven solution.

Water supply is periodic, infrequently located along block faces, often unavailable, and when available, is pumped under very low pressure. Water is still commonly trucked into the colonias at a relatively high price, and the quality is generally lower than that available through the public system. Most of it is drawn from shallow surface wells which are contaminated by surface pollutants.

Waste disposal is not provided for by a public system of collection. Solid waste often accumulates in vacant lots and in the streets. When collected locally, it is often deposited in some large open area in the colonia or in some remnant of the lake to decompose. Serious problems with vermin and disease often result. Internal household waste is often improperly disposed of in pits or malfunctioning sewer systems.

Road improvements are a low priority in the Texcoco colonias. Major corridors within the newer subdivision are paved, e.g. Avenida Central in Nezahualcoyotl; but they account for only one in twenty platted streets. For most colonists who begin their work-trip on foot or bicycle this is not a great problem, yet is a source of inconvenience, dust and mud. Paved streets are an unmet expectation of the colonists' purchase agreement.

Open spaces have been required by the federal subdivison law at regular intervals for markets, recreation, public meeting spaces, and schools. The spaces are provided but usually amount to barren windswept fields. Marketplaces are not clean or maintained. They offer little variety, poor quality foodstuffs, and high prices.

3) Colonist Predation

The colonist falls prey to a great many opportunists who take advantage of new migrants who are remote in many ways from the civilization of the central city. Local businesses fix prices for foods, household products, and services substantially above those of the central city markets. Respondents claimed that they traveled frequently to the Merced market to purchase goods; but, in fact, they spend a good deal on products bought in small quantities from local convenience stores.

As was mentioned previously, the first to take advantage of the näive colonist is the developer. His use of confusing terms of trade, contract agreements, and pressure tactics intimidates the colonist who assumes the developer has the buyer's best interests at heart.

When established in a temporary makeshift dwelling and yet unadjusted to living in the suburban colonial environment, the colonist falls prey to many charlatans supposedly representing the government, tax agencies, public utilities, law enforcement organizations, etc., who demand payment for some hypothetical lien on the property or service being rendered. Often auxiliary police demand payment for use of public water supplies and for illegal hookups to power poles.

For a long period of time the colonist lives in a fear of being in violation of some law or of holding an invalid deed. He accepts these conditions, however, for these are a small price to pay for the promise of a new life and the pride of having achieved what none of his ancestors could dream of: ownership of land, a home and a future.

IMPACTS OF SUBURBANIZATION OF MEXICO CITY

The accelerated rural-urban migration and consequential suburbanization of Mexico City during the 20th century is on a scale beyond most major world capitals. The growth of the central city at a rate far beyond its next largest city (termed macrocephalous or primate structure) is a study in Malthusian projections. The metropolitan population grew from 369,000 in 1900 to 1.1 million in 1930, 2.9 million in 1950, 8.8 million in 1970 and should be almost 14 million by 1980. Projections by El Colegio de Mexico indicate a 1990 population of about 20.8 million and, in 2000, over 25 million. In two decades assuming a continuation of present trends, Mexico City will be the world's largest city. The impacts upon a city with an infrastructure intended to support 5-10 million will damage the city's systems and its people.

Conditions in Mexico City deteriorate monthly, due to the extreme sensitivity of the Mexico City basin and the inability of city employment and housing facilities to absorb population. Unikel (1970) lists a few of the growing concerns including underemployment, high cost of living, growing contamination of the air, increasingly irritating noise levels, increases in crime, population aggressiveness, enormous loss of time due to traffic congestion and the problem of central city subsistence. Villarreal (1976) adds the exponential increase in cost for water supply, the substandard housing occupied by almost 50 percent of the population, rapid increase in vehicle use, and high annual growth rate of *colonias proleteria* (Netzahualcoyotl at 26 percent).

GOVERNMENT POLICY RESPONSE

The Federal District has established a long-standing policy and resulting programs to reverse rural-urban demographic trends by promoting rural-regional development that might deflect or reverse population centralization. Its policies for regional growth pole development have not been successful. The Secretary of Hydraulic Resources' goals of rural agricultural development, industrialization of rural regions, and creation of new urban areas have not been achieved.

The National Urban Development Program of 1978 (PNDU) has many of the same objectives. Its philosophy is that population centralization can be reversed through a program of 1) discouragement of growth in Mexico City through public service taxes, tariffs, and disincentives to industry, 2) selecting priority development zones in the nation which due to their particular resource characteristics and locational advantages will become growth centers, 3) development of cities which have large regional service thresholds, 4) promotion of intercity transport, 5) development of support centers for dispersed rural groups, and other objectives.

CONCLUSIONS

The problems of growth in Mexico City are the problems of

failure to develop a program of balanced national development. The compounding of locational advantages of Mexico City has resulted in an inertia very difficult to reverse.

The National Development Plan proposes policies targeted for the central city as well as policies designed to increase regional attractiveness to development. The question is whether or not these tax, tariff, and disincentive policies will work. Such policies are very difficult to implement effectively and the history of differential regional incentives illustrates this. Even with additional taxation, the large profit margins accruing to the locational advantages of Mexico City would be overwhelming.

Regional development objectives and central city disincentives have the further disadvantage of a great lag time for implementation and market response. Mexico City cannot afford to wait twenty years for a trend reversal.

An effective policy must include major immediate incentives for industrial relocation and public subsidy of relocating the employee base to some new region. The policy must also include a major effort for government decentralization. The PNDU proposed a weak policy of regional administrative balance. The government should remain centralized but in some new location. With no difficulty, the federal government could phase a relocation of its own offices to some nearby regional center, e.g. Querétaro, Pachuca, or to the site of a new capital town somewhere within the central highlands.

The massive urbanization problems for migrants and Mexico City noted in this study have been created by the immense relative attractiveness of Mexico City to rural inhabitants. Until Mexico achieves major successes in regional employment and income convergence, the tendency will be for more rural-urban migration and escalating urban problems. A decisive effort at decentralization must be made promptly to avoid the urban oppression of the rural migrant that is forecast for the 21st century.

REFERENCES

Avalos, Rodolfo Jimenez. *Regimen Juridico Y Adminstrativo de las Colonias Proletarias del Distrito Federal.* Mexico: UNAM, 1962.

Butterworth, D. "A Case Study of the Urbanization Process Among Mixtec Migrants from Tilantongo in Mexico City." *America Indigena,* Vol 22(3), 1962.

Brown, J. *Patterns of Intra-Urban Settlement in Mexico City: An Examination of the Turner Theory.* Ithaca: Cornell Univ. Latin American Studies Dissertation Series No. 4, 1972.

Collins, William. "The Evolving Spatial Pattern of Metropolitan Residential Growth in Mexico City, Mexico 1930-1970." Univ. of Cincinnati, unpublished dissertation, 1974.

Kemper, Robert. *Migration and Adaptation,* Vol. 43. Sage Library of Social Research. Beverly Hills; Sage Publications, 1977.

Reforma al Ley Federal Agraria. Mexico: January, 1972.

Rossi, Peter. *Why Families Move: A Study in the Social Psychology of Urban Residential Mobility.* Glencoe, 1975.

Unikel, Luis S. "Los Dilemas del Crecimiento de la Ciudad de Mexico." *Revista Interamericana de Planificacion.* Vol. 13, No. 49, 1979.

Villarreal, G. G. "El Desarollo Urbano de Mexico: Diagnostico y Perspectivas." *Revista Interamericana de Planificacion.* Vol. 10, No. 30, 1976.

TRANSCENDING RURAL-URBAN BOUNDARIES:
A COMPARATIVE VIEW OF TWO LABOR RESERVES AND FAMILY STRATEGIES[1]

Terry Hoops and Scott Whiteford

The growing literature on urbanization, development, and agriculture in Latin America portrays an image of rigid boundaries between the city and the countryside. While the city's geographical limits are clear, the other definite lines have tended to blur some of the critical linkages between urban centers and rural areas. Equally significant, rural to urban migration is usually portrayed as unidirectional and bipolar.[2] This paradigm includes the implicit assumption that once migrants enter a new environment, they change their social organization and patterns of work. We do not deny the importance of rural-urban distinctions, but we hope to point to a critical dimension they hold in common which has been previously neglected. In this article we will argue that many migrants by moving to the city do not in fact shift from one form of socioeconomic structure to another but remain part of a labor reserve that traverses rural-urban borders, as does the capitalist mode of production. Few households in a labor reserve, rural or urban, have a single dependable source of income to sustain them through the year. They are forced to combine a variety of strategies over the year to maintain themselves, often at a subsistence level. These strategies are critical to the perpetuation of a labor reserve in the countryside as well as in the city.[3]

Commercial agriculture in Latin America has expanded, using the labor of the peasant sector, which has served as a labor pool. When not selling their labor, peasant families allocate their time to subsistence agriculture—a survival tactic. By competing with each other for temporary employment and using family labor for the subsistence production of food crops, they reduce the cost of their labor for the capitalist employer. This is not a static situation. A series of factors, including population growth, deteriorating land, loss of land and irrigation rights to commercial agriculture, and poverty give rise to migration to the cities. As Alain de Janvry points out, "The functional dualism between peasant and commercial sectors in Latin American acriculture implies the increasing proletarianization and impoverishment of the rural masses" (de Janvry n.d.:39).

Many of the rural poor who move to the cities of Latin America remain part of the "labor reserve." Here the mixed household economic strategies so crucial for the survival of the peasant and the maintenance of the labor reserve continue to play an important role, although they assume new forms. Mixed strategies are a necessary adaptation to conditions of low pay and underemployment, and serve to support a large population at a precarious subsistence level. Most families would prefer to be fully employed, yet they have not been able to get the jobs. Thus the adaptations necessary to cope with the problems of the dependent capitalist economy generate the responses that perpetuate the system. "It is the extremity of their needs, the necessity of taking, if not willingness to take, any wage labor that may become available that renders them a pool of reserve labor (Uzzell 1980:11). While production is individualized (wages are paid to individuals), both consumption and reproduction fall within the domain of the household. Wages of family members are often pooled to maintain the family, including those members who are unemployed (children, the temporarily unemployed, the sick), providing security for the individualized laborer. Equally important is the role of the family as a unit of reproduction of labor, both on the daily basis (subsistence) and the biological reproduction of labor.

Our case material is drawn from two regional capitals: Querétaro, Mexico, and Salta, Argentina. Both are former colonial centers and have grown rapidly in the last twenty years. With rich agricultural hinterlands, both cities have served as commercial centers. In the last twenty years Querétaro has become increasingly industrialized, in contrast to Salta, whose economic base remains commercial agriculture. Families in labor reserves located in the two cities utilize different strategies reflecting these differences, but play similar roles in the productive process. The growth of the two cities has been largely the result of migration from rural areas, and has been accompanied by an increasing diversity of economic strategies among the migrant population. In many cases, family work strategies include both rural and urban work. Both populations fit many of the traditional definitions of marginality. Some theorists have defined marginal populations as populations excluded from the political decision-making process. Others have emphasized the economic component distinguishing between those "who participate in industrial production and its associated benefits and those who do not" (Lomnitz 1977:10). Explicitly or implicitly the term carries the assumption of non-functional populations.[4] The paper treats these populations as integral parts of an economic structure, in which both employers in the city as well as the countryside depend upon a flexible source of labor.

QUERÉTARO

Querétaro, capital of the state Querétaro, is located approximately 200 kilometers north of Mexico City. Its historical importance, recent growth and industrial development has been greatly affected by its strategic location between large commercial and industrial centers of the north, especially Monterrey, and those of the south, which include not only Mexico City, but also Puebla, Toluca, and several other cities. Until about 20 years ago, Querétaro's primary economic activities were agricultural. This was reflected in the political and economic dominance in the city of several large land-owning aristocratic families, some of whom trace their ancestry in the city back to colonial times (Whiteford, 1964). Their presence, along with an especially influential church structure, gave the city a decidedly conservative atmosphere and agricultural orientation. Beginning in 1936, however, these families began losing portions of their lands to ejidos as a result of the land reform policies of the Cárdenas administration. Although expropriation affected only portions of large land-holdings, and these portions tended to be of poor quality and low productivity, the process of expropriation marked the beginning of the decline of the predominance of these families.

The introduction of industry greatly transformed the character of the city over a period of time. The most significant stage in the process of industrialization began in 1963, when the governor began openly recruiting both national and transnational enterprises. Perhaps half a dozen industries were already established at the time; today approximately 40 large and medium-sized industries hire approximately 23,000 to 25,000 workers.[5] Very little of what is produced is intended for Querétaro's consumption but rather is exported either to other parts of Mexico or to foreign markets. Industrialization brought with it a fourfold population increase in the city, from about 60,000 in 1962, to about 250,000 today.[6] Ecologically, much of the surrounding land previously devoted to agriculture was transformed into new low-income neighborhoods, squatter settlements, enormous government sponsored worker-housing projects, and middle and upper income "fraccionamientos"; in the old colonial core of the city, new commercial centers were established, large colonial homes were subdivided into multiple small ones, and tenement slums multiplied. Our study focuses on one ejido that has been partially taken over by a squatter settlement. Because of fluctuating demands in the local labor market, and the low wages paid by the local industries because of overabundance of labor, members of the ejido have had to diversify their economic strategies to make them less vulnerable. Our study examines particularly how economic activities surrounding membership in the ejido serve as one of the prinicple means for defense against these conditions by ejidatario familes.

Ejido Casa Blanca is located on the southern edge of Querétaro, and straddles both sides of the Pan-American highway, which serves as the crucial link between northern and central Mexico. The land upon which the ejido is located, about 1137 hactares, is for the most part hilly, rocky, and dry. The principle crops grown on ejido land are maize, *frijol,* and during the rare years of abundant rain, garbanzo. The ejido has no irrigation,[7] a feature typical also of most other ejidos in the area. Other traditional economic activities of the ejido include herding and mining, chopping and selling wood (though its supply was soon exhausted). Several ejidatarios own plow animals which they rent to members of various ejidos. Goats and cattle are also kept by a few members. Generally animals were provided though government funds or brought with ejido funds, and were distributed to the individual members.[8] Stones and lime (*cal*) were sold to building contractors, and *Tepetate* production is contracted to an independent miner for a share of the profit made from it.

The incomes or subsistence goods derived from these economic activities were never in and of themselves sufficient to provide for the subsistence needs of the ejidatarios and their families, forcing them to seek sources of income outside those provided from within ejido membership guidelines. Land reform laws establish that members of an ejido must productively farm the land that they are given. The *parcelas* of Ejido Casa Blanca, however, produced far too little to be the sole source of family subsistence, primarily because of the lack of irrigation.[9] Other types of work often provided far better income and working conditions, and often led the ejidatarios to abandon their *parcelas,* or, in spite of its illegality, to rent them out to other ejidatarios, and to seek employment elsewhere, usually in Mexico City. Until the early 1960s, the benefits of membership in the ejido were far outweighed by the demands it entailed. These demands included farming the land oneself (no rentals were permitted by the Agrarian Reform law), and carrying out the various requirements of the Department of Agrarian Affairs, which was in charge of ejido affairs, without compensation. Furthemore, loans for assistance in agriculture from the government were hard to obtain, and ejido funds were controlled by a federal agency[10] making access to the funds difficult. Finally, marketing their crops was extremely unprofitable for the ejidatarios, who, as a result of dry farming, were forced to sell them during seasonal periods, giving an advantage to irrigated crops, which could be harvested and sold during the off-seasons.[11] The unprofitability of practicing agriculture on ejido land led to the large-scale abandonment of *parcelas* by ejido members. Of the 87 ejidatarios first given land in 1936, only 31 continued to farm their *parcelas* in to 1941, and the remainder were deprived of their ejido rights. This trend continued through 1962, when the results of a census directed that 20 ejidatarios be deprived of their ejido rights for having abandoned their *parcela* for more than two years; and another 42 heirs were deprived of their rights either for the same reasons or because their parents had failed to complete the legal actions establishing them as heirs. Following the 1962 census, 56 new *campesinos* were given rights to *parcelas,* many of them qualifying for the rights because they had farmed the *parcelas* given them for over two years before the census.[12] Those ejidatarios who did maintain their membership did so either because they were able to farm several *parcelas* simultaneously through share-cropping arrangements, or because they were too old to do other work adequately. By the early 1960s, however, the situation on the ejido was reversed, and as the rights of membership began providing access to new valuable sources of income, the advantages of such membership began outweighing the disadvantages. As migration into the city swelled the demand for land and housing, the ejidatarios began illegally selling parts of their *parcelas* to the incoming migrants. They first began selling plots of land they had received as a result of petitions to the Department of Agrarian Reform[13] for extensions of the residential sector of the ejido. The plots received in this fashion usually measured 40 x 40 meters, and when sold, were subdivided into several smaller plots. A large proportion of those who bought land originally were relatives of the ejidatarios. As demand for land grew, ejidatarios began selling off their *parcelas* without first petitioning for residential extensions. According to one ejidatario, sale of the land proved more advantageous than farming. Plots were sold to various classes and for a variety of prices, depending especially on the relationship of the buyer to the ejidatario. At times land was exchanged for favors. The buyers included various members of different social classes. Most ejidatarios also kept several plots for themselves, which they either distributed to members of their families, or which they rented out.[14] Land sales resulted in the population growing from about 500 in 1962 to an estimated 50,000 today in the neighborhood.

In 1975 CORETT[15] took control of the neighborhood lands, and on request of the ejido, expropriated 400 hectares of ejido land although only 210 of those were urbanized. The ejido received an indemnity of 2,000,000 pesos for the expropriation, as well as 20% of the price of all lands sold by CORETT.

(All who had bought lots from the ejidatarios had to buy them from CORETT also.)

As urbanzation has spread over the ejido, the nature of ejido membership has been radically transformed; as a result, solicitations for membership have greatly increased. While expropriation has ended most land sales by ejidatarios, other benefits accruing from ejido membership have provided valuable new opportunities to ejidatarios. Among them are that the ejidatarios continue to receive indemnification for expropriated lands. Also, CORETT, which still maintains contact with the ejido, has promised to buy for the ejido a hacienda with irrigation.[16] Finally, ejido membership still provides access to government agencies through the political structure of the ejido. The role of the president of the *comisariado ejidal* has greatly increased in importance in its function as broker, both formerly in the selling of land, and at present in providing access of the ejido to various governmental agencies. The access is crucial not only for agricultural purposes, but also for providing information concerning available job opportunities, while the *palanca* (influence) of these agencies assists in realizing these opportunities.

While in outward appearance ejido family strategies of livelihood differ little from those of their urban neighbors, in fact their membership in the ejido adds a new dimension to these strategies, transforming their nature. Ejido membership becomes the focus of family economic activities, since it provides a stable and somewhat secure means of supplementing family incomes. The responsibilities of ejido membership usually rest with older men or women in a household, freeing other residents to pursue other sources of employment. Sources of income derived from ejido membership include rents from houses and land obtained when the *parcelas* were divided. Added income is produced through share-cropping arrangements. Furthermore, relief from the obligations of ejido membership has enabled most ejidatarios to work in other jobs, several work in the service sector—for example, for the police— while others hire themselves out as *jornaleros* (day laborers), most often performing construction work. Herding continues to provide a very small income for one or two ejidatarios. Finally, the benefits mentioned in the preceding paragraphs provide other sources of income. However, income derived from the ejido continues to be insufficient as a sole means of subsistence for member families.

Although they are still constrained by the requirements included in membership, new alternatives allow ejidatarios to escape them as much as possible. Those whose land is already expropriated   no longer have to farm, a condition that has led several members to donate their land to the city. Furthermore, the constraints can be avoided by putting control of cultivatable *parcelas* in the hands of women, who legally can rent the land out or sharecrop it; and, while illegal, similar practices by older men are usually overlooked. Often older men will refrain from naming heirs for as long as possible, thereby acquiting family members from obligations incurred in membership. Finally, sharecropping, despite its risks, is also widely practiced by other members who don't fit into the above categories.

The ejido ususally consist of the ejidatario and his or her spouse, unmarried children, and often married sons, their wives and children. A close system of cooperation exists between members of the household; as a result of the process of urbanization, however, cooperation between ejidatarios, even those who are close relatives, has virtually ceased except in the necessary governmental functions of the ejido. Family members will often live together in the house of the ejidatario, or in several houses in the same neighborhood that had once belonged to the ejidatario. Other members of the families of the ejidatarios will pursue employment strategies similar to their immigrant neighbors'. Their houses will often have small stores in the front rooms, which nonworking members can attend to. There are at least 600 such *tiendas* in the neighborhood. Other family members may tend stalls in the neighborhood market, or sell wares of food in the streets. Women often work as servants or cooks for other families in Querétaro. A variety of jobs arranged on a daily basis are also available to family members. Almost all small children of ejidatario families attend public schools.

Most important, this family arrangement allows one or more of its members, usually young men, to seek jobs in the industries in Querétaro, or in "support service" jobs. As Ward (1975) points out, this type of family economic organization enables industry to draw off from this population the best laborers for very low wages. Almost all the households of ejidatarios have one or more members, usually young men, who work in the industries of Querétaro or in "support service" jobs. Furthermore, due to the unstable conditions of the Mexican economy, industries are forced sporadically to lay off or hire large groups of workers. Doing so is often simplified by providing workers with only short-term contracts that do not guarantee renewal.[17] The instability of this labor force has made independent unionization difficult, although workers in several industries are represented by government unions. The hiring practices of these industries contribute to the maintenance of low wages and serve to protect the industries from labor unrest. An interviewed personnel director explained that his company preferred to hire young men with families who would not cause any labor problems because they could not risk losing their jobs. He also said that industries prefer to hire farmers who have been "unspoiled" by labor problems in other jobs. The wages paid are often inadequate to meet subsistence needs of the workers' families, forcing them to depend on income provided for by mixed family strategies.[18]

According to several ejidatarios, such mixed family strategies, as well as benefits from ejido membership, have provided a better standard of living than before urbanization. The feeling is not shared by all, however, since social and economic differentiation between ejidatarios has also increased since urbanization.

In conclusion, while ejidatarios have maintained membership in the ejido, suggesting that their source of livelihood is primarily agricultural, they have in fact pursued a number of different work strategies related to the urban context in order to make a living. The strategies are reflected in the household structures predominant among ejido members, and in the cooperation between those family members. The stategies are also reflected, on another level, in the form in which urbanization on the ejido took place. Finally, these strategies contributed to the dominant economic system by providing to industrial capitalism the large flexible labor reserve pool that it needed in order to grow.

SALTA

Salta has historically been a trade center linking northwest Argentina to Bolivia. Fertile land in the city's hinterland is planted with sugar cane, tobacco, and grapes, while cattle range the less arable areas. Agricultural production is dominated by a Salta-based oligarchy that owns the major plantations and farms. The city has grown without an industrial base, with much of the migrant population finding work in the service sector. By 1970 the city population had reached 185,000. The majority of the migrants come from the small towns in the region, but a significant number come from Bolivia.[19]

The plantations, which were established at the end of the nineteenth and the beginning of the twentieth century, require seasonal labor to expand their production. In response to the scarcity of cheap labor, plantation owners in the 1930s and 1940s either bought or rented highland farms. They forced the peasant families who lived on these farms to send members of their families to work on the plantations six months of the year. The impact on the highland communities was devastating. Food production fell as labor was withdrawn from work at crucial points in the agricultural cycle. Local craft production was almost eliminated as skilled artisans were forced to work in the *zafra.* Local markets were transformed, and families became dependent on the cash economy to buy many products farmers produced locally. Low wages paid on the plantations, intensifying the growth poverty of the communities, generated increased permanent migration out of the *hacienda* regions. Many migrants settled in Salta. Others continued working in the zafra.

After 1940 the owners of the sugar plantations lost some of their political power. A series of strikes erupted on the plantations, and the first efforts were made to form unions. In an effort to replace labor that was moving to Buenos Aires and to break the unions, the plantation owners mounted a major recruiting effort to bring Bolivian workers to Argentina, many without legal papers.[20] After the sugar harvest, many Bolivians remained in Argentina, taking work in the city as well as on farms. Over the years a large labor force of Bolivian families settled in Argentina. For many of those who settled in Salta, rural work remained an important source of periodic or seasonal income, and they remained part of the labor reserve for rural as well as urban employers.

The opportunity structure in Salta and the countryside includes a number of structural conditions. Employment for most family members without special skills, education, or capital is low paying and undependable. To make the situation even more difficult, labor laws are seldom enforced, especially in the case of foreign workers. Faced with a structure in which they occupy a precarious position, families are forced to develop a multifaceted strategy of survival. This strategy and its underlying assumption could be called a strategy of least vulnerability.

For most of the families, a sense of vulnerability permeates their world view. They are painfully aware of the socioeconomic constraints on their efforts to establish a secure livelihood. While they see Argentina as a land of abundant resources with more employment opportunities than Bolivia, few have found secure niches. Their concerns are reflected repeatedly in conversations that inevitably turn to inflation, the lack of unions, the scarcity of good jobs, the qualities of employers, and work opportunities in other areas. Jokes about how people manage to get back at a bad employer are a great source of mirth. The fear of debilitating illness or injury haunts many families that depend on their energy and strength to earn a living. Since employers explicitly prefer young men, aging is perceived as a major threat. The Bolivian migrants of the study occupy a middle ground between two extremes described in the literature of Latin America: the fatalistic urban poor on the one hand, and the extremely optimistic migrants on the other hand. Most of the Bolivian migrants indicate that they are confident of being able to cope with a difficult situation. While they acknowledge their precarious position, they feel that by being careful, clever, and hardworking they can survive, and possibly improve their lives over a long period of time.

A variety of factors influence how particular families interpret their situation and subsequently deal with it. Families whose members include illegal immigrants clearly feel the most vulnerable. Many have been threatened with being reported to the police and subsequently deported if they joined unions or attempted to protest substandard wages or failure to pay. This problem is not restricted to the illegal migrants. In a sample of 40 legal migrants, 15 reported employers who still owed them money, and only two felt they would be paid. In some cases the employers came from out of town, hired the workers, finished the job, and left the city without making final payments to his workers or leaving a forwarding address. In other cases, powerful local individuals hired illegal immigrants and either delayed payments or paid extremely low wages. Women as well as men talk of a high rate of nonpayment. Four out of 30 women reported being fired without pay, being blamed for theft or breakage they did not do.

Families with large numbers of small children who cannot work and couples over fifty years old who do not have established work feel especially vulnerable. The least threatened, given equal material resources and special skills, are families with a maximum number of children of working age who have implemented a variety of adaptations or tactics. Tactics explicitly recognized as important include: patron-client relationships, holding multiple jobs even if only temporarily available, small-scale entrepreneurial efforts, maintenance of land and kin ties in Bolivia, raising of animals and gardening, and formation of active social networks in Salta to gain access to jobs.

These tactics are utilized through the cooperation of households, usually extended or nuclear families. Women play a critical role as do children and, occasionally, grandparents. Women are paid less than men in both the city and the countryside despite making a major input in the production process. On the plantations they work trimming cane leaves, but only their husbands are paid. On tobacco farms women who work sorting and poling leaves are paid less than men who harvest. Children too are hired in the tobacco harvest and earn less than women for the same task. Because of the exploited position of women, household work decisions revolve around the work opportunities for men, and the women's work is viewed as supplemental even though it may be more dependable, as for example, when the women work as maids. This has been noted in other parts of Latin America (Bossen 1979).

Patron-client ties are an important tactic for the poor in

Salta. Cutting across class divisions, patron-client relations are used to adapt to the limited mobility that characterized dependent development (Rothstein 1979:25). The ties link individuals in the labor reserve to employers, giving a temporary employment relationship a more permanent dimension. Many workers conscientiously seek a "good patron." By working very hard at low wages, many workers feel they can develop a reputation with the employer as a reliable, productive, and unobtrusive worker and possibly be kept on the job or rehired. This tactic may also be reinforced by naming the employer as a godparent to a child, although urban employers seldom feel this entails strong obligation. When successful, this particular tactic may give the worker some stability, but at a price of lower wages and possibly worse working conditions than he might have in another less permanent job. At the same time it gives the employer much control over the worker at little cost. The vertical ties between the employer and the workers function to make the workers more vulnerable in another sense. It reduces class consciousness, and reduces the possibility that horizontal ties will be formed between employees, Bolivian or Argentine, that might lead to organization and pressure for wage increases, additional employee benefits, or possibly movements for even more profound change.

Part-time self-employment is an important tactic to reduce dependence on employers as well as to cover periods of unemployment. Employers commonly underpay their workers, or renege on payments: because of the employment structure in the city, they know they can always find more workers. Others simply leave town without paying when the work project had been completed. Workers, aware of this potential danger, try to reduce the risk by inquiring about employers' reputations. But more importantly, they try to develop work alternatives that can get them through periods when they otherwise might have work for an employer of unknown or questionable quality. For this reason, family members will often work long hours at their self-employment, with meager returns on their labor, because it may be better than taking a risk with an employer.

At times, self-employment may create additional jobs which can absorb the labor of family members when they are not working. One example is the family store. Although it may bring in scant income, hardly paying for the inconvenience and long hours of waiting for customers who buy little because of price inflated by their inability to buy in bulk, the store may be maintained; despite the low return on each unit of labor, it represents possible insurance against the inevitable periods of unemployment.

Another type of self-employment is gardening and animal raising. In regional centers like Salta, the poor may own enough land to grow food for themselves and occasionally for sale; this is usually more difficult in the large primate centers. Like the family store, these are labor-intensive projects. In some cases these gardens and animals (fruit trees, vegetables, chickens, turkeys, ducks, guinea pigs, goats) can be used in times of crisis—such as unemployment—to feed the family and possibly extended kin or friends. Produce is also important in creating social ties with individuals who will help in times of crisis: one of the main methods of establishing long-term friendships and reciprocity is the exchange of home-grown produce, which is preferred to buying gifts.

For those migrants who had land in Bolivia, however small, the maintenance of the village ties was more than symbolic. The possibility of returning to Bolivia was for some a goal but for others a life jacket in case their efforts in Argentina did not work. Many sent remittances back to parents or children even though they did not expect to return to Bolivia to live for long.

Social networks are of great importance to families who form the labor reserve. The networks serve to help the families find employment as quickly as possible. On the other hand, they provide employers with a means of hiring and firing on short notice, taking advantage of the conditions of the labor market. In many cases, families carefully develop their networks, a strategy intended to increase their access to information about employment possibilities or even to gain access to jobs. This process generates friendships but also serves to divide the urban poor who are competing for limited employment opportunities.

Familes do not emphasize all of these tactics equally nor are they equally successful. There is a series of factors that influence their decisions as well as the outcomes. On an individual level, there are important differences in skill and resources.

Equally important for foreign workers is whether they have work papers or are illegal. An illegal migrant is obviously more vulnerable. On the family level, families at the point in the family cycle where they have a high ratio of healthy working-age members, in contrast to dependents, have a distinct advantage over families with predominantly young children. There are also differences in the degree to which the family members or household members are willing to contribute jointly to the maintenance of the group. Yet despite these differences, employment decisions and their implementation are seldom purely individual acts; instead a family or household acts on the basis of the groups' needs and resources.

CONCLUSION

We have examined two populations whose members' economic strategies combine both rural and urban activities despite the fact that they reside in cities. In neither case does residence in the city foreclose the importance of agricultural work. Both populations fit the traditional definition of marginality; they are characterized by under and unemployment, a lack of political power and deprivation of the benefits of the modern sector of the society. Yet the members of these populations are not marginal; rather, they play an important role in the structures of the different dependent capitalist economies in which they participate.

Transformation of the rural society through penetration of the market economy and expansion of commercial agriculture forced many of the families who had been subsistence agriculturalists to take seasonal work in commercial agriculture and eventually to seek work in the city. Neither the urban ejidatarios who were incorporated by the expanding city nor the Bolivian migrants who moved to the city were able to find secure employment. In both cases they remained part of a labor reserve of underemployed workers who competed with each other for temporary work in agriculture, industry and the service sector.

Lacking job security and union protection, the workers are subject to short-term employment bearing the brunt of the expansions and contractions of the economic system. The low income neighborhoods of Querétaro and Salta lack many public services reflecting the lack of political power and low incomes of their inhabitants. Equally important, the neighborhoods have replaced villages as the locale of family subsistence maintenance. It is in the neighborhoods that families use mixed strategies as their forefathers had used family labor in the countryside in an attempt to cope with poverty. Differences in the strategies of the two populations discussed herein reflect the distinct economies of the two cities as well as their hinterlands. Equally important at another level of analyses are family factors such as household composition, position in the family cycle, and family resource base. In both cases the populations remain part of a process which maintains and reproduces a class of people who provide short-term labor for both rural and urban capitalist enterprises while they support themselves through periods of unemployment.

The populations we have examined in this paper do not represent a social class that is being integrated in a slow but evolutionary manner into the modern economic and social sector of their nation. Rather, we must conclude that their position will only improve as the economic and political structures to which they are subject are radically transformed.

NOTES

1. Terry Hoops appreciates the support from the Inter-American Foundation which funded his research in Querétaro in 1978, and Andrew H. Whiteford under whose National Institute of Health grant he workd in Querétaro in 1976. Scott Whiteford is grateful for the support received from the Ford Foundation in 1971 and the National Science Foundation in 1974 for his work in Salta. In addition, Hoops grew up in Salta and Whiteford worked in Querétaro. The authors are listed alphabetically.

2. For a discussion of the weaknesses of the bipolar model see Uzzell 1976.

3. It should be noted that while we hold that the internal organization of this population and its articulation to the greater economic structure enables it to function as a labor reserve within the framework of capitalism, we are not implying that this function was its raison d'être; in other words, its function alone does not explain the cause of its existence. The historical factors which gave rise to the formation of the labor reserve must be studied within their particular historical contexts. This analysis

lies outside the scope of this paper.

4. "Marginality theory" has been criticized by various authors. Perlman, (1977), for example points out that " . . . the 'marginality' paradigm is based on an equilibrium model of society . . . . Marginality theory assumes that in a functioning system the interconnections between sub-portions tend to be mutually satisfactory and beneficial to all. It is perfectly possible, however, to have a stable system which is balanced to the advantage of some precisely through the explicit or implicit exploitation of others. Exploited groups in such a situation are not marginal but very much integrated into the system, functioning as a vital part of it" (pp. 244-5). For further discussion and alternative perspectives, see Peattie 1974, and Babb 1979.

Several dependency theorists, equally critical of that perspective, speak of marginality in terms of the labor reserve. (c.f.: Babb, *ibid,* Murmis 1969, Nun 1969, and Quijano 1974). They place this marginalized labor reserve as a socioeconomic formation, or form (or mode) of production separated from, yet dependent upon, the dominant capitalist system. In contrast, from our perspective, the labor reserve is not marginal; its appearance as being so is the result of its contradictory class position, in which it provides cheap labor, goods and services to capitalism in a similar fashion as the "full" proletariat, yet it is denied full incorporation into the capitalist relations of production, and its crucial position within capitalism is constantly negated by that system.

5. The data comes from CANACINTRA: Camara Nacional de la Industria de Transformacion.

6. Approximate unofficial figures, based on conversations in the census office in Mexico City and in the "palacio de Gobierno" in Querétaro.

7. Two wells were dug in the 1960s but both failed to provide water. Explanations of the failures are abundant: crookedly drilled wells, faulty or stolen pumps, a corrupt contractor, and the like.

8. Thirty-six goats were given to each ejidatario in 1965 in compensation for Burócrata land project which was expropriated by the state government. Only one substantial herd remains; according to accounts, others were sold off, eaten, or died in epidemics.

9. According to a newspaper account (*Noticias,* June 2, 1973), the average ejido hectare produces 4-500 kilos of maize. According to two ejidatarios from Casa Blanca, an ejidatario might be able to make the equivalent of $15,000 off one harvest, hardly sufficient to support one family for about 100 days.

10. FIDEICOMISO

11. CONASUPO, an agency that attempts to maintain higher prices for agricultural products, buys a minimum of two tons of maize at a time, making it virtually impossible for ejidatarios to sell them, according to the several ejidatarios interviewed.

12. It should be pointed out that the above figures represent a process which took place over a long period of time and only came to a head when a census was finally taken. The census, which should be legally carried out every two years, was not, in this case, carried out for at least a decade.

13. In 1971, it became the Secretaria de la Reforma Agraria.

14. In 1971, approximately 2,000 people invaded and settled 30 acres set aside for community neighborhood services. Discussion of the invasion is outside of the scope of this paper; however, it should be noted that it resulted in strong conflict between the ejido and the leaders of the invasion. The latter organized a patrol system for the invaded area, and surrounded it with barbed wire. The governor ultimately took personal control of the situation to resolve the conflict.

15. The federal agency that regulates invaded ejido lands.

16. During my stay in Querétaro, the ejido leaders were looking at a hacienda that comprised 70 hectares of irrigated land and a crop of unharvested alfalfa. The hacienda which they were to receive was to be considered private property, rather than state-owned as in the case of the ejido.

17. In interviews with workers of one industry, I was told that their contracts had to be renewed every 80 days. Workers of another industry stated that their contracts were for 28 days.

18. Various workers interviewed from different industries stated that they were paid the federal minimum wage (105 pesos daily—less than $6 U.S.), others, particularly those with more seniority, often made twice that amount. Various families interviewed calculated the minimum cost of living in Lomas de Casa Blanca for a family of four to be approximately 200 pesos a day. Workers generally agreed that the wages they received were inadequate to sustain their families.

Representatives of industry hold, of course, that the wages they pay are adequate. The personnel director mentioned above, as well as the director of the Querétaro branch of a national organization for industrial representation, denied that the poverty conditions of Lomas were in any way related to the wages residents received. In fact, such poverty conditions existed because there were no industrial employees in the neighborhood,

I was told; they were not employed due to "deviant (social and mental) character." I was unable to obtain from them any lists of workers. All my evidence was very much to the contrary, however. The industry which the personnel director represented alone picked up five or six busloads of workers a day from the neighborhood for its three shifts, and I was informed by workers that many others who did not ride the busses found other means of transportation.

19. The advantages of foreign labor for employers are multiple. The workers are docile (fearing deporation), cheap, often willing to take below minimum wages, expendable when services are not needed, and mobile (Ward: 1975:18).

20. Estimates of the number of Bolivians in Argentina or Salta vary because many are illegal. In 1970 the range was 105,000 to 500,000. The Director of the Regional Office of Migration felt at least 70,000 Bolivians lived in the province, with over half in the city of Salta. The official census list only 26,341 foreigners in the whole province. See Whiteford (In Press) for Bolivian labor on plantations in Argentina.

BIBLIOGRAPHY

Babb, Florence E. "Market Women and Peruvian Underdevelopment. Paper presented at the annual meetings of the American Anthropological Association, November, 1979.

Bossen, Laurel. "Sexual Stratification in Middle America." Paper given at XLIII International Congress of Latin Americanists. Vancouver, Canada, 1979.

de Janvry, Alain. "The Agrarian Question and Reformism in Latin America."

Lomnitz, Larissa. *Networks and Marginality: Life in a Mexican Shantytown.* New York: Academic Press, 1977.

Murmis, Miguel. "Tipos de Marginalidad y Posición en el Proceso Productivo." In *Revista Latinoamericana de Sociología.* 5:2, July, 1969.

Nun, José. "Superpoblación Relativa, Ejército Industrial de Reserva y Masa Marginal." In *Revista Latinoamericana de Sociología.* 5:2, July, 1969.

Peattie, Lisa R. "The Concept of 'Marginality' as Applied to Squatter Settlements." In Wayne A. Cornelius and Felicity M. Trueblood, eds, *Latin American Urban Research*, Volume 4, Beverly Hills: Sage Publications, 1974.

Perlman, Janice. *The Myth of Marginality: Urban Poverty and Politics in Rio de Janeiro.* University of California Press: Berkeley, 1977.

Quijano Obregón, Anibal. "The Marginal Pole of the Economy and the Marginalised Labour Force." In *Economy and Society.* 3:4, November, 1974.

Rothstein, Frances. "The Class Basis of Patron-client Relations." In *Latin American Perspectives* 6:2, Spring, 1979.

Uzzell, Douglas. "Ethnography or Migration: Breaking out of the Bipolar Myth." In *New Approaches to Migration.* Edited by Dave Guillet and Douglas Uzzell. Houston: Rice University, 1978.

_____ . "Mixed Strategies and the Informal Sector: Three Faces of Reserve Labor." In *Human Organization.* 39:1:40-49, 1980.

Ward, Antony. "European Capitalism's Reserve Army." In *Monthly Review,* November, 1975.

Whiteford, Andrew Hunter. *Two Cities of Latin America.* Garden City, N.Y.:Doubleday & Company, Inc., 1961.

Whiteford, Scott. *Workers from the North: Plantations, Bolivian Labor and the City in Northwest Argentina.* Latin American Monograph Series. Austin: University of Texas Press, in press.

URBAN-RURAL DIFFERENCES IN THE
SELECTION STRATEGIES OF COMPADRAZGO:
A CONTROLLED COMPARISON*

Carl Kendall

A recent article has questioned the significance of rural and urban contexts of the performance of and selection strategies in *compadrazgo* (Middleton 1975:473), referring to an issue based on the work of Redfield (1941:220-221;222).[1] This article reviews the history of this question and presents a comparison of some indicators of urban and rural *compadrazgo* structure and use. The paper argues that the rural-urban distinction needs careful consideration before application.

REVIEW OF THE LITERATURE

Redfield noted a greater number of ceremonies used to initiate ritual kinship in rural as compared to urban areas and also greater responsibility of *padrinos* and the overwhelming importance of the *compadre-compadre* bond. He observed also the choice of kin to serve as godparents, and the use of parental terms of address for godparents. *Compadrazgo* was less important in urbanized Chan Kom and Dzitas; and, finally, in urban Mérida *padrinos* were chosen just for the secular benefits that might accrue to the parents and godchild.

*Research presented below was sponsored by the Wenner-Gren Foundation for Anthropological Research, Inc. (1972-1973), The Department of Anthropology, University of Rochester (1972-1973), and the American Philosophical Society (August 1975). Support for write-up was provided by the Facultad de Ciencias Sociales, Universidad del Valle de Guatemala (1978). The author gratefully acknowledges this support.

Attempts to confirm Redfield's observations in other contexts resulted in Paul's efforts to link kinship and ritual kinship (Paul 1942, and Ravicz 1967). A correlation was found between choice of kin to serve as godparents and the intensity of the kin relationship. In rural areas, kin were more frequently chosen as sponsors; in urban areas, non-kin were frequently chosen. The former are known as "intensive" choices as opposed to the latter "extensive." The selection strategy employed seemed to be an excellent indicator applicable to the investigation of *compadrazgo.*

Wolf and Mintz attributed the differences (i.e., differences which might correspond to those observed by Redfield) in *compadrazgo* performance and *compadre* selection in Barrio Poyal and San José, Puerto Rico to strategies of *compadre* choice under different economic circumstances (1950:359ff). In Barrio Poyal, urban in nature and encompassing great disparities of wealth and status, parents frequently choose sponsors of a higher socio-economic level; this is called vertical choice. In San José, a mono-class isolate (to use Wolf's term), parents choose their socio-economic equals. This pattern is called horizontal choice.

Presumably economic class differences between *compadres* destroys something of the ritual kin relationship (Ingham 1970). But yet another set of studies have contended that *compadrazgo* is an instrument of social solidarity in the face of urbanization and increasing economic differentiation (Foster 1953:1,9; Foster 1969; Freidrich 1958:25; Lewis 1963: 129,130; see especially Stein 1961:117; and even Wolf and Mintz 1950: 356). No one position seems to satisfy the ethnographic paradoxes generated by current investigations of ritual kinship (cf. Deshon 1963:576,579; Ingham 1970:281; Osborn 1968; van den Berghe and van den Berghe 1966:1236,1242; Pitt-Rovers 1958; Middleton 1975, among others.)

Incompatibility of research design and the large number of field sites discussed with reference to *compadrazgo* make controlled comparison difficult (Eggan 1954:743-746). This valuable tool has not yet been applied to *compadrazgo.* The paper focuses on rural-urban differences in *compadre* choice in the *municipio* of Esquipulas, Guatemala, a site conducive to controlled comparison, and with indicators derived from the works of Paul, and Mintz and Wolf.

RESEARCH SITES

Esquipulas, a compact town of 9,000 inhabitants, is the *cabecera* or center of the *municipio* of the same name in the Eastern Guatemalan highlands. It is the largest pilgrimage center in Central America with more than 1.5 million visitors annually. Pilgrims swell the population of the city every January through April and spend several million dollars a year in Esquipulas. Needless to say, great differences in wealth are found in the permanent population of Esquipulas. Differences of class, ethnic group, occupation, national origin, and economic status are great among both pilgrims and permanent population. The city has undergone considerable change in recent years, e.g. compare the 1973 population when the study was made (Table 1) with that noted above.

The *aldea* of San Isidro, in the same *municipio,* is a small scattered community of 519 inhabitants located twenty miles by dirt road and footpath from Esquipulas. The aldea is inhabited by *Ladino* small farmers who grow corn and beans for their own consumption and raise livestock and grow tobacco for cash. Economic differentiation among the households exists, of course, but in comparison to Esquipulas, stratification by class of other variables is slight. Table 1 presents some characteristics of the two communities.

DESIGN OF RESEARCH

Questionnaires were prepared to deal with the indicators cited above and additional variables. Preliminary questions dealt with the number and kind of *compadrazgo* ceremonies, the form of *compadrazgo,* the rights and duties of participants in these ceremonies, and a subjective statement from each informant concerning his reasons for forming the *compadrazgo.* Responses to all but the last question were essentially identical in Esquipulas and San Isidro.

A complete census was then conducted in Esquipulas and San Isidro. Detailed information was sought with respect to each household member and all *compadrazgo* relationships of the homeland.

Fieldwork was designed to test: 1) if differences in rural-urban *compadrazgo* form and elaboration could be found within an environment conducive to controlled comparison; 2) if rural-urban differences in the *compadrazgo* function could be noted; and 3) if rural-urban differences in *compadrazgo* selection strategies could be measured, and if any correlation between the above points could be found.

The field site was selected to control for variables of ethnic affiliation and cultural history. In addition to comparison of censuses, interviews were conducted in both San Isidro and Esquipulas to determine the context of the ceremonies, emotional impact of the relationsip, and other qualitative parameters.

TREATMENT AND ANALYSIS

No differences in the number of ceremonies, rules of participation, or content of ceremonies could be discovered between rural San Isidro or Esquipulas.

One feature that separated the two communities was the residence of Protestants in Esquipulas who did not participate in the *compadrazgo.* Urban centers are mixed with respect to religious affiliation while rural towns tend to bud off religious dissidents to form new communities.

For quantitative analysis, ninety-eight households were randomly selected from the Esquipulas census for ease of comparison with the San Isidro population. Only male baptismal sponsors were tabulated. This treatment necessitates some justification. The problem of the size of the total population is not a trivial one, for the total number of linkages contains, at a minimum estimate, 3,125,000 links—not the sort of material for hand calculation. As has been pointed out by Barnes (1972:7), large networks of this sort are difficult to work with, and much insight may be gained with a partial network, or with a few selected first-order relationships. Especially for parameters involved in this study, evidence of highly selected individuals should be easily visible through preliminary questionnaire analysis and also through informal discussion. Evidence of vertical or horizontal choice would be equally visible.

For purposes of verification and correlation of socio-economic status in the measurement of horizontal or vertical choices only locally resident *compadres* were tabulated (see Table 2).

TABLE 1
CHARACTERISTICS OF THE TWO COMMUNITIES JUNE, 1973

	Esquipulas	*San Isidro*
Total Community Population	4,863*	519
Households Involved in the Study	98	99
Sample Population	488	519
Mean Household Size of Sample	4.98	5.24
Access to Roads	yes	no
Electricity	yes	no
Piped Water	yes	no

*census of permanent residents conducted November 1972

TABLE 2
CHARACTERISTICS OF COMPADRAZGO SELECTION
IN SAN ISIDRO AND ESQUIPULAS

	Esquipulas	*San Isidro*
Total Baptismal Sponsors	525	586
Total Baptismal Sponsors Dwelling Locally at Time of Sponsorship	379	87

MEASURE OF HORIZONTAL CHOICE

One measure of horizontal or vertical choice of *compadres* given the pyramidal nature of the distribution of social status might be to test how often certain people are chosen. As might be expected, certain people serve repeatedly as godparents. Three hundred seventy-nine Esquipultecos served as sponsors a total of 525 times. This multiple selection was fairly well distributed through the godparent population, but 28 (7.3 percent) of the cited residents compadres served 174 times, or 33 percent of the time. This is a vertical choice selection pattern. In contrast to what might have been expected, however, San Isidro also has a vertical choice selection pattern. There, eight persons of the eighty-seven named local *compadres* served in eighty-five of the 236 sponsorship occasions in which locals served (29.7 percent). Furthermore, eleven persons served in 106 sponsorship occasions (45 percent). In both Esquipulas and San Isidro these most-chosen individuals included the wealthiest men in town as well as others chosen for reasons of community-acknowledged moral status. Of course, in San Isidro these most-chosen, wealthy men were also heads of large families; this was only partially true for Esquipulas.

It might be argued that results presented for San Isidro are anomalous due to the large percentage of non-local choice. Local versus non-local choice has not been an important indicator in previous studies, however, and this paper deals with only two of the many posssible indicators of intensity of relationship. In addition, most of the non-local choices for San Isidro with the exception of the selection of the kin discussed below, were resident either in Concepción, Honduras or Esquipulas, both urban centers. This would lead us to believe that such choices would be vertical. The horizontal-vertical parameter will not easily help us distinguish *compadre* selection in the two towns.

MEASURE OF INTENSIVE CHOICE

Quantitative analysis of the intensive-extensive dimension of contrast does, however, reveal a difference. In San Isidro, 156 (26.6 percent, of the 586 total choices are affinal or consanguinal kin. The most commonly selected are FB, FZ, MB, and MZ. Intensive choice is diminished in Esquipulas; of the 525 total choices, sixty-six are intensive *compadre* choices. San Isidro may thus be said to practice a more intensive *compadrazgo.* Several other significant parameters of choice undoubtedly influence this outcome. Perhaps the most significant is the fact that a local choice in San Isidro is much more likely to be, by chance, an intensive choice. This is because most of the permanent population of San Isidro is connected by ties of blood or marriage. On the other hand, local choice in Esquipulas is much less likely to produce an intensive choice because of the social distance encompassed in an urban setting, although intensive choice may be pursued as a strategy. I hypothesize that in the cases of non-local intensive choice the siblings shared rights to land and/or had recently migrated from a nearby non-local site. The dimension of local and non-local choice, with its emphasis on cooperation necessitated by co-residence in a community or locale, must be separated from the selection of kin, just as domestic group must be separated from family in the analysis of domestic organization.

CONCLUSION

This paper addresses the impact of urban and rural environment of the institution of *compadrazgo*. In terms of the social indicators usually applied to the institution, the rural and urban environment seems to have little or no effect on the institution of *compadrazgo*. The major difference in the two towns was the selection of kinsmen to serve as batismal sponsors; this pattern of intensive choice was found more often in rural San Isidro than in urban Esquipulas. The significance of this finding is brought into question by the fact that local choice of ritual kinsmen in San Isidro or other rural communities in eastern Guatemala is more likely to produce an intensive choice. Since access to land in San Isidro is controlled by kinship or marriage it might be hypothesized that potentially disputing kinsmen are attempting to resolve their problems through intensive kin choice, but only 236 of the total 586 sponsor occasions utilized fellow residents. In any case the impact of the institution of *compadrazgo* is slight or non-existent in these two communities. Local versus non-local choice (with a meaningful application in an urban context) and the optative conditions in each case of intensive choice would be important links in this puzzle.

In the case of Esquipulas and San Isidro, the impact of the rural and urban environment on the institution of *compadrazgo* would seem to be confined to certain spatio-temporal effects and perhaps spurious features that do not produce different types of *compadrazgo* in each environment. The patterns of intensive choice within the communities are instructive. Some of the wealthiest families in Esquipulas, precisely because they have something to lose in disputes, practice intensive choice

(Kendall n.d.). This finding is similar to the findings of Lewis in Mexico City (1963) of rural patterns of interaction in an urban context.

IMPLICATIONS

The study points to the need for a more sophisticated application of the ideal types grouped under the bifurcate distinctions common in Mesoamerican studies. If urban and rural environments do not reveal the distinctions predicated by these types, that is, if rural environments demonstrate urban characeristics and if urban environments manifest rural characteristics, it is preferable to strip these characteristics of their geographical or spatio-temporal markers. What needs to be identified are the networks (Nadel 1957) or the domains of interaction (Forte 1969) that are being characterized by "urban" and "rural" and allow them to be applied conjointly in the analysis of institutions and society.

NOTES

1. See Wolf and Mintz (1950) for a comprehensive review of the literature up to 1950. Other sources are Gudeman (1971) and Kendall (1974).

2. *Compadrazgo* is the institution of ritual kinship promoted by the Catholic church in its Spanish variant. The institution can be visualized as a triangle linking sponsors of ritual events such as baptism, parents, and offspring. The sponsor and parents call and refer to each other as *compadre*, co-father or *comadre* co-mother. The sponsors are called *padrino* and *madrina*, godfather and godmother while the child is called *abijado* or *abijada*, godchild. The importance of the institution is strongly felt in Latin America. Work on *compadrazgo* since Paul (1942) has demonstrated that characteristics of persons selected to serve as *compadres* such as socioeconomic status are important features of *compadrazgo* use and structure, as is discussed below.

3. The figure of 9,000 cited here is the estimate of Carlos Pacheco, ex-deputy candidate and mayor of Esquipulas, for the permanent year-round population of Esquipulas. The figure in Table 1 included only those Esquipultecos who resided in Esquipulas year-round in 1972. A much larger number of people claim Esquipulas as their residence, but migrate for work.

REFERENCES

Barnes, J. A. *Social Networks*. Reading, Massachusetts: Addison-Wesley, 1972.

Deshon, S. "Compadrazgo on a Henequen Hacienda in Yucatán: A Structuralist Reevaluation." *AA* 65: 574-583, 1963.

Eggan, F. "Social Anthropology and the Method of Controlled Comparison." *AA* 56: 743-760, 1954.

Fortes, M. *Kinship and the Social Order: The Legacy of Lewis Henry Morgan*. London: Routledge and Kegan Paul, 1969.

Foster, G. M. "Cofradía and Compadrazgo in Spain and Spanish America." *Southwestern Journal of Anthropology* 9: 1-28, 1953.

_____. "Godparents and Social Networks in Tzintzuntzan." *Southwestern Journal of Anthropology* 25: 261-78, 1969.

Freidrich, P. "A Tarascan Cacicazgo: Structure and Function." In V. F. Ray (ed.) *Systems of Political Control and Bureaucracy in Human Society*. Seattle: University of Washington Press, 1958.

Gudeman, S. F. "The Compadrazgo as a Reflection of the Natural and Spiritual Person." Proceedings of the Royal Anthropological Institute of Great Britain and Ireland for 1971: 45-67, 1971.

Ingham, J. M. "The Asymmetrical Implications of Godparenthood in Tlayacapan, Morelos." *Man* (n.s.) 5:281-289, 1970.

Kendall, C. *Filiation and Brotherhood: Compadrazgo in Esquipulas*. Ann Arbor: University Microfilm Corp, 1974.

_____. Intensive Ritual Sponsor Choice and Kinship.

Lewis, O. "Some Perspectives on Urbanization with Special Reference to Mexico City." In Aidan Southall (ed.) *Urban Anthropology*. Oxford: University Press, 1963.

Middleton, D. R. "Choice and Strategy in an Urban Compadrazgo." *American Ethnologist* 2:461-4, 1975.

Mintz, S. W. and E. R. Wolf. "An Analysis of Ritual Coparenthood (Compadrazgo)." *Southwestern Journal of Anthropology* 6:341-68, 1950.

Nadel, S. F. *The Theory of Social Structure*. London: Cohen and West, 1957.

Osborn, A. "Compadrazgo and Patronage: A Colombian Case." *Man* (a.s.) 3:593-608, 1968.

Paul, B. D. *Ritual Kinship: With Special Reference to Godparenthood in Middle America.* Thesis, University of Chicago, 1942.

Pitt-Rivers, J. "Ritual Kinship in Spain." *Transactions of the New York Academy of Sciences* 11(20): 423-31, 1958.

Ravicz, R. "Compadrinazgo." In R. Wauchope (ed.) *Handbook of Middle American Indians.* Austin: Unviersity of Texas Press, 1967.

Redfield, R. *The Folk Culture of Yucatán.* Chicago: University Press, 1941.

Stein, W. W. *Hualcan: Life in the Highlands of Perú.* Ithaca: Cornell University Press, 1961.

Van Den Berghe, G. and P. L. Van Den Bergh. "Compadrazgo and Class in Southeastern Mexico." *AA* 368:1236-1244. 1966.

IV
Perspective

DEVELOPMENTAL DILEMMAS AND PARADOXES: A PERSONAL PHILOSOPHICAL NOTE

Peter Dorner

Development is a many-faceted and somewhat forbidding subject. I do not address the topic specifically in a Latin American context but in an even more general one. There are three principal and basic points:

(1) to outline three different dimensions or means of involvement in developmental processes

(2) to review some of the growing literature treating development issues in a global context

(3) to emphasize the lost opportunities resulting from insufficient efforts to provide for the growth and enhancement of human capacities

Knowing what the problems are, the questions to ask, depends a great deal on the perspective from which one is looking at the world. A little over thirty years ago I was a farmer on a small dairy farm in northeastern Wisconsin. On the farm one tends to think in physical terms: it is easy to see and to define accomplishment and non-accomplishment. If you are behind a team of horses and a plow and you plow a furrow down a long field and look back, there is a real sense of accomplishment and it is easy to see and measure. It is open to public observation and demonstration. Even the horses seem to appreciate what is being done and after a while they need very little guidance. This physical visibility as a measure of achievement holds for many tasks on the farm and in occupations generally that are self-directed and involve tangible materials and results.

The limitations of such physical involvement on the local farm level is that there are influences beyond the farm boundaries that affect very directly, and often most drastically, what the farmer can and cannot do. And I am not referring to weather and climatic hazards. Farmers are accustomed to these risks, and they take various precautionary measures to protect against them. It was the more mysterious goings on somewhere else that affected the prices and costs and family opportunities that were not understood.

In the years of the great depression of the 1930s, I was a young boy and I saw and I felt how my parents agonized over the fact that it wasn't at all clear how they would be able to come up with the land taxes—let alone the interest payment on the mortgage. Plowing a straight furrow, having a good herd of dairy cows and a nice pen full of fattened hogs were of no avail to counter these external and shadowy forces that made it impossible to get the money to buy even the barest of necessities.

The paradox and some hint at an explanation to this mystery was provided by John Steinbeck depicting the destitute conditions of the displaced and bankrupt farm families of the Southwest, specifically Oklahoma. The following colloquy from *The Grapes of Wrath* is between one of Steinbeck's "Okies" and a tractor driver whom he has threatened to shoot for knocking over his buildings and plowing up his land.

"It's not me. There's nothing I can do" (says the tractor driver). "I'll lose my job if I don't do it. And look—suppose you kill me? They'll just hang you, but long before you're hung there'll be another guy on the tractor, and he'll bump the house down. You're not killing the right guy."

"That's so," the tenant said. "Who gave you orders? I'll go after him. He's the one to kill."

"You're wrong. He got his orders from the bank. The bank told him, 'Clear those people out or it's your job.' "

"Well, there's a president of the bank. There's a board of directors. I'll fill up the magazine of the rifle and go into the bank."

The driver said, "Fellow was telling me the bank gets orders from the East. The orders were, 'Make the land show profit or we'll close you up.' "

"But where does it stop? Who can we shoot . . . . ?"

The Okie could not shoot the industrial revolution. He could not shoot our failure to devise a public policy that would put that revolution to the advantage of our whole population. (Griswold p. 148).

Moving from the local, physical world and trying to understand these mysterious happenings beyond the boundary of the farm, I went off to school to get some book learning. How beautiful and satisfying it was to have these mysteries explained with a logic that appeared beyond reproach. They weren't mysteries at all. One simply had to have a braoder and more inclusive view of how people and institutions functioned within an intricate webb of interrelationships tieing the economy and the society together. While we could not physically see and test the results of action at this macro level, as one could at the micro level of the farm, the logic of the explanation was convincing.

And so, even before I got really wise (*i.e.,* before I had the Ph.D.) I became a university professor, I taught in the classroom, carried out research, worked with students as well as with farmers and managers of agriculturally related business firms and cooperatives. I understood their problems, and now I had the theoretical vision to explain those mysterious happenings beyond the farm boundaries which they could only feel but could not understand.

But as the years passed and my experience of direct involvement with farm work became more remote, especially with the rapid changes in farm production and marketing techniques, farm size, and farm price and cost relationships, I began to lose touch with that complex physical world. My theoretical knowledge outgrew and came to supercede the first hand practical knowledge of the problems that farmers were actually experiencing. It left me increasingly uneasy, but then my knowledge of the "system," my theoretical grounding in economics, and my knowledge of U.S. institutions served me well—if not in providing an answer then at least in providing a method for finding an answer to real, experienced problems. Some farmers were very responsive to such analytical suggestions, but others were not. Well, after all, you couldn't reach everyone; some were just ignorant and would never learn. Likewise some of the policies coming out of Washington often seemed terribly naive and mixed up—almost as mysterious, even with my newly acquired theoretical vision, as those other mysteries beyond the line fence on the farm.

Then, a little over twenty years ago, I had my first real experience working with people and carrying out research in different cultures with different social systems and institutions than I had previously experienced. My first such contact was in my Ph.D. dissertation research on the natural resource and land tenure issues of the American Indians. Several years later I worked on land reform issues in Chile and in other countries of South and Central America. These experiences were unsettling in many respects, and they led to a major reprogramming of the computer of my mind. I learned to appreciate the many things we take for granted and the assumptions underlying our objective analyses and our knowledge. These assumptions, frequently, though not always, serve us well in the institutional context within which they were developed, but can lead us far astray in other contexts.

Finally, and to bring these personal reminiscences to a close, twelve years ago I had the opportunity to work for over a year with the President's Council of Economic Advisors in Washington. In that position one is very close to and involved in the processes of making public policy judgments and decisions. It's a bit frightening to think that one's judgments, offered so freely in the classroom and even in professional writing, might actually be taken seriously and acted upon with the potential to affect—for good or for bad—the lives of millions of people. After a year, I longed to return to the irresponsibilities of being a university professor. Please do not misunderstand my use of the term "irresponsible." I am using it only to differentiate between the luxury of speculating, theorizing, and researching in an attempt to understand complex issues and relationships on the one hand, and the need to make judgments and decisions which lead to policy action whose many consequences for different groups can never be foreseen with any great precision or detail. After that experience, I became more tolerant, and policies no longer seemed quite so naive and illogical, given the many pressures, conflicting interests and demands which somehow had to be reconciled.

What this personal note is intended to convey is the basic divisions of labor in the entire developmental enterprise. There is the world of physical work and action; there is the world of ideas—the intellectual enterprise; and there is the world of public decision making—the public policy enterprise. These are not isolated activities; they are closely linked and interdependent. Most of us function to a degree at all levels, but we do specialize and concentrate at one level—most of us at the intellectual, academic level—*i.e.* the world of ideas. There are different skills involved, different concepts, and different levels of knowledge. These different levels are all vital to the survival of civilized society, and a recognition of the role and importance of these different functions—*as well as their limitations*—should be sufficient ground for approaching this complex task of development with a sense of humility. Will Rogers must have had something like this in mind when he said, "We are all ignorant, we're just ignorant about different things." Or, more recently, Sam Levinson, whose humorous remarks frequently attempt to call attention to the wisdom in the common sense of ordinary folk, observed, "You don't have to be in Who's Who to know What's What."

It is easy to be critical about the world of physical work. Many of the people in this area are uneducated, and many improvements could be made if people would change their ways of doing things. But being uneducated is not to be equated with being ignorant. Physical work is itself an experience in learning and education. Peasant farmers have many insights into the conditions that most directly affect their lives, and we must try to learn from them and in turn offer them an understanding as to the implications of their insights which we should be able to do given our broader theoretical view of the processes with which they are so intimately involved.

It is also easy to be critical of policy makers and the people in the rapidly growing bureaucracies. And there is much to be critical about. And at times, I suppose, development efforts do resemble an approach such as Professor Eugene Meehan has described in his analysis of public housing programs in the United States. Meehan maintains that the "horse" theory of social improvement remains as the best guide to the progress of such programs. That is, if the task of improvement

> . . . . is taken as a problem of transferring grain from the public grainery to the unfortunate sparrows, it is performed habitually by feeding the grain to an intervening horse—often capable of heroic feats of constipation. The system is operated by horses and guided by awareness of the benefits that accrue to horses; the sparrows are necessary, but only to justify feeding the horses. And anyone seeking to feed the sparrows directly is quite likely to be kicked through the walls of the stable in which the principal horses are housed. (Meehan 1976, p. 51)

It is well to recognize that within the context of this parable, we are all closer relatives of the horses than of the sparrows.

We must appreciate the difficulties of public policy decisions and their implementation, and our own limitations with respect to these decisions. I would like to quote from a 1930 piece by Harold Laski, "The Limitations of the Expert," which I believe remains highly relevant:

> But it is one thing to urge the need for expert consultation at every stage in making policy; it is another thing, and a very different thing, to insist that the expert's judgment must be final. For special knowledge and the highly trained mind produce their own limitations which, in the realm of statesmanship, are of decisive importance. *Expertise,* it may be argued, sacrifices the insight of common sense to intensity of experience. It breeds an inability to accept new views from the very depth of its preoccupation with its own conclusions. It too often fails to see round its subject. It sees its results out of perspective by making them the center of relevance to which all other results must be related. Too often, also, it lacks humility; and this breeds in its possessors a failure in proportion which makes them fail to see the obvious which is before their very noses. It has also, a certain cast-spirit about it, so that experts tend to neglect all evidence which does not come from those who belong to their ranks. Above all, perhaps, and this most urgently where human problems are concerned, the expert fails to see that every judgment he makes not purely factual in nature brings with it a scheme of values which has no special validity about it. He tends to confuse the

importance of his facts with the importance of what he proposes to do about them. (Laski 1930)

We are all part of this intellectual *expertise* enterprise. But despite its limits, of which we should be fully cognizant, I state my own conviction unequivocally that research without any restriction and the freedom of expression and publication are *the* critical functions. If they are stifled and restricted it will lead us backward and in the direction of a new dark age. Yet, we must be humble and recognize our limitations in offering full-blown solutions to complex public policy issues, and we must retain contact with the world of physical work and experience.

I will now turn, after all this philosophic meandering, to my reaction to some global issues and analyses that I had opportunity to study as a result of cochairing the "Wisconsin Seminar on Natural Resource Policies in Relation to Economic Development and International Cooperation."* Within the past fifteen years or so, there has been increasing recognition that development, although basically a national undertaking, has global dimensions which appear to be growing in importance. The increasing dependence of many nations on ever growing importations of food, and that of others on the growing importation of petroleum; the power and reach of transnational corporations; the changing power relationships among nation states and groupings of states; growing concerns over resource scarcity and environmental deterioration; all these and more have led increasingly to viewing development issues and constraints in a global context.

Compounding the problem, of course, is the fact that natural

---

*This seminar was co-sponsored by the University of Wisconsin-Madison, the Organization of Arab Petroleum Exporting Countries (OAPEC), the Arab Fund for Economic and Social Development (AFESD), and the Kuwait Fund for Arab Economic Development (KFAED). Arab scholars and students and University of Wisconsin Professors and students met three times weekly throughout the 1977-78 academic year, then spent another year writing. A book length manuscript is being published by the University of Wisconsin Press. In the remainder of this paper I draw on materials from my introduction to that volume.

resources are distributed very unevenly among countries and frequently bear little relation to population densities and developmental aspirations or current levels of living and consumption patterns. Consequently, substantial quantities of most natural resources or their immediate products move in international trade. Thus, there is a renewed and growing controversy over the terms on which these natural resources and resource commodities are traded for other goods—e.g., manufactures, capital goods and equipment, technical skills and services, etc. And within this overall setting, there are new demands for more equitable, humane, and efficient modes of development, both within and among nations. This development is to occur in a system of constraints which include finite natural resources, ecosystems with poorly measured yet definite limits for absorbing the shocks and the by-products of growing populations and geometrically expanding resource use, and political systems that attempt to resolve pressing social problems by inducing rates and kinds of economic growth that cannot be sustained indefinitely.

In reviewing the vast literature on various aspects of these global issues, one is struck by the wide divergence in conclusions and positions that emerge from different analyses. On the one hand are extreme positions projecting doom and catastrophe and instilling fear. If enough people come to believe in these predictions and conduct their lives accordingly, such prophecies can become self-fulfilling. Fear paralyzes the intellect and leads to despair—especially among the young who have, after all, a longer future than the middle aged and the old. In the depths of the depression of the 1930s, President Roosevelt reminded the U.S. that "The only thing we have to fear is fear itself." There is a profound difference between perceptions of the future which instill fear (projecting dangers which are imaginary or dangers which cannot be avoided) and perceptions of the future which arouse caution and concern about current events and likely future events and so induce creative responses and provident measures to prepare for that future. Some of the "shock treatment" literature of opinion is produced by scientists and marketed in the name of science. One is often surprised at the profundity of pronouncements and the alleged global wisdom that can be extracted from a modicum of understanding of how the real world actually functions. There is a role for such "shock" literature. It is the same role played by the leaders of any popular movement. Perhaps no movement of this kind can get off the ground without leaders who take a legitimate point of concern and extrapolate that point to an exaggerated and even irrational conclusion. This is a crucial role and an important function, but I do not believe that this is the best role for serious researchers and scholars who must seek to retain a sense of proportion and provide an objective view not only for themselves but for the public at large.

It is indeed the responsibility of scholars and scientists to help inform the public and the people who make public policies. There is no question that individual nations and the international community face grave problems that urgently need attention, but science does not bestow clairvoyance. We cannot, in most cases, see or predict with much accuracy very far into the future. Projections of catastrophe usually have no solid evidential basis. There is a danger that the general public as well as people in government will become immune to all warnings of science (whether or not they are warranted) or will turn hostile and fail to grant credibility to any and all conclusions of scholarly research. It is like the little boy crying wolf— after a number of warnings of catastrophe which are not borne out by experience or which are contradicted by evidence, any shock value that such speculations might have is soon lost and people fail to pay attention at best or turn outright hostile toward the source of such warnings.

There is an opposite extreme of unqualified and unfounded optimism. Some people prefer to live in a world of dreams and to be lulled into complacency. A variant of this (a position in search of a scapegoat) is expressed by those who have a vision of Utopia which depends for its realization solely on the elimination of a set of actors (or actions)—dictators of the left or right, or multinational corporations, or the consumption habits of the wealthy, or the breeding habits of the poor, or scientists, or politicians, or OPEC, etc. Subscribers to this overly-simplified view of global society are more often than not revealing a suppressed desire for the power to shape events to suit their private purposes. Again, there is a profound difference between blind faith that some miraculous intervention will somehow see us through to ever greater achievements, and a faith in human intelligence (with appreciation of its limits), concrete experience, and past accomplishment.

In dealing with these global issues, there is a strong tendency to get lost on the abstract sea of high and noble purpose where the imagination is freed from the stabilizing influence of experiencing the consequences of the courses of action being proposed. No one is immune to these tendencies. The very intricate nature of most of these issues and the impossibility of comprehending in any fundamental sense the physical, social, economic, cultural, and political conditions guiding people's lives in this still vast world, suggest a course of caution and humility.

One must, however, enter yet another caveat. Although the "truth" (or a workable compromise) may lie somewhere within the broad spectrum of possibilities encompassed by the pessimistic and optimistic extremes, there are many valid reasons why serious studies of these issues will reach conclusions that diverge widely. There is no single objective truth about the policy questions inherent in these global issues.

Policy always deals with the future; it is always necessary to make certain assumptions and estimates about many behavioral variables and their interaction. Projections of past trends of resource use and environmental degradation do indeed lead to a gloomy outlook for the future. Other analysts counter that increasing scarcity of finite resources will be reflected in higher prices and costs which will curb consumption, stimulate technological developments to economize on the scarcer resources, and indeed induce people to change their consumption habits. The contention here is that sheer physical projections of resource availabilities ignore the most fundamental resource—human knowledge and intelligence. Science, it is suggested, has changed emphasis and direction in the past and it can (indeed it must) do so in the future. And although any new course in science and technology will inevitably be destructive of some human habits and institutions, the creations of science and technology also provide new optimism and new alternatives. Future developments in science and technology cannot be foreseen. If they could, we would not need research. There is always an element of faith with respect to the future constructive uses of science and technology, but human experience throughout history has shown the creativity of human intelligence in dealing with the physical universe and in shaping and reshaping behavior, institutions, and techniques in living within the physical universe. Has the modern era locked people into patterns of growth and dependence in which this demonstrated capacity for creative adaptation has been weakened? Differing assumptions about some of these intangibles can lead to divergent views about future prospects and appropriate policies.

A basic and inescapable problem in treating these global issues of natural resource policies and economic development is that of time. No serious student would contend that there are *no* physical limits to natural resources of the earth, or that there are no limits on the earth's ultimate capacity to support biological systems. But how close are we to approaching such limits and how much time can be allowed in planning to adjust to them? Assumptions vary widely as do policy prescriptions rooted in these different assumptions.

Another issue that leads to diverse prescriptions also depends on assumptions about human adaptability and the time span under consideration. It is the issue of growth in human populations. Rhetoric to the contrary notwithstanding, and with a few exceptions, most nations are concerned with population growth. Very few if any treatises on economic development ignore the issue. Although there seem to be few defenders of continued rapid growth in population, the Third World nations, where population growth (and often current density as well) is highest, remind the industrial nations that growth in numbers is only one side of the population question. The other side is rates of use and levels of consumption of natural resources by the wealthier populations in the industrial countries. The majority of the world's people live in the developing countries, but the minority living in the developed industrial countries consumes a highly disproportionate amount of the natural resources moving in international trade.

The contrast is clear. One view holds to the assumption that only by controlling population numbers and growth rates can the poor of this world hope to improve their status and physical wellbeing. The other view holds that while this is often necessary and accepted, unless the rich control their levels and rates of growth of resource consumption, there will be insufficient resources for the poor to improve their position and, in any event, they will be unable to compete for the needed resources—many of which *are* growing scarcer.

Differing analyses and prescriptions are grounded not only in differing assumptions, but in differing political realities and power relations and positions among the nation states. A common view of people in the industrial countries is that they never got anything for nothing. They worked hard for what they got; let others do likewise. Yet in the minds of many, there is an uneasy feeling that the industrial countries have gained disproportionate advantage from their leadership in science and engineering and the multitude of techniques for "conquering and controlling" nature. On the other hand, there is a feeling of near certainty by many in the developing world that the industrial states' advantage and current high levels of material consumption are the direct result of colonization and exploitation, over many years, of the developing world. Divergent policy prescriptions are not purely analytical matters of assumptions and empirical conclusions, but also matters of interpretation of history and of political relations among equally sovereign yet not equally powerful nation states.

In any discussion of evaluation of policy for the future it is never quite clear to whom prescriptions are addressed. Individuals are all, to a degree, trapped by their own culture and its institutions. Yet the changes that must occur will indeed be based on the decisions of millions of individuals and families— whether reducing the number of births, lowering rates of resource use and consumption, adopting new values and pursuits to displace resource-intensive styles, etc. However, inducing the necessary change in the decisions of tens of millions of individuals so that these will move society in a new and consistent direction can only be achieved by restructuring national institutions and incentive systems and not only by appealing to individuals voluntarily to change their ways. People do live and act at the local level, but their alternatives and opportunities are shaped significantly by events at regional, national and international levels.

Even policies devised and implemented at the level of the sovereign nation state are inadequate to encompass the problems. Just as the physical environment links all people of the globe in its intricate web in interrelations and interdependencies, so too do increasingly complex economic and political interrelations and interdependencies both expand and restrict the possibilities for nations to act. Natural resources are imbued with a "public interest." In a simpler era when life's functions were provided for on a smaller scale and with near self-sufficiency at local levels, resource use and conservation issues could be more readily encompassed by local action. However, with ever greater complexity, scale, and mutual dependencies, the concept of the public in defining that "public interest" has come to include ever larger numbers over increasingly wide geographic areas. Some of these complex issues cannot be resolved at the national level, but require international cooperation, negotiation, and agreement.

The way in which the world is now structured, institutionally, does not provide enough feedback to discipline powerful decision makers, be they private or public, to make their acts consistent with the larger (sometimes global) public interest. Decisions and actions taken by economically powerful private interests or nations may have widespread and costly consequences for people in remote parts of the globe, yet those making the decisions may be unaware of the far-reaching influence of their own acts. Even if they are aware of these consequences, they do not feel their real costs. It is only as these costs (which are now widely diffused) are reflected back and borne by the private firm or the nation which incurred them that their self-interest will be transmitted to smaller organizational units throughout the system and will eventually serve to redirect the actions of millions of individuals at the local level. In earlier and simpler times, incentives and sanctions could be devised and changed at the local level. In today's complicated world of mutual dependencies and disparate economic, military, and political powers held by ever larger decision making units, this process of institutional and incentive reconstruction must include first and foremost those powerful actors who help by their decisions to shape the opportunity structure of individuals the world over.

Issues of natural resource policies in relation to economic development and international cooperation generate quite different views because appropriate data are often lacking, assumptions regarding future adustments and adaptations differ, and because historical and political perspective and interpretation also vary. Substantial agreement does exist about the needs for more balanced development which conserves resources, for increased transfer of resources from rich to poor, and for structural changes in present configurations of economic and political power—both within and among countries—to meet these needs. Diverging views, however, arise when concrete proposals for action to adust to these generally recognized conditions are put forward.

A world of more than 150 independent, sovereign nation states compounds the complexity of these problems. Most substantive policies in economic and social development and resource use are made at the level of the nation state, and the nations of the world are extremely diverse with respect to population size and density, technological development, per capita income, natural resources under national control, economic and political organization. This tremendous diversity notwithstanding, a greater unity of purpose and a more balanced global development *are* required if the people of this world are to avoid ever more destructive confrontations and are instead to move toward a system where conflicts are defused and resolved through joint deliberation and negotiation.

In closing, I want to return to the more practical world of local action—whether that be action by the local community or the nation state. People do live and work at the local level. As Wilfred Owen noted several years ago,

> There once was a nation of 200 million people that was the most powerful country in all the world. At the national level the inhabitants were very rich, but at the local level they often turned out to be quite poor. And as luck would have it, they all lived at the local level. (Owen 1967)

Some economic and social problems are strictly domestic; many others have inescapable components and complications which can be resolved only by the people and government of a particular nation. It is illusory to think that countries can do little until external problems of international order and international trade are settled. Sef-help *is* important. Charity *must* begin at home. An improved distribution of income *and especially of opportunity* within countries is an obligation of every nation, and that responsibility cannot be delegated without loss of a nation's sovereignty. It is equally defensive and deceptive for industrial countries to contend that they can do little to help until all internal structural reforms have been accomplished by the developing countries. Both faces of this argument are self-serving excuses of the rich and powerful— not the poor and weak—within and among nations.

It must be re-emphasized the *redistribution of opportunity*— rather than a mere redistribution of current income without a change in the opportunity structure—is the core of the problem. The redistribution of current purchasing power to those incapable of working will remain necessary in all societies. But to look upon that sort of redistribution as in any sense approaching a solution to problems of massive poverty, unemployment, and inequality is grossly to misinterpret the functions of government. Even if it is possible to alleviate the worst poverty through post-production distribution, people cannot simply be placed "on ice" until such time as they are needed. People must be engaged in worthwhile productive activities in order to develop the skills, capacities, and discipline which a productive agriculture and industry require. Output, employment, and distribution objectives must be combined and harmonized within the same policy, and that harmony may be impossible without a redistribution of property and opportunity and related structural changes. National reforms in the internal order are vital ". . . in order to pass on whatever gains are achieved internationally to the masses rather than to a handful of privileged groups. It is also vital in order to gain credibility for the demand for a new international economic order. We cannot very well ask for equality of opportunity internationally if we in the Third World deny the same equality of opportunity to our own people. That is why it is vital that we undertake, in the next phase, major reforms in the internal order" (ul Haq 1976, p. 49).

But developing nations can and must see major opportunities as well as domestic obligations and responsibilities. And the greatest uncaptured opportunity within most of the developing countries is development of the human resource. Natural resources in the purely physical sense are finite; human intelligence and skills, so far as we know, are not. It is indeed a tragic waste that so many millions of people have had no opportunity to be challenged to develop their human capacities—both the powers of the mind and the skills of physical dexterity. Even the untutored and unsophisticated mind has much to contribute, given the opportunity. All individuals are potentially creative. Human skills and capacities, developed through formal schooling *and* work opportunities, are any nation's true and basic renewable resource. The motive force in the development process is not provided by investment plans and projects of public administrators and private entrepreneurs, important as these are. The informed self-interest and the growing skills of the mass of farmers and urban workers, and their creative human energies, are the real impulse for any long-term progress.

The human resource plays a dual role. Man is a resource as well as the user of resources. Every individual is both user and used, the interested and the object of interest, the reason for development and the means of its realization. Labor is sometimes treated as simply another input in the production process. It is that and it does represent a cost to be entered in the calculations of planning and project evaluation. But how easy to lose sight of the fact that development must be by and for all the people and that opportunities and incentives and skills are needed that it can be so. A society shortchanges itself if it draws upon no more than a small fraction of its potential human creativity, the basic renewable resource. Basic literacy and jobs are requisite if the mass of people now in the fringes of development is to become the valuable national resource it could in fact be, and if it is to improve upon its own condition in the process. There will always be some men and women who do not care to respond to opportunities or test their capacities, but all should be given the chance to develop their potential abilities to the fullest.

Providing opportunities to people is not solely a matter of national interest. The extended human family draws upon the creative genius of its members from all races and all areas of the globe. We of the living generation are the beneficiaries of the human resources, the knowledge and skills, nurtured by past generations. We are apprehensive, and appropriately so, over the welfare of future generations lest our indulgent consumption dissipate some critical resources and jeopardize the future of our children and grandchildren and generations beyond. Yet we do need to retain perspective and include the human resources of the present among our concerns. What is the most valuable of the collective social assets that we pass on to our heirs? We are the future generation of generations past; what were the most valuable assets we inherited? Among them were undoubtedly accumulated and dependable knowledge and skills, institutions, and social organization. The resources of any society include and indeed are defined by its acquired skills—technological, managerial, professional, and organizational—the intangible capital embodied in the living generation.

Short-term interests may often govern the acts of individuals, but society needs a leadership, a vision, and a strategy that protects and encompasses the interests of future generations. The current generation *must* make long-term economic and social investments for future generations. The present generation is most short-sighted if those who happen to hold advantage (no matter their nation) neglect their responsibility for the investments which will benefit the heirs of the poor. Security is not a need confined to the aged of this generation; it is important to the working population of today so that they may give their children the education and investment which they will need to fully appreciate, utilize, and build upon their inheritance from all past humanity. It is in this way that the security and opportunities of the current generation extend to the future.

Much is heard today about development being a "zero-sum game"—that whatever one nation gains another must lose or, in a broader sense, that all the material "progress" made to date by means of science and technology is a delusion based on reckless consumption of "geological capital" in the form of coal, oil, mineral deposits, and the very soil of our sustenance. It is a truism that exponential growth in consumption of resources cannot continue indefinitely, yet many believe that the very recognition of these limits is an important first step, that the problems are not yet of catastrophic proportions, that it is not too late to deal with them, and that it is possible to find new directions in science and technology and human preferences. Whatever the conclusion with respect to these issues might eventually be, it is a certainty that there is no zero-sum game, in either narrow or broad sense, in human knowledge and intelligence. Knowledge grows not in isolation and preservation but in use and distribution.

The strategic importance of developing the human resource is, of course, not confined to the developing countries. The industrial nations share these opportunities and responsibilities. Here we must think not in terms of categories of nations but in terms of people. People everywhere, in all nations rich and poor, have aspirations and needs and potential creative contributions which cut across conventional political borders. The needs of the poor, especially, are immediate and compelling; the conditions in which they find themselves are not generally of their own making or choosing; their contributions, if they are encouraged to make them, will not be confined to their own welfare but will be shared by humanity in general—by the current generation and generations unborn.

REFERENCES

Griswold, A. Whitney. *Farming and Democracy*. New Haven: Yale University Press, 1948. Griswold is quoting from John Steinbeck, *The Grapes of Wrath*. New York: The Viking Press, 1939, pages 51-52.

Laski, Harold J. "The Limitations of the Expert," *Harpers Magazine* Vol. 162, No. 967. Reprinted in *Specialists and Generalists: A Selection of Readings*. U.S. Senate Subcommittee on National Security and International Operations, 90th Congress, 2nd Session 1968. Washington: U.S. Government Printing Office.

Meehan, Eugene J. "The Rise and Fall of Public Housing: Condemnation Without Trial." Paper prepared for the Annual Meeting of the American Real Estate and Urban Economics Association, Washington, D.C. May, 20-21, 1976.

Owen, Wilfred. "A Fable: How the Cities Solved Their Transportation Problems." Washington D.C.: Urban American Inc., 1967.

ul Haq, Mahbub. "The Third World and the International Economic Order." Development Paper 22. Washington, D.C.: Overseas Development Council, 1976.

World Food Forum Proceedings. The Inaugural Event Commemorating the 100th Anniversary of the USDA, 1862-1962, May 15-17, Washington, D.C., 1962.